William Johnson Galloway

Advanced Australia

A short account of Australia on the eve of federation

William Johnson Galloway

Advanced Australia

A short account of Australia on the eve of federation

ISBN/EAN: 9783337312039

Printed in Europe, USA, Canada, Australia, Japan

Cover: Foto ©ninafisch / pixelio.de

More available books at **www.hansebooks.com**

ADVANCED AUSTRALIA

ADVANCED AUSTRALIA

A SHORT ACCOUNT OF AUSTRALIA ON THE EVE OF FEDERATION

BY

WILLIAM JOHNSON GALLOWAY, M.P.

METHUEN & CO.
36 ESSEX STREET, W.C.
LONDON
1899

PREFACE

BEFORE giving to the publishers these notes of my journeyings during the early part of this year in Australia and New Zealand, the greater part of which appeared, during the months of March and April, in the hospitable columns of the *Manchester Courier*, I have taken some trouble in revising and correcting them, to the best of my ability, from the latest available official returns. I am therefore indebted for many of my facts, and for most of my figures, to a class of documents available to all, but probably, in this country, perused by few —the publications of the several Colonial Governments. But, in putting together, as it were, the leaves of my notebook, I have not intended to write either a work of reference or a volume of travels; and my book makes as little claim to literary merit as to statistical completeness. To deal with the agriculture, as yet only in its early stages, of Bunbury and the Mallee, of Gippsland and the Darling Downs, of Colac and Tasmania, would require all the knowledge of another Arthur Young; while who should treat fully, as well as intelligibly to the general, of the mining industries of Ballarat and New Zealand, Mount Morgan, " the Towers," Broken Hill, Mount Lyall, Kalgoorlie, and Chillagoe, must have the silver tongue of a mining expert, as well as the treasures of his wisdom. The provincial peculiarities of " Tassies " and cornstalks, gum-suckers, crow-eaters, sand-gropers, and " wait-a-whiles," might furnish many jests to your globe-trotting philosopher, or to a witty reporter. But as

PREFACE

I am neither a journalist nor a philosopher, I have attempted no more than to convey to the reader how Australia, on the eve of Federation, impressed a chance traveller; as an exporter, especially, of raw produce, as a possible home and outlet for our surplus population, as a field for the observation of political experiments, and as a member, generally, of the Imperial body-politic. Much may be learnt from Colonial legislation: if we only learn, sometimes, what to avoid. Local option, old-age pensions, payment of members, the referendum, all the panaceas of the demagogue, are in full operation in one or another of these practically republican (but very English) States. One and a half millions they spend by the year on education, as against our ten millions in England. Yet the output of their State schools, as we shall see, is not a whit more satisfactory than that of our Board schools, perhaps in some ways even less. Pensions ranging as high as 26s. 3d. weekly are proposed in at least one colony for persons over 55, to be provided by a tax on bread. (See Appendix E: Old-age Pensions, N.S.W.) On the whole, Australia offers, perhaps intentionally, but small encouragement to our emigrants now. Of the fourteen thousand visitors who arrive annually from Europe, barely the lesser half remain as settlers. Yet Queensland and New Zealand have reverted of late to assisted immigration; and there are openings everywhere and at all times for the suitable newcomer—lawyer, farmer doctor, artizan, or domestic servant. But it must be remembered that all trades profess themselves overmanned; that the producer has the only real certainty; that production in a new country is a very rough business; and that unskilled energy can only command a success which is likely to be moderate, at the price of unmitigated hardship. The best craftsman, in agriculture as in other trades, has particular advantages in a community where the level of technical knowledge is low. But the best craftsman, in any trade, will probably not wish (unless it be for reasons unconnected with business) to leave England. Few of our middle-class families are guilty, nowadays, of the cruel folly of sending their youngsters off to Australia as, "jackeroos" or "remittance-men," to find their level in an environment which gives them no fair chance. We prefer to send them to South Africa instead. But there are still always men and women in every social rank to whom Australasia appeals as offering an opening, which they fail to see at home, for the free exercise of their faculties. And if, in my attempt, however obscurely, to estimate these colonies from this point of view, I have sometimes been guilty of more frankness, perhaps, than would be altogether discreet if it were my fortune to be domiciled there myself, it will surely be allowed in my excuse that to do otherwise were to darken counsel.

For the rest, I enjoyed great hospitality throughout the colonies: and I shall always feel towards them, as a result of my tour, the increased amity which, amongst men of the same blood, is the natural result of a better understanding. To Mr Kingston, the Premier of South Australia, Sir George Turner, the Premier of Victoria, Mr Reid, the late Premier of New South Wales, and Mr Seddon, the Premier of New Zealand, as well as to a host of other leaders of political and social thought, I have to express my most heartfelt thanks for the untiring courtesy with which they assisted my natural desire for information.

The Friendly Societies spared themselves no expense nor trouble to make my visit both pleasant and instructive.

Nor can I forget the kindness with which the several Governors received me; a reception partly due in some cases to a previous personal friendship, but in all mainly, as I could perceive, to my humble connection with the Imperial Parliament.

Finally, I have laid particular, but not, I think, unnecessary emphasis, in the last chapter of the book, on a point which I regard as of vital importance to the future of the Empire; the necessity, I mean, under the coming Federal Constitution of Australia, of maintaining unimpaired the judicial prerogative of Her Majesty the Queen, and the right of every subject, whether at home or in the colonies, to appeal, in the last resort, to the Privy Council of the realm. This is a question less striking, indeed, but perhaps, ultimately, of not less constitutional importance, than that which is now finding its solution in South Africa.

CONTENTS

CHAPTER I

WESTERN AUSTRALIA 1

The Long Trail—The Australian Atmosphere—Albany—Perth—Hunt's Dams—The rush to Bayley's Find—The noble army of prospectors—The City shark—Output and dividends—Timber—History—Politics—Federation improbable.

CHAPTER II

SOUTH AUSTRALIA 24

The Bight—The City of Churches—Democratic experiments—Orange v. Green—The Cabinet—Wakefield—Wheat—Wine—Copper—Prospects.

CHAPTER III

VICTORIA 39

Free passes—The Murray snag—Ballarat—Breeding gondolas—Dimdamnboolah—Melbourne—Cable trams—The Yan Yean—Lord Brassey—Politics—Protection — Factories Act — The first flock—Bendigo—Mining—Agriculture—Education.

CHAPTER IV

TASMANIA 63

The Garden Island—Potatoes, contentment, and jam—Unmarried females—Sleepy Hollow—Land-settlement—Land-values—Economic Federation.

CHAPTER V

NEW SOUTH WALES 70

The Harbour—The Queen City of the Pacific—Steam trams—Colonial shirt-sleeves—Art—Journalism—Architecture—The pastoral industry—The troubles of Job—Land-settlement—Mining—Australian gems—Light railways—Politics—Future.

CHAPTER VI

QUEENSLAND 88

Owls to Athens—The Darling Downs—An Australian Manitoba—A hill of gold—A home industry—Chilled meat—Artesian bores—Sugar-bounties — Liberian coffee — Population — Land-settlement—Agrarian outrages—Free emigration—The reverse of the medal—Finance.

CONTENTS

CHAPTER VII

NEW ZEALAND 107

The economical Anglo-Saxon—Wellington—Auckland—Past and Present—The Vogelian policy—The Fjords—Sulphur baths—The Governor and the Cabinet—The Land-system—Frozen meat—Mining—Revenue—The Labour Laws—Divorce—Local Option as a fact—The Native-born—Assisted Emigration—The Maories, the Normans of the Pacific—Gold-dredging on the jugular.

CHAPTER VIII

OLD AGE PENSIONS IN PRACTICE 134

The Act of 1891—An income of £18—Infamia—10,000 Pensioners—No alien need apply.

CHAPTER IX

THE NEW COMMONWEALTH 146

Inducements to federate—Service's Council—Parke's Convention—The awakening of the Native-Born—Reid's Conference—The Convention of 1897-8—The reference to the people—The check—Amendments—Success at last—Western Australia stands out—Imperial Federation—Colonial contingents—The Privy Council.

CHAPTER X

A POINT IN THE COMMONWEALTH BILL . . . 175

The silken bonds—Hegemony and the Royal prerogative—Canadian loyalty—Australian difficulties—The Colonial Kingdoms—Democracy and the old Kings—The subordination of the Bench—A saving clause required.

APPENDIX (APPENDICES A TO J) 181

ADVANCED AUSTRALIA

CHAPTER I

WESTERN AUSTRALIA

MOST voyages are not travelling, now-a-days; but merely existence on a mail steamer. Again, more than one hundred and fifty globe-trotters pass through the Suez Canal every week on their way to Australia; and though the number is not in itself overwhelming, imagination boggles at what would happen if every globe-trotter committed his voyage to print, as most of them do to paper. Yet, on the other hand, not to keep a stylograph in your board-ship coat-pocket were the merest profligacy. For, east of Suez, a man sometimes raises, not only a thirst for "pegs," but a hunger for information; because, though the world is undoubtedly shrinking, and the (till '95) inaccessible desert places of (for example) Kalgoorlie are now graced by an excellent club, which is within an easy thirty days of London, yet there are such things, even now, as local atmospheres. And an outward Australian liner carries about with her somehow, stowed away in her inner consciousness, a local atmosphere of the Bush which she dons with her suit of awnings somewhere about the Red Sea. You have left Charing Cross behind you at the starting-end of the long trail, and the talk henceforward, under the patronage of the

twin Australian heroes, Mr Lansell and the late Mr
Tyson, is all of squatting and gold-mining, "the Gulf"
and "the Block," and a hundred other stimulating
technicalities, with their resultant yarns, in half an hour.
Ten days of this sort of thing after leaving Colombo,
and you are in Western Australia : " W.A," as its inhabitants and neighbours usually call it ; or, as it is dubbed
by journalists, "the Golden West." Western Australia,
in effect, is a colony which has been brought very prominently under the notice of the English public during
the past four or five years, on account of the remarkable
gold discoveries which have taken place there. But no
traveller, who is not also an explorer and is prepared
to devote years to the task, can hope to take anything
but a hasty glance here and there in passing at this
great area, which comprises nearly one-third of the
whole Australian continent, and is equal to one-fourth of
Europe, with Great Britain and Ireland included.

The first point at which the mail steamers touch, after
crossing the Indian Ocean, is King George's Sound.
Albany, on the north side of Princess Royal Harbour,
within the Sound, is a pretty little town of about 4000
inhabitants, some 340 miles from Perth. It has a rising
timber trade, and is by way of being a sanatorium ;
though perhaps its chief support is drawn from the two
or three hotels on the harbour front, and the shillings
spent there by passengers. As a coaling-station, it is
of great strategic importance, and is garrisoned by a
battery of permanent artillery, maintained at the joint
expense of the colonies. An enemy's fleet which should
set out to attack Australia would find its coal supplies
exhausted by the time it reached the southern portion
of the continent, and would be practically helpless ; hence
the fortifications, by which in time of war the coal stored

WESTERN AUSTRALIA 3

here would be preserved for the use of the British ships. Albany lives in continual fear of being superseded, as a port of call for the mail steamer, by Fremantle; and indeed it cannot be looked on, at present, as offering a favourable field for the investor in corner allotments.

To reach Perth, the capital city of the colony, a railway journey of some thirty hours in a north-westerly direction is necessary. This line was constructed by the West Australian Land Company, and was opened in 1889. The company received from the Government a grant of 12,000 acres of land for every mile constructed, to be selected within a distance of 40 miles on either side of the line, with half the frontage to the railway reserved to the Government. The line has recently been taken over by the Government for £1,100,000. There are other private, or land-grant lines in the colony, chief amongst which is the Midland Railway, running back north to Geraldton. But the system has in most cases given dissatisfaction to all parties concerned — Government, investors, settlers, and the travelling public.

Whilst Sir John Forrest is in power, it will be utterly useless for the most philanthropic of concessionaires to propose to build railways for the colony. The colony has undertaken the work itself, through contractors, and has achieved an astonishing record for cheapness and celerity of construction. The gauge is 3 ft. 6 in. in all cases, and the line was open in March 1898 as far as Menzies, a mining town to the north of Kalgoorlie, 450 miles away in the interior of the Eastern Desert. Warned by the extravagance which some of the other colonies have displayed in regard to the cost of their earlier railways, and assisted, no doubt, by the absence of all physical difficulties except the scarcity of water, the Government has so contrived that its railways are run at a profit of 4½%, the best result in Australia. One of the projects of the future, the distant future no doubt, is to connect the Kalgoorlie line with the most westerly extension of the lines in the colony of South Australia. When that is done, the traveller landing at Perth will be able to travel by rail right through the continent from west to east. The capitals of all the other colonies—Adelaide, Melbourne, Sydney, and Brisbane—are already connected by rail.

The city of Perth, which a few years ago contained a population of only 9,000, has since the gold discoveries sprung up to 40,000 souls. It is situated on the Swan River, about twelve miles inland from Fremantle, and under the shelter of a bold hill, Mount Eliza, which is crowned by the public park. The view from the summit, looking across the river, which widens opposite the city into the two lakes of Perth and Melville Waters, divided by the long flat promontory of Mill Point and fed by the broad and winding stream of the Canning, is picturesque enough : but otherwise the city generally is squalid and dirty; and it cannot be said to have anything especially attractive in its sandy surroundings. It possesses, however, some handsome buildings, and some fine streets. St George's Terrace, where the Western Australian Bank and public offices are situated, is a fine avenue. Government House, where Sir Gerard Smith, the Governor, lives, is a handsome and commodious residence. The Town Hall is also a fine building, standing on a slight eminence. An electric tram service is in process of completion.

The first subject to which I naturally directed inquiry in this land of gold was the subject of gold-getting and gold output ; the present position of the industry and its prospects. The eyes of gold miners in all parts of

WESTERN AUSTRALIA 5

Australia have for many years been turned to the great inland territories of Western Australia as a region possessing great possibilities of mineral wealth. Sir Roderick Murchison's name is on its map. So far back as 1865, a capable young surveyor named Hunt penetrated with horses and a waggon to the country east and south of what is now Kalgoorlie, and reported country "probably auriferous." He had happened on a wet season; but his achievement was still most remarkable, and his track, and even one of the dams he constructed, were of much use when the country was opened up more than thirty years afterwards. He found the valuable district of the Hampton Plains, and seems even to have reached, with a flying party, the still very remote region of Kurnalpi. Hargreaves, the celebrated prospector from N.S. Wales, was given £500, about this time, to inspect and report on the colonies' mineral resources. But he was only shown the coastal districts, and his report was discouraging, though some quartz which must have come from near Coolgardie was taken to Sydney in 1866. In 1869, again, another young surveyor, John Forrest (now the Right Hon. Sir John Forrest, the Premier), discovered and named Mounts Malcolm, Margaret, and Leonora; each of them now the centre of rich mining districts to the north of Kalgoorlie; and in 1871, Alexander Forrest, his brother, the present Mayor of Perth, camped for a time at a *gnamma*-hole which must have been close to Bayley's find and the Tom Tiddler's ground of Fly Flat.

The word "rush" is used in Australia to describe the great rush of miners from one goldfield to another when news of rich finds is published. Western Australia has had several "rushes," and the bleached bones of many of the pioneers lie all over the continent. Kimberley, in the far north, had its rush in 1896; but fever and the difficulties of transport crushed its prosperity, though mining is still carried on there by a few persistent adventurers who live on, as is usual with such haunters of derelict goldfields, in the hope of good times to come. It was not till July, 1892, that Bayley and Ford, two prospectors whose headquarters were at Southern Cross, a struggling camp then on the remotest fringe of civilisation, pushed out along Hunt's old track to Coolgardie, and discovered a very rich reef, which was afterwards known as Bayley's Reward Claim. In one year half a ton of gold was obtained from this mine by the most primitive processes. The fame of the yields spread, and then one of the greatest "rushes" ever known in Australia occurred.

The whole mining, or migratory and prospecting population of Australasia set out in hot haste for the fields, and was followed by all the wastrels and failures who had been left "on their uppers" by the bursting of the Melbourne land-boom. The tract which ran eastward through the primeval bush was a curious sight in those days. Heavy waggons, laden with flour, chaff, and whisky, lumbered axle-deep through the mud, drawn each by its team of a dozen great horses in single file —for 1893 was a wet season—and each accompanied by its string of "swampers" who paid perhaps almost their last 30s. for the privilege of walking alongside for ten days and having their swags of a hundredweight carried on the top of the load. Big Broken Hill men, and ruined speculators from all the colonies, went up with their own buggies or teams; alluvial men walked up with little more than their water-bags; "Kimberley wheel-barrows," or one-wheeled cart nondescripts drawn by a human team, were a fashionable, if not a very efficient, means of transport; and one man, a German, actually packed a flour barrel with stores, pierced the whole concern with an axle, and rolled or dragged it the whole painful way to Coolgardie. Men walked blindly into the unmapped desert in search of an utterly imaginary Golconda of the moment known as Mount Youle, and found Kalgoorlie, and then did not know what they had found. Every one who could afford it carried his own condenser, because the only permanent water "out back" was salt. The extraordinary reports that came down to the coast were but half believed for some time in Perth itself. Miss Flora Shaw, who was investigating Australia for the *Times*, was not allowed even to visit Western Australia, and the London papers ignored the rush as long as they could. But a few of the better informed, chiefly from Piccadilly, of all places, found their way out, and met with their reward. They were followed by "mining experts," newspaper correspondents, "agents of the Rothschilds," and the rest. Everything that could be sold or floated was floated or sold, in Adelaide, or locally; in London, or to the French. Prospectors on foot and on horseback, with camels and on bicycles, spread themselves all over the interior; living and looking for gold where a few years before well-equipped expeditions of experienced and scientific explorers had found it difficult to penetrate. Boilers and machinery were dragged through the silence and desolation of the bush to far outlying mines, which in some cases have been left once again to desolation and silence. For before long the boom subsided. The excitement of the market had passed. That strange community of the prospectors of Australasia, the best gold-finders of the world, whose coming to any country is always followed by discoveries which without them might have remained for ever overlooked, and who had reserved, as it were, this greatest of antipodean "rushes" for their most striking and perhaps for their final manifestation, scattered themselves to the four quarters of the earth. They may be found at Klondyke, in New Guinea, in Siam, in China, or in South Africa; but they have left the Western Australian goldfields, as yet only half exploited; and without them new discoveries will be made but slowly. They have left behind them, however, a large population of wages-men and others on the fields, who are steadily developing the mines for the European capitalist. Coolgardie, which is situated about 240 miles east of Perth, has had to give place to Kalgoorlie, its neighbour 25 miles to the east again, as a gold producer and the principal centre of the goldfields. The fame of the large telluride lodes of the Boulder group has spread to London and Paris, and the immigration of thousands of new citizens (chiefly from the sister colonies) to the goldfields has been followed by the investment of millions of European capital in the purchase of mining shares.

I do not propose to write a history of gold mining in Western Australia, but will in preference devote some attention to the results up to the present. There can be no doubt that many of the mines which were floated as companies were utterly worthless. This always happens in Australian mining, and is in some measure due to the fact that all mining is of necessity an uncertain and peculiar business. A scientific prospector, with all the learning of the geological schools at his finger ends, may err widely, whilst an ignoramus blunders on to a rich lead or a highly payable reef. No man can see beyond the end of his nose. "Where it is, there it is," runs a Cornish mining proverb. Position, too, is often worth gambling upon, though it is as often misleading. Whenever a really good mine is found, there are sure to be scores of

WESTERN AUSTRALIA 9

others floated in its vicinity. Alluring prospectuses are drawn up, and neat plans are published, showing on paper that the reef runs directly through the property offered to the public. The Great Boulder line was caricatured, in the *Sydney Bulletin*, as an octopus. An amusing story is current in Western Australia, which shows what the residents there thought of the way in which the British public were, in their opinion, "got at" by the mining company promoter and his London confederates. A very rich patch or "blow" of quartz was found by a prospector near the surface. Off went a promoter who had obtained a share to London to float a company, taking the quartz with him, which was thickly studded with gold. The shares were eagerly subscribed for, and a board of directors appointed, which sent out orders to work the mine at once, and get out a crushing. Months elapsed, and there was no return from the rich property; and then a peremptory telegram was despatched: "Crush at once and wire result; surprised at unexplained delay." This elicited a prompt response at once as follows: "Cannot crush till you send back the reef." The only quartz which the mine yielded was that which had been taken to London to float the company.

The story is a parable: but it must be remembered, in fairness to the colonial vendor, that "wild-cat" properties are usually handled and floated in the City by shady professional promoters, who for the most part are looking for wild-cats, and whose misdeeds are not to be visited on the colony. And, moreover, the ignorance, or impatience, of London Boards of Directors who do not know the difference between a developed mine and a prospecting shew; who sometimes, apparently, suppose themselves to be buying the one at the price of the other; and who often allow their English consulting engineers, quite unacquainted, perhaps, with the nature of the ore to be crushed, to saddle them with expensive mining-plants before the reef is opened up, is likely to be at least as ruinous to the prospector, who has parted with his lease, possibly, for valueless shares, as to the London investor who is loudest in his abuse. The only safety, for all parties concerned, lies in the combination of a Board which knows something of business with efficient local supervision. Mining, altogether, is an extraordinary industry. But almost more extraordinary than the ignorance of London Boards, and the recklessness of British investors, is the haphazard way in which engineers and managers are selected. And one's ordinary calculations as to human motives and conduct are sometimes quite upset by the unscrupulous calm with which an incapable, inexperienced, careless, drunken, or dishonest manager will sacrifice the hundreds of thousands (may-be) of his company's capital to his own petty advantage, or to secure another quarter's payment, perhaps, of his salary of £500 a year. It is far easier, and often more immediately profitable, to mutilate than to make a mine. On the other hand, it is not, perhaps, so generally understood as it might be, that under the conditions of mining in Western Australia, £30,000 for developing, or £50,000 for equipping, a mine, is by no means too large an allowance of working capital.

But, if there have been many failures in mining ventures in Western Australia, there have also been extraordinary successes. During my stay in Australia a company was wound-up by voluntary liquidation; or, to speak more accurately, the winding-up was completed, for the assets were so huge that it had taken more than a year to conduct the operation. Its history reads like a version of the "Arabian Nights Entertainments," and is a justification of the sanguine hopes that the deserts of West

WESTERN AUSTRALIA 11

Australia would turn out an El Dorado. The original capital was only £150, subscribed by a syndicate of ten speculators in Adelaide, the capital city of the colony of South Australia, who each risked the price of a second-hand bicycle to send a prospecting party to Coolgardie, in June 1893. A little more than four years afterwards, when the liquidation commenced, the assets consisted of 25,000 Associated shares, 10,000 Lake View Extended, 100 Lake View South, 200 Royal Mint shares, and £1513 in cash, and there were no liabilities. The value of its holdings were a couple of months since :—In the Great Boulder, £1,662,500 ; Lake View Consols, £2,812,500 ; Associated Mines, £2,475,000 ; Ivanhoe, £1,875,000 ; Kalgoorlie Mint, £100,000 ; Lake View South, £220,000 ; Lake View Extended, £65,750 ; Great Boulder, No. 1, £65,000—total £9,275,750. There have also been distributed to the shareholders £3,421,000 in shares and £950,000 in dividends, making a gross return of £13,646,750. That these are not mere paper values—such fairy coinage as that which makes millionaires in a month in what is known as a land boom and, before it can be realised, turns into insolvency schedules— is shown by the fact that the above mines have already produced 17 tons of gold, to the value of £2,250,000 sterling. The process by which one man's investment of £15 is in five years turned into £1,364,675 has, as I have said, its other side, and many wasted millions are to be placed to the debit of the account. But the thousands who lose their small stake can generally afford to do so, or, at any rate, suffer so little that they prefer holding their tongues to admitting that they have been the dupes of a glowing prospectus and the victims of a glib promoter. So the game goes merrily along, and there is always money forthcoming for the schemes that can point to such results as those given above, and tickle the public ear with the suggestion that there is a chance —if it be only a five million to one chance—that a new investment may in like manner multiply twenty-thousand-fold annually. It is rather a grim comment upon the fate of the pioneer miner that the chairman of this syndicate, at the meeting which adopted the final report, in accepting a vote of thanks, moved to express gratitude to the discoverer of this enormous wealth. He would forward the motion, he said, by letter; "as he understood that Mr Pearce, the original prospector, was now at Klondike trying his luck." This Pearce it was who "pegged out" the Great Boulder, the Lake View, and the Ivanhoe; and thus founded the present Boulder City. Paddy Hannan, who found the alluvial at Kalgoorlie, was lately rescued from indigence by the mayor of the town which once bore his name, who secured two allotments for him as a sort of endowment. And Bayley, who started Coolgardie, is dead. But the average man is blind to the reverse of the picture, and, tempted by such glittering bait as that contained in the above statement of accounts, will risk health, life, and savings on the chance of drawing a dazzling prize.

The output of gold from Western Australia has been disappointing to many eager investors; but this is accounted for to some extent by the very difficult nature of the country, especially in respect to water supply, and it has taken a long time to manufacture and erect the adequate machinery for extracting and treating the ore. But for the year 1898 the returns have shown a remarkable increase. The output of gold for October in Western Australia was 116,824 ounces, value £444,000. This, compared with the largest previous monthly output, 93,395 ounces, showed an increase of 23,429 ounces.

WESTERN AUSTRALIA 13

The export of gold from Western Australia for the last ten months of 1898, the latest date at which the figures were available, when I left the colony, amounted to 841,625 ounces. The importance of that statement will be made apparent when I say that for the whole year of 1896 the total output was only 281,265 ounces. Therefore, in two years they have increased the output no less than 560,300 ounces. It was estimated by the Premier of the colony, Sir John Forrest, that the output for the whole year of 1898 would exceed one million ounces.[1] Sir Gerard Smith, the Governor, went further than that, and said that the output for the year 1899 would reach one and a half million ounces of gold. Should Sir Gerard Smith's estimate be realised, and I do not think there is any reason to suspect that it is an extravagant one, then the value of gold produced next year will be close upon £6,000,000.[2]

Kalgoorlie gold is particularly pure, and has more than once fetched £4, 4s. 4d. per ounce. Speaking roughly, the annual dividend forthcoming from Western Australian mines may now, perhaps, be computed at about one and a half millions sterling, or rather over £1 to the ounce of reef gold recorded; a figure which should be much exceeded in the future, but which, as it stands, is a very handsome return on the amount of British capital actually expended in the colony. The amount absorbed in the way of margin or commission by London promoters and the like is quite another story. But of the nominal capital of

[1] I have since ascertained that the output for the whole of 1898 was one million and fifty thousand ounces, valued at close on £4,000,000 sterling. But see Appendix I.

[2] The official returns for January—June 1899 give 692,875 ounces: value, £2,632,927 (compare £1,788,636 for corresponding period of last year). August returns give 145,000 ounces, or £552,000; the second largest monthly export on record.

twenty millions, not all was paid up, and comparatively little reached Western Australia.

The greater part of the area of Western Australia is dry, sandy, desert country, which would seem to be the natural home of sandal-wood and quandongs, and where most of the gum-trees are " piped." And yet so vast are the resources of the colony that there is an area of forest country in its south-western portion which is equal in size to the whole of Great Britain, and which contains a mass of marketable timber which is, perhaps, only equalled in the famous red-wood districts of North California. The classic description of Australian forest scenery was written by Marcus Clarke, the author of the most widely-read Australian novel, " For the Term of His Natural Life." He says: " The dominant note of Australian scenery is a weird melancholy. The Australian mountain forests are funereal, secret, stern ; their solitude is desolation. They seem to stifle in their black gorges a story of sullen despair. No tender sentiment is nourished in their shade. In other lands the dying year is mourned. The dying leaves drop lightly on his bier. In the Australian forests no leaves fall. From the melancholy gums strips of white bark hang and rustle." Perhaps, as is averred by later writers, this description partakes too much of the gloom of the writer's own imaginings, but the traveller is not likely to dispute the truth of what has been so poetically expressed. The forests of Australia are, to a large extent, wanting in the umbrageous wealth which is the glory of the sylvan recesses of other lands. The trees, those, that is, which have a value for timber, run up in narrow tapering stems to a height of from 70 feet to 100 feet without a limb ; and then there is a small head, with thin, long leaves widely scattered, and affording little shade. But many of these forest giants are impressive from their very size. The giant tree of Western Australia is the Karri. The bark is smooth, yellow-white in appearance, and peels off every year, giving the stem a clean appearance. On an average these trees grow to 200 feet in height, 4 feet in diameter, 3 feet to 4 feet from the ground, and about 120 feet to 150 feet to the first branch.

Trees of the size indicated are what one usually meets with in the Karri forests, but much larger specimens are, of course, run against now and again. For instance, on the Warren River, it is not unusual to meet with trees which go 300 feet in extreme height, over 180 feet in height to the first limb, and from 20 feet to 30 feet in circumference at the base. It is certainly a matter of local record that some years ago a resident on the Warren River lived and partially raised a small family in the hollow of one of these fallen monarchs. It appears that the tree was hollow and fell, and was afterwards further worked out and lined by the enterprising settler as a dwelling for his family, until such time as he was in a position to build the modern edifice which now stands not far from the site or remains of the primitive habitation. The old tree was destroyed and effaced from the place by a recent bush fire. This specimen was said to be over 300 feet in length, and some 12 feet in diameter at the base. Whilst on this subject, I may mention that the tallest trees in Australia, and, as it is stated, in the world, grow in the colony of Victoria. There were local traditions of the existence of trees in Gippsland 500 feet high, which would have quite eclipsed the giant *Wellingtonias* of the Yosemite ; but these were based on mere guesses. Officers of the Survey Department made a search some years ago, and careful measurements of the tallest trees to be found, and the greatest height of a living tree was found to be 330 feet. A prostrate tree nearly 350 feet in length was discovered. The Jarrah tree of Western Australia, which is by far the most valuable for commercial purposes, and of which immense forests exist, is not nearly so picturesque in appearance as the Karri. The trees are rugged in appearance, and the general effect, taken in mass, is sombre. In the best forests the trees run from 50 feet to 60 feet in height to the first branch. There is a large and growing export of this timber to Europe, and the industry promises to be one of the most successful that has been established.

At Jarrahdale, which is about thirty miles from Perth, on the South-Western Railway, one company has five sawmills working night and day to execute the orders from England and elsewhere. Recent flotations of these Jarrah and Karri companies have been to some extent over-capitalised. But amalgamation and other measures are in a fair way to put this matter right; and it certainly seems to be the case that the chief difficulty in connection with the trade is to secure enough vessels to ship the timber in. Jarrah is unrivalled for piles, etc., in water or wet ground, and for wood paving. The French, for some reason best known to themselves, prefer karri for this latter purpose, but it is not highly esteemed in Western Australia, and on the deck of Port Melbourne pier, which is partly laid with it, it did not seem to me to have worn well. Jarrah resists the attacks of white ants, for which reason it is much used, especially in the goldfields country, for railway sleepers.

With the inrush of population caused by the gold discoveries agriculture has advanced rapidly. The mines have been developed principally by new arrivals from the other colonies and from Europe, but the local population has reaped a harvest in the increased demand for vegetable

WESTERN AUSTRALIA 17

and cereal products. Fruit-growing has been undertaken on a considerable scale, and with every prospect of success. The pearl fishing industry in the north is an important source of employment. This great colony stretches from temperate to tropical latitudes. It was in the north of Western Australia that Grien, otherwise " De Rougemont," laid the scene of his romantic adventures. I can vouch for it that no credence was given in the colonies to his stories ; and as the cable messages came from London announcing one marvellous fabrication after another the whole continent laughed in derision. As soon as the man's portrait was published he was recognised at once.

It was only in 1890 that constitutional government was granted to Western Australia. The history of the colony before 1890 has yet to be written, and will indeed, recent as most of it is, take some writing. From the mutinies, wrecks and maroonings of the early Dutch navigators on the Abrolhos and the like, to the rescue of Fenian prisoners from Fremantle by the American ship *Catalpa* in 1876, and even to the doings of the late Mr Deeming at Southern Cross, it is full of startling episodes, though they are mostly tinged with that sordidness which is somehow a characteristic of Australia—the Whitechapel of the colonies. Originally considered a dependency of the Dutch East India Company, and, like New Zealand, nearly annexed by the French in the early decades of this century, the colony was planted, at the instance of Captain Stirling of New South Wales, and Mr Peel, an adventurous capitalist related to the statesman, in 1829. The plan of their syndicate was to settle 10,000 emigrants in the country, who were to grow beef and pork for the Royal Navy, horses for the Honourable East India Company, and cotton and tobacco for the world at large, each on his two hundred acres of land. In return the

B

syndicate was to have a proportionate grant of two million acres for itself. The plan miscarried; the colony languished; even to this day bacon, beef and horses are imported, and cotton and tobacco are unknown crops; and in 1840 a fresh start was attempted, in strict conformity this time with the principles of the unspeakable Wakefield. The failure of the settlement of Australind, settled on his kid-glove-colony system, is an even better proof than the Adelaide fiasco of the folly of transplanting ready-made polities, and of believing that supply will find its own demand. It is an example, also, of how London Boards of Directors can wreck their colonial properties by listening to irresponsible advisers who have "been there." In 1849 the despairing colonists fell back, for twenty years or so, on convict labour; and when, in 1870, Responsible Government, of a sort, was granted, Lord Carnarvon demurred to making it Representative, on the ground that, of 8000 adult males in the settlement, 5000 or 6000 had been transported. However, from this time the colony began to progress. Throughout the 'seventies, the Forrests and others were adding vast stretches of back country to its available assets. The picturesque figure of Sir John Forrest will be well remembered in this country, where he was a distinguished visitor on the occasion of the Queen's Jubilee. Sir John is a man of simple and straightforward speech, of fine physique, and of great courage. He first became known throughout Australia as a daring explorer of the great central unknown land, when, in 1870, he and his brother, Mr Alexander Forrest, journeyed from Perth to Adelaide, occupying about eight months in the expedition, travelling through a great deal of unexplored territory, and examining the whole country between Esperance Bay and the South Australian border. The party was accompanied by two aboriginals, one

WESTERN AUSTRALIA 19

of whom claimed, on his return, that he, and not his white leader, should have been the central figure of the public reception at Adelaide. " Me take 'em through," he said. However, Sir John was rewarded by the Government with £75, and "Billy" had to rest content with a mere £12, 10s. 0d.

Four years afterwards, the explorer led another, and a remarkably successful, expedition into the central parts of the colony, penetrating that immense tract of country from which flow the Murchison, Gascoyne, Ashburton, De Grey, Fitzroy, and other rivers falling into the sea on the western and northern shores of the continent. He had the disadvantage of travelling with horses instead of camels ; but he persevered, in spite of immense difficulties, in a waterless country. He discovered a large area of rich grazing lands, and gave a full and most valuable report of the country traversed. The hardships and dangers still to be encountered in this work of interior exploration are shown by the fact that two years ago one branch of an expedition, which made a diversion from the main body, perished in the desert ; and it was only after months of search that the bodies were found.

Sir John Forrest was the first Premier of the colony, and he still holds the position, though, for various reasons, every one of his colleagues has been changed. He has been most energetic in pushing forward railways into the interior of the country, so as to serve the goldfields ; Menzies, as we have seen, having been reached last year, and great extensions, to Leonora on the north, and to Norseman on the south, being on the Government programme for this session. One of the prime necessities of the goldfields is an efficient water supply. When this is provided, hundreds of mines that are now idle, owing to the ores being of too low a grade to pay the heavy expenses of treatment, will prove to be able to work at an excellent profit. A great scheme, for which an expenditure of £2,500,000 has been authorised, has been devised by the engineer-in-chief, Mr O'Connor, and approved by other engineers of high standing. This scheme includes the construction of a reservoir to impound the waters of the Helena River; and its pumping to a height in the Coolgardie district, and distribution thence by gravitation. The preliminary works are being carried out; but, as faults have been found in the strata where the reservoir has been started, and as it is no easy matter, even with the aid of the most powerful pumps, to make twenty-five million gallons of water daily flow uphill for several hundred miles, more than two and a half millions sterling will, probably, be required in the end.

In the period, then, of less than nine years since Representative Government—a period the latter part of which has seen the rise of the population from forty to one hundred and seventy thousand, more than half of the manhood of which is settled in the desert of the lately unknown interior, where great mining plants, telephones, electric lights, and palace hotels have replaced the mia-mias of a few wandering blacks; and which has seen the expansion of the revenue from £400,000 to nearly £3,000,000 (£2,478,000 for the present financial year; being £275,935 *less* than in the preceding year), and of trade from £2,000,000 to over £10,000,000; the energies of the Government have been chiefly occupied in pressing matters of administration, in providing for the necessities of the new-comers, for means of transit to their homes, and for water for their mines; in a policy of works, that is, which has been denounced by those who have benefited from it as a policy of sop. Hence Western Australia has not yet had time to devote itself to those

WESTERN AUSTRALIA 21

experiments in democratic goverment which I shall have occasion to notice in my references to the other colonies. Considerable opposition was offered in the Imperial Parliament to granting the demand of the colony for self-government, and a long agitation was required before that boon was granted. An objection, which seemed natural on the face of it, was taken to handing over, to what was practically a mere handful of people, a million square miles of territory. But territory is of little value without population to develop it; and, under the direct government of the Crown, Western Australia was making little if any advance. Wisely, the power of self-goverment was granted. Nominally, the executive power is vested in the Governor, who acts upon the advice of a Cabinet composed of six responsible Ministers. The constitutional rule, throughout Australia, as in England, is that the Crown does not act without the advice of the Cabinet; and it does not change the Cabinet unless the representatives of the people express a want of confidence in it.

Sir Gerard Smith, K.C.M.G., the present Governor, was appointed in 1895, and has proved himself to be a fairly popular representative of her Majesty. He is a courteous and kindly gentleman; and a pleasantly fluent speaker. The social duties of an Australian Governor are most arduous and exacting; though not, in ordinary times, obviously important. He is expected to preside at all functions, and to visit nearly all the provincial towns on the occasions of the holding of annual agricultural shows or races; which things involve a great deal of travelling, and a great deal of public speaking. When Lord Hopetoun was Governor of Victoria, he complained that the one crumpled rose leaf of his life in that colony was the fact that he was expected, on all occasions, to "turn on the tap," meaning the oratorical tap. Sir Gerard Smith performs this part of his functions very agreeably and acceptably ; and if he has had to learn that it is not within the scope of his commission (as he supposed before he went out), to attend to the drainage of Coolgardie, he is probably, on consideration, all the better pleased. At the same time, it was fortunate for the colony, and particularly fortunate for its Premier, who had his trade to pick up, that the difficult period of transition, after self-government was granted, fell under the administration of the late Sir William Robinson, who was possibly the best and certainly the most able of our old school of colonial Governors.

Western Australia, despite its rapid growth, is suffering, locally, from a severe depression, the reaction from the recent boom. From a variety of other circumstances, it is scarcely the place at present for the new settler. It only remains, therefore, to repeat that the output of gold has increased from 207,000 ounces, or less than £800,000, in 1894, to 1,050,183 ounces, or £3,990,697, in 1898 ; and £2,632,927 for the first six months of 1899 ; that most of the dividends come to England (wherefore the colonists will probably try in the future, like Victoria and Queensland, to keep their good things to themselves); and to add that, if some mines have been mutilated or mismanaged, that is perhaps largely because, while in Queensland, New South Wales, Victoria, and South Australia, the consumption *per* head *per annum* of liquor is the equivalent, in proof alcohol, of just about 2 gallons, and in Tasmania of 1½, in Western Australia it amounts to over 3.

It seems unlikely, on the whole, that this colony, whose history is entirely different from that of the other side of Australia, and whose population and economic conditions are so different, will join the Federal Commonwealth at once, or without holding out at least for some pledge in regard to the completion of the Trans-Continental Railway. It is

WESTERN AUSTRALIA 23

the object of the great harbour works at Fremantle, and the settled desire of Sir John Forrest, his Ministers, and everyone interested in Perth, to make Fremantle the first and last port of call for the European mail steamers. The construction of this railway would be a reversion to the earlier policy of the colony, expressed by a Select Committee of the Western Australian Parliament in 1884, and revived by Dr Boyd in 1886; from which the construction of Anthony Hordern's Albany line was a departure. It is not likely to be attained for a long time under the Commonwealth, unless a distinct arrangement is made before federation is concluded, as Adelaide would probably object; and by the proposed constitution her objection would be fatal. Again, it is the desire of the Minister of Agriculture and the older settlers not to take any definite step till the local agriculturists have tightened their hold on the local market, which would mean a delay of four or five years. Sir John Forrest, on the other hand, is pledged to refer the question to the people; and though it appears that every effort will be made, even by enfranchising the women of the coastal districts for the occasion, to counterbalance the preponderant adult male vote of the goldfields, yet it seems possible that in a Referendum the voice of the Outlanders, who cannot be expected as yet to be over-jealous of the special advancement of this colony in particular, will carry the day. But I will recur to this question in a subsequent chapter. The draft Commonwealth Bill has been submitted to the criticism of a Select Committee of the local Parliament, and will go to the people with the Committee's amendments, if at all. In Western Australia, alone of the Australian colonies, politicians are unpaid. They are therefore unusually independent of their constituents. And the Government as a whole, in spite of Sir John Forrest's pledges, is clearly hostile to Federation,

Chapter II

SOUTH AUSTRALIA

LEAVING Albany by the mail steamer, three days are occupied in crossing that portion of the Southern Ocean which is known as the Great Australian Bight; three days, usually, of bright sun, leaping porpoises, and stiff breezes. The Leeuwin, just behind us, is known to old travellers as one of the most unpleasant corners in the world. The landing in South Australia is effected at Largs Bay, whence a run of half an hour by rail brings one to Adelaide, the capital city of the colony, known sometimes as the city of churches. I may say at once that the name South Australia is not at all an appropriate one, for the colony does not occupy the southernmost portion of the continent, and its territory stretches right away to the Gulf of Carpentaria on the north. This nomenclature is very misleading to residents in Great Britain, and the most ludicrous mistakes are made in the addresses of letters intended for the various colonies. Thus, letters come to Australia addressed, " Melbourne, Victoria, near Sydney, South Australia," which is just about as correct as would be the address, " London, England, near Paris, Ireland."

The frontage, so to speak, of Adelaide to the sea is distinctly sandy and torrid; and would be even more desolate in appearance, if that were possible, than the coasts of Western Australia. But the city proper is situated on the Torrens River, about seven miles inland,

It is in the midst of a broad fertile plain, from which a few miles northward a range of hills rises abruptly; these are ascended by the intercolonial railway. The population of the city proper is about 40,000, and including the suburbs within a ten mile radius it amounts to 130,000. The colony was founded on the lines of an ideal polity, the invention, as usual, of Mr Wakefield: and was subsequently reconstructed by circumstances. The capital was laid out in the year 1837, and named Adelaide by the special request of King William the Fourth, after his consort. It is built nearly in the form of a square, and by the foresight of its surveyor was almost surrounded by what are termed "park lands" half a mile in width. There are also five fine squares for ornamental purposes. The river Torrens, originally a dingy stream, divides the city into North and South Adelaide, which are connected by five massive iron bridges. An embankment across the stream has turned it for a mile or two into a beautiful sheet of water. The cleanliness of the city is a very pleasing feature. This effect is heightened by the fact that a light-coloured stone, of excellent quality for road-making, is found in abundance in the neighbouring hills. In hot weather the white appearance of the streets is perhaps somewhat trying to the eyes, but it strikes the stranger very agreeably. There is also a perfect system of underground sewage. The streets are straight and broad, and run at right angles to each other. King William Street is two chains in width; and in it the principal buildings are situated, such as the Town Hall and the Post and Telegraph Offices. On North Terrace, which overlooks the river, the Parliament Houses are situated. The façade is of white marble, quarried at Kapunda, in the colony. Here also is situated the Adelaide University and the Exhibition building; the latter, a fine structure, erected at a cost of £50,000, to commemorate the jubilee of the colony in 1887. In the building there is now an interesting museum, and a spacious, well-lighted art gallery, in which is housed a well-selected collection of valuable pictures. The residence of the Governor also fronts North Terrace, and stands in spacious grounds. The beautiful Botanic and Zoological Gardens are close to the city. To this charming retreat I was attracted early, and frequently returned. The area is about 130 acres; and it has been very tastefully laid out, local and tropical plants being grown in profusion. It is a very popular resort for the inhabitants, and I need not say is highly appreciated in summer. For nine months in the year the climate of Adelaide is very pleasant, but in summer there is no blinking the fact that it is decidedly hot. The temperature ranges up to 110 degrees in the shade, and on rare occasions runs several degrees higher. The air is, however, very dry, so that this great heat is not oppressive as might be expected. There is an excellent and abundant water supply, obtained from the Mount Lofty ranges before mentioned. These latter also form an agreeable summer retreat, and many of the well-to-do citizens have residences there.

Passing to political topics, the traveller finds in South Australia one of the most democratic constitutions in the world. The colony boasts that it leads the way in Australia in radical legislation, and runs a dead heat, in most matters, with New Zealand itself. The boast is probably justified. Politics, at all events, with church-going, seem to be the principal recreation of the Adelaide man, as gambling in Kalgoorlie mining shares is his business. There are two Houses of Parliament, known respectively as the Legislative Council and the Legislative Assembly. For the latter, which is the popular chamber,

SOUTH AUSTRALIA

no property qualification whatever is required of either candidates or electors. The qualifications of a member of the Council are that he must be thirty years of age, and a natural-born or naturalised subject of the Queen, and that he must have been a resident of the district which he represents at least three years. Electors must have a freehold of £50 value, or a leasehold of £20 annual value. The Council has not the weight nor influence of the unpaid Upper House of Western Australia, nor of that of Victoria.

For the Assembly no man has more than one vote, and every man twenty-one years of age who has been for six months on the roll is allowed the privilege. Three years ago the franchise was granted to women, and they now stand on exactly the same footing as men with regard to voting for members of either House. Not overlooking the fact that with regard to the exercise of political functions married women are at times placed under a disability, the Act with great and tender foresight provided another method of recording the votes of those who are from physical causes unable to go to the poll. The high hopes entertained by some as to the purifying effect upon politics of the women's vote, and the fears entertained by others as to evils attendant on its exercise, have in neither case been realised. Women have voted at one election, and the result was that no change at all could be attributed to the effect of their vote. They went to the poll in large numbers, attracted no doubt by the novelty of the privilege, but the result was such as would have been anticipated had men alone voted.

The members, in Adelaide as in the neighbouring colonies, do a great deal of talking for their £300, or thereabouts, a year; though there has not been, so far, fortunately, very much for them to talk about. However, each community has made courageous efforts to tackle the social problem, and many useful lessons may be picked up by the globe-trotting politician.

The Australian colonies are in the future sure to become more and more the scene of experimental legislation. Their government has practically been handed over to the labouring classes and small shopkeepers, who form the mass of the community. What is called the Radical section are almost everywhere in a majority. One colony is not prepared to learn from another, nor to allow an experiment to be made elsewhere, and accept or reject it according to its results after a reasonable trial. So far, there have been practically no foreign complications to interfere with free internal evolution, or to distract attention from the purely economic struggle. Everywhere the working man has full power, and a very hearty disposition, to try all conceivable or suggested means to better himself. The fact that there are Radical laws on the statute-book of one colony is the means of raising a clamour for the adoption of similar measures elsewhere. Only an extended trial can disclose what the result of any measure will be, but whatever legislation can do for the improvement of the position of the working classes in Australia will be done. In all the colonies there is a demand for rapid extension of the functions of the State. The railways are nearly everywhere the property of the State, and it is now claimed that the mines should be. The State is expected to find work for the unemployed, and to dictate a minimum wage to all its contractors. In all the colonies there is a demand for the provision of pensions for the aged poor. In New Zealand such a system has been adopted, and in some of the other colonies legislation is promised. In South Australia, as well as in New Zealand, there is a law by which the State intervenes in labour disputes, hears evidence, and makes an award. If the award be against the employer it may be enforced, unless he chooses to surrender his business. But it cannot be enforced against the men ; for, as has been remarked, " you cannot imprison a nation."

Great attention has been given in all the colonies to the subject of education. Up to a certain age it is given free by the State ; and children, within certain age-limits, who are not privately educated, are required to be sent to the State schools by their parents under pain of increasing fines for neglect. At the last census there were, in South Australia, in round numbers, 80,000 children of school-going age—five to fifteen years : and of these 47,000 were attending State schools and 13,000 private schools. The system is secular, and four and a half hours a day are devoted to instruction. Before and after those hours Bible reading may be given if the parents desire it. When the education system was established it was decided that the secular principle was the complement of the compulsory one, for, as children of all sects and of no sect are compelled to attend school, it was thought that they should not be forced to receive religious instruction which would be repugnant to the beliefs of their parents. It may be mentioned here that the Roman Catholic and the Orange element is strong in all the colonies. It might have been thought that this old-world element of discord would have been left behind or forgotten, but it is not so. The Roman Catholic vote is a thing to be reckoned with in all elections, whether they be of committees of charitable institutions, of municipal councillors, or of legislators. The orange and green elements are manifested in divisions in the police force, and in dissensions in the lower ranks of the public service. It was hoped that if the children of Roman Catholic and Protestant parents could be mixed together in the same schools, a mutual feeling of respect and goodwill would grow up, and the divisions would be gradually obliterated. This hope has been largely frustrated by the opposition of the Roman Catholics to the State schools. They assert it as a principle of faith that religion and education must go together; and, except in the remote country districts, they have maintained, at great cost to themselves, separate schools. They complain bitterly of the injustice of a system by which they are compelled to pay their share as taxpayers to the support of schools they cannot take advantage of. There are constant demands on their part for a separate grant for their own schools; demands which have been, so far, in South Australia at all events, without effect, Thus one result of a system which, it was hoped, would bring Roman Catholics and Protestants nearer together has been to embitter the feeling between them. Though religious teaching is forbidden, the school books abound in lessons of a high moral character; truth, honesty, kindness, industry, manliness being enjoined on almost every page, while selections from the best poems of our language are frequent. Yet, in the net result, it may perhaps be admitted that the national character, as the native-born generations, educated on this system, grow up, is showing signs of a leaning towards the purely materialistic. The Roman Catholics reap the reward of their devotion, not in politics nor billet-hunting alone. Protestantism, indeed, seems rather moribund as a religious force in Australia; has in many ways almost become a mere convention of respectability. And the Australian face, which is generally fairly typified amongst the semi-professional cricketers who visit England, is perhaps more intelligent than cultivated; as, indeed, is natural in a community where everything tends to be levelled to a conformity to the ideals of what, in England would be the lower middle-class.

SOUTH AUSTRALIA 31

The Right Honourable C. C. Kingston is the Premier of the Colony, and has occupied that position for nearly five years. He is a barrister by profession, and has long been a leading man in South Australian politics. He is a man of powerful physique, and is considered a forcible debater. His style is very incisive, and at times his attacks upon his opponents are so severe that he has become involved in many bitter personal quarrels. He is a Radical of a somewhat extreme type in politics, and has hitherto managed to keep the support of that section in Parliament which directly represents the labour interests. I also met Mr F. W. Holder, the treasurer, who is a gentleman of striking personality. He possesses very wide information, and very considerable powers of expression. An ardent and powerful supporter of federation, he has a great belief in the future of Australia, and has the power of kindling in others his own enthusiasm. Mr Symon, Q.C., who is not a member of Parliament, but was elected a member of the recent Federal Convention, is one of the leading figures in the intellectual life of the Colony. He is a man who would make a mark anywhere in his profession; and, though unaccustomed to parliamentary forms, he stepped at once into a leading position in the deliberations of the Convention. His Excellency, Lord Tennyson, the son of the poet, is Governor and Commander-in-Chief of the Colony, having lately succeeded Sir Thomas Fowell Buxton. I may mention that the appointment of Governor carries also that of Commander-in-Chief of the forces. But the position is practically a nominal one. The Governor does not directly interfere in the management of the forces. In this matter, as in all others relating to the internal affairs of the Colony, he acts solely upon the advice of his Ministers for the time being. The Governor was absent during my visit; and Chief Justice Way was acting as Lieutenant-Governor. It is a position he has often held before: and it is said that if, under the Federal Commonwealth, the provincial governors are chosen from amongst Australian notables (a change which would, in my opinion, be, for many reasons, highly inadvisable), the Right Hon. Sir S. J. Way, with Sir John Forrest in West Australia, and Chief Justice Maddon in Victoria, will be about the first to be offered the position. Which is perhaps the reason why a clause has been inserted in the constitution specially incapacitating judges from holding it.

Of course Adelaide is not South Australia, and one who has a desire to become acquainted with the resources and the people of the colony must not confine himself to its metropolis.

When the colony was established in 1836 it comprised only about one-third of its present territory, viz., the portion lying between the Southern Ocean and the 26th degree of south latitude. But in 1863, the Government of the colony having undertaken to found a new habitation in the northern territory, all that portion of the colony lying due north of the original grant was added to the area, which now comprises upwards of 900,000 square miles. The Northern Territory has never been self-supporting: and in recent times has been rather a hunting-ground for European concessionaires, who looked forward to developing it, if at all, with coloured labour. This process will probably be put a stop to under the Commonwealth. The Australian working-man would rather that his tropical possessions stayed empty for ever, than that they should support an Asiatic population. The original settlement in the South, as has been said, was established on principles eloquently expounded by Mr Edward Gibbon

Wakefield, who was esteemed a high authority in such matters. His main idea was to allow Crown lands to be sold only in limited quantities, and to the favoured few. The mass of the population was to be kept strictly in the employ of the members of this artificial landed class, who, by settlement and high farming, were to be able (how, and by close recourse to what market, Mr Wakefield never troubled to explain) not only to pay good wages, but to keep themselves in civilised comforts. Nothing was so foreign to the ideas of this philosopher as to allow every man who landed in an unpeopled, untamed, and almost unlimited waste to make the best he could of its vast, though attenuated, resources. This, however, is precisely what the new settlers at once attempted, though they set about it in the least practical of ways, by trying, in effect, to make a living by taking in each other's washing. Neglecting to cultivate the soil, about the first thing they did was to start what is known by a term which is, like the thing itself, of American origin ; namely a land boom. Here, said the colonists to themselves, is an enormous territory. We, the fortunate first-comers, have got possession of sites which must become extremely valuable when the colony becomes populated, which will speedily happen. So they set to work trafficking in allotments of land, which went up to fancy prices. Large fortunes were made, on paper ; and all went swimmingly, until before long these wealthy owners of desirable building-sites found themselves on the brink of starvation. No one was producing anything. Had it not been for the timely arrival of a shipload of stores, the enterprise would have ended in a terrible disaster. But the danger brought the people to their senses, and they set to work in earnest. South Australia is now a great agricultural community, where it pays to harvest a crop of wheat of no more than

c

five bushels to the acre; but where the average production is considerably more than that, for the colony comprises a very large area of splendid wheat-growing land. The cheap system of cultivation and harvesting which is carried on enables the farmer to make good profits from light crops. The land is more fertile than, and as easily tilled as, the prairies of Western America, while a cheaper system of harvesting is adopted. The peculiar dryness of the air enables the stripper, which is a combined reaping and threshing machine; to be used, while on the American prairies the grain has to be reaped, bound, stooked, carted and threshed. There is no winter such as is known in Europe; but May to September are practically the spring, and October, November and December the summer or harvest months. The drawback to production is the deficient or uncertain rainfall. A great deal of the northern territory is sterile, uninviting desert, which will possibly never be of any service; but there are also great breadths of pastoral and agricultural land; and the tapping in recent years of vast stores of artesian water in the northern parts of Queensland and South Australia gives hopes that, in a not distant future, the periodical Australian droughts will be deprived of their terrors, for the farmers will be able to keep their cattle and sheep alive. Already in Queensland there are bores sunk which give a total flow of artesian water of upwards of 200,000,000 gallons per day, and authorities speak of the supply as being practically inexhaustible. Great rivers sink almost away in the interior plains; for instance, it is said that the Darling River carries into the Murray only one-sixteenth of the water which it receives in its course. In the discovery and use of these subterranean resources lies one of the greatest hopes for the future development of the vast central area of Australia.

There is no great chain of mountain ranges to gather the surplus moisture in the form of snow, and send it down to the parched plains just at the time it is required for irrigation and pastoral purposes. But there are vast elevated table lands, composed of porous material, which receive the semi-tropical downpour of rain that finds its way in great subterranean channels across the continent to the southern sea. And it is these stores which are now being tapped with so much advantage.

All the colonies have passed through a most disastrous period of drought during the last four years, and consequently the pastoral and agricultural interests have suffered severely. About one and a half million acres are put under wheat every year in South Australia; and in ordinary seasons a yield of eight to ten bushels per acre may be anticipated. This, of course, returns a handsome profit to the farmer; but during recent years, for the reason stated, the average yield has sunk below the remunerative point, viz., to a little over four bushels to the acre. The wheat, on account of the heat and dryness of the climate, makes a very high quality of flour; and, therefore, it realises the best price in the world's markets, fetching in the London market, like the Victorian article, considerably more than English, Indian, American, or New Zealand produce.

The soil and climate are exceedingly well suited for the growth of the vine, the fig, and the olive. The wine industry has already attained considerable proportions. The soil is nearly everywhere a rich red alluvium, overlying limestone, and upon this latter the vine flourishes luxuriantly. There are about 18,000 acres of vines in full bearing, mostly in the warmer districts, which produce a rich full-bodied wine. But in the cooler portions of the colony, towards the south, and in some of the hilly districts, the more delicate clarets and hocks are produced. If a thoroughly profitable export trade can be established, there will be an almost illimitable field for its development, for almost all over the colony vines grow freely. Already these wines are becoming known in the English market, about 300,000 gallons being exported annually. The orange also grows well; and within a few miles of the city luxuriant groves may be reached, where the rich yellow fruit is seen shining in abundance through the dark glossy leaves. Olive oil of good quality is manufactured, and the dull sage-green foliage is to be seen on every hand, for the tree is largely cultivated. Once started, it seems to grow without further trouble. Of course, the local demand is limited; and up to the present the oil has not been manufactured to such an extent as to enable it to compete outside the colony with the product of the south of Europe, or rather with that cotton-seed oil which is commonly sold as Italian to the undiscriminating Briton. What can be done with olive oil in Australia has been shown in the neighbouring colony, at Perth, where the Roman Catholic Bishop lately sold and shipped a limited quantity, for flavouring purposes, to Italy itself; a method of sending "coals to Newcastle" which is not without its parallel elsewhere in Australia, as we shall presently see. But, in industries such as these, cheap labour is the great essential: and it is a satisfactory thing, after all, that labour cannot be obtained at the same rate here as in European countries.

The mineral wealth of South Australia is not so important a factor in the community's wealth as in some of the other colonies; but in the early days some of the richest copper mines of the world were discovered and worked here. The famous Burra Burra mine yielded

10,000 tons of pure copper in three years, and even better results were obtained from the Wallaroo and Moonta mines. For some time, the price of copper having fallen, the industry was practically non-existent, but the recent sharp revival has brought about a very different state of things. The two last-named properties are again working to a profit, and many old mines have been revived, and new ones opened in the Far North. Smelting is carried on very economically and profitably near the coast: and large quantities of refractory gold ores from Kalgoorlie have been sent here in preference to Cardiff, though, once on shipboard, their additional freight to Wales would have been of small moment.

There is a public debt of £23,000,000, which is at the rate of £62 per head of the population, and the annual interest-charge is £940,000. About £12,000,000 has been expended in railways and tramways, and there has also been large expenditure in harbour improvements and other public works. The colony bears its heavy burden manfully. There lies before it the hope of a steady and prosperous future; for, with its enormous areas of rich soil, it may expect to support a very large population in comfort, if not in affluence. The present population is about 320,000, but there would be no difficulty in feeding ten times as many in this fertile land. Yet there is no prospect, at present, of assisted immigration. This is a "means of betterment" which fails to appeal just now to the mind of the South Australian working-man. He sees in it, indeed, chiefly a means of increasing competition in his labour market. And upon the whole, the young adventurer, the capitalist, and the farmer who insists on changing his sky, will perhaps be wise if they give South Australia the go-by; not because it is not a possible, though democratic, paradise, but because they can do better elsewhere.

The trade of South Australia, in common with that of the rest of the colonies, is now showing strong signs of recovery. During 1897-98 imports decreased in comparison with the previous year to the extent of £935,000, and exports by £791,000, giving a total shrinkage of trade of £1,736,000. During the last twelve months imports have increased by £28,000 and exports by £684,000, an advance, in all, of £712,000.

CHAPTER III

VICTORIA

THE journey from Adelaide to Melbourne, the capital city of the Colony of Victoria, or the Cabbage Garden, as I heard a candid, but, I fear, jealous, Sydney man name it, can be made either by train or steamer; and, as time was an object to me, I chose the former method. The train leaves Adelaide about seven o'clock in the evening, and arrives in Melbourne shortly before noon the next day; the length of the journey being 483 miles, 196 of which are in South Australian territory, and the remainder in Victoria. Sleeping berths were provided, and the trip was most comfortably made. Our colonies are famous for their hospitality, and do not belie their reputation. On my arrival I was presented with a free pass over all the railways, and in many other ways during my visit I had proof of the proverb that a prophet hath least honour in his own country. These free passes, however, are taken quite as a matter of course by Colonial politicians; every sitting member in each of the provincial Parliaments wearing a gold token on his watch-chain, which entitles him to free transit not only over the Government lines of his own colony, but (by courtesy) over those of the whole continent. The privilege was considerably abused at one time, and was even extended to the wives and other connections of the members. During the first few miles of the journey the scenery is very picturesque, for the line climbs the Mount Lofty range by a circuitous route. Deep ravines are crossed on lofty iron bridges, and the shoulders of the hills are tunnelled through frequently; so that the scene is constantly changing, and one passes from an extended view of the great plain on which Adelaide is situated, with the city in the middle distance and the Southern Ocean beyond, into total darkness, to emerge a minute later and catch a passing glimpse of a long winding mountain gorge.

Sixty miles from Adelaide the river Murray is crossed. It is a slowly flowing river of about one-third of a mile in breadth, and of about 1,700 miles total length. It is navigable for steamers for the greater part of its course, considerable sums of money having been spent by the three colonies of South Australia, Victoria, and New South Wales, through the respective borders of which it flows, in "snagging"; that is to say, in clearing from its bed the huge red gum trees which have fallen into its waters. The red gum is a valuable species of eucalyptus, very tough and durable, from which the felloes of wheels are made. It is also one of the most lasting timbers known for pier building. These trees grow close to the banks of the river, and, being gradually undermined as the earth is washed from their roots, they fall in and become what is known as a "snag." The word has been given a wider meaning, and a politician, for instance, who has been baulked in some effort is said to have run against a snag. Too many snags spoil the politician. The control of the Murray River and its tributaries formed one of the great inducements to (as well as one of the difficulties in the way of) federation; the apportionment of the respective rights of New South Wales, Victoria, and South Australia to draw off water for irrigating and other purposes having given rise to bitter disputes. New South Wales is said to have threatened to cut off the stream at the head, and Victoria claimed some credit for not intercepting the whole supply before it reached Adelaide. But of these things I shall have to speak in dealing with Federation as a whole.

The principal town through which the train passes on the way to Melbourne is Ballarat, where I broke my journey ; famous in the gold-digging days, and contesting with the equally well-known Bendigo the honour of being the chief provincial centre of Victoria. It has a population of about 40,000. This place was in 1851 and the years immediately following one of the richest alluvial goldfields in Australia. It was here that the diggers took up arms to resist what they considered an unjust tax imposed upon them. The famous Eureka stockade was formed, which was carried by storm by the police and troops and forty or fifty miners were killed. The whole dispute really took its rise in the unnecessarily rough treatment meted out to the diggers by the police. All over the Anglo-Saxon world both police and wardens have learned to understand diggers better since then ; and it is probable that the Ballarat riot, if handled properly, would have been no more serious than the manifestation which occurred at Kalgoorlie some two years ago. Peter Lalor, an Irishman, the leader of the insurgents, lost an arm in the fight. A price was put on his head, but he evaded arrest, and lived to become Speaker of the Legislative Assembly. A statue of him now stands in the main street of Ballarat. Ballarat has been a great gold producer from its discovery to the present time, and has produced, from first to last, over seventy-two millions sterling in gold. Its deep leads, or buried auriferous river-beds, are examples of cheap mining; twenty of the leading properties having returned amongst them £6,000,000, and having paid two and a half millions in dividends, while making calls of only half a million. The chief mining here, however, is in quartz. So heavily impregnated with gold is the water in the deep levels of these Victorian mines that the old hands working in them have a superstition that, when exhausted, a level has only to be left unpumped for a few years to be worth working again; and some barrels of water taken from below, hermetically sealed and shipped to Paris, are recorded, when opened after a storage of some years, to have been found to have precipitated several nuggets. Ballarat, which is a most unusually clean and pleasant place for a mining town, is remarkable chiefly for its wide, tree-planted streets and for the municipal lake of Wendouree. An economical town-councillor, criticising a proposal to beautify this lake by procuring some gondolas to float on its waters, is said innocently to have proposed to " get a pair of them and trust to Nature." As the centre of a large and very flourishing agricultural and pastoral district, Ballarat is not dependent on mining alone, but has as its near neighbours the farmers of the forest of Bungaree, as well as being within an (Australian) day's drive of the famous and hospitable squatters of Colac. It was the former whom the present Mayor of one of the municipalities into which, according to Australian custom, the place is divided, immortalised, when he thundered at an excited meeting, during a Parliamentary election, as " Men of Ballarat, *and savages of Bungaree!*" And it was not so very far from here that a weary sundowner, disgustedly conscious of the failure of his most lurid adjectives to convey the full tedium of his dusty tramp from the one town to the other, started a new vogue in colonial swearing by sand-

wiching his oaths. He had walked all the (bloomin')
way, he said, from Dim - (dam) - boola to Warrackna-
(bloomin')-beal. The Botanical Gardens are decorated
with marble statuary, bequeathed to the city, for the
most part, by mining speculators. One group, the Flight
from Pompeii, by Benzoni, cost over £4000.

A journey of about sixty miles further lands one in
Melbourne, one of the two principal cities south of the
Equator. It was named after Lord Melbourne, who was
Prime Minister of England at the time it was founded,
in the year 1836. It had then only a handful of enterprising settlers, and its remarkable growth has been one
of the wonders of the century; for in fifty years it has
developed into a city of nearly half a million inhabitants,
with property of the net annual value of £15,000,000.
The latest estimate, for 1897, gives the population of
Melbourne and suburbs at 458,610 (as against Sydney's
417,250). During the boom period of a few years ago
it rose to 470,000. But the burst of the land boom
was followed by the reconstruction of the Banks: and it
will be long before rents, even near the centre of the
city, recover themselves, for the simple reason that its
suburbs are full of empty houses and shops.

One of the first things that struck me in Melbourne
was the splendid means of communication, throughout the
whole place, in its system of tramways, the best, and
the most costly, in the world; far superior to anything
we can show in England, and only paralleled by the
similar system in San Francisco. We are not likely
to see anything like it in England, in any case. For
this was an extravagant luxury of the boom times; and
both Sydney and Perth, in choosing their new tram
systems, have bowed to the demonstrated fact that
electricity, while nearly as good, is much cheaper than

the cable system to instal. The cars run through all the principal streets, communicating with the various suburbs, and they take you, apparently, anywhere for threepence. (A threepenny bit used to be the smallest coin in circulation in Melbourne.) There is a double line of rails, and I ascertained that there are now 54 miles of this double track in operation. The cars are neat structures, and are fitted with perforated wooden seats. One car is enclosed and one open; they start and stop without a jerk; they glide into almost instant motion at the highest speed compatible with safety; they are cool, and clean; and they are in every way suitable to the climate, and have proved very popular since running was commenced twelve years ago. The motive power is an underground cable, worked by large stationary engines about midway along each journey. I visited some of the engine-houses, and saw the splendid machinery, the enormous wheels round which the cable revolves, and the great engines doing their work almost silently. One objection to the cable system of cars is that if there is an accident to the machinery, or if a cable breaks, the whole of the cars on the line are stopped till the repairs are effected. When first the lines were opened, there were occasionally such stoppages, causing inconvenience to travellers, who, depending on them to reach a railway terminus to take perhaps a long journey, were disappointed. But now, I am informed, owing to the greater experience of the drivers (or "gripmen," as they are called), stoppages are unknown, and the ordinary citizen relies on his tramcar with as much confidence as, and perhaps more than, on his train. The company has in use over 90 miles of wire rope, costing about £40 per ton. The total amount expended on tramway construction was £1,600,000. The company obtained running powers over the streets from Parliament for thirty years. At the end of the lease the lines become the property of the various municipalities, without any charge, excepting that the tram stables have to be taken over at a valuation. Twelve years of the lease have now expired, so that in eighteen years this magnificent revenue-producing property will pass to the municipalities. As the income from traffic receipts amounts to over £330,000 a year, and the working expenses to less than £200,000, the wisdom of the policy which dictated these terms in favour of the municipalities will be at once apparent. The company sets apart a certain amount of its revenue for a sinking fund, so that at the end of its term its debt will be liquidated.

The streets of Melbourne are broad and straight, and hence they are well suited to the tram traffic. The main streets are 99 ft. in width, and between each two of those broad thoroughfares runs a narrow one, which bears the name of the principal street, with the prefix " little " added—as Collins Street, " Little Collins Street "; Bourke Street, " Little Bourke Street "; and the like. Until a few years ago, many of the relics of the very early days could be seen in the streets, small and dilapidated weatherboard shops holding their place in the midst of more pretentious structures. But within the last twelve years a great portion of the city has been rebuilt, and only a few of these antiquities can now be discovered. The other extreme has, indeed, been reached, for there are no by-laws of the city regulating the height of buildings, and therefore there was no restraint upon the builders, who, during the boom period, ran up structures from 90 ft. to 100 ft. high, and of ten to twelve stories. These stand up like towers here and there, and are a disfigurement to the architecture of the city, which, as a general rule, is very handsome and stately. There are many fine buildings, both for business and public purposes. The Town Hall is a large edifice, occupying a central position: and the city appears to be thoroughly well governed;—to be proud of and contented with the dignified and efficient traditions of its mayor and councillors, who, while occasionally, perhaps, using municipal politics as a stepping-stone to public life, have never allowed their desire for popularity to override their duty to the ratepayers. No scandals as to corruption of municipal officers or councillors have occurred. The streets are well kept and well lighted. Electric lighting companies commenced the work; but recently the city established a plant of its own, and it has now made arrangements to buy out the private companies, and to supply electricity not only for street lighting but for private use.

Melbourne has an abundant water supply; a matter of the very first concern in a warm climate. It was carried out by the Government at a cost of about three and a half millions, and was a splendidly paying concern. So lavish is the use of water that it was stated that, during one very hot day of my stay, the consumption rose to 120 gallons per head of the population, without exhausting the supply. A great work now in progress is the sewage of the city. This is being carried out by a specially constituted authority named the Melbourne and Metropolitan Board of Works, upon which all the municipalities are represented. The Melbourne water supply was handed over to it, Yan Yean reservoir and all, together with the responsibility for £2,400,000 borrowed by the Government for the construction of additional works. At the time this was handed over, it was thought that there would be sufficient surplus revenue from the water to enable the sewerage to be effected without any additional rate; but this has proved to be too

VICTORIA

sanguine a view, and an additional rate of one shilling in the pound will be required on all the sewered portions of the city. The works are now well advanced, and parts of the city are already connected with the sewers.

It is a curious fact that several of the suburbs of Melbourne, being anxious, in the boom times, to borrow money (as, being separate municipalities they were entitled to do), changed their names, apparently for the benefit or conviction of the British investor—as, for example, from Sandridge and Emerald Hill to Port Melbourne and South Melbourne. It might almost be hoped that they will now, having achieved their end, go back, like Sandhurst, which is now once more Bendigo, to their older titles.

Lord Brassey is Governor of Victoria, and he resides in a large mansion near the city, in the midst of well laid-out grounds. Government House is quite a landmark, for it is situated on an eminence, from whence it can be seen for miles. Lord Brassey still indulges his taste for the sea. He performed a noteworthy feat of seamanship in sailing out to take up his duties in his fine yacht, the *Sunbeam*. He also owns a smaller boat, and is president of the principal sailing club. He is noted for his many and weighty speeches on a wide range of topics. As the leader of society in Victoria, Lady Brassey is very popular.

There are, as is usual in the colonies, two Houses of Parliament; the Legislative Assembly being the popular chamber, and the Legislative Council the representative of property and stability. It is in fact the ratepayers' house, as only owners of property to the extent of £10 annual value, and lessees of £25 annual value, have votes. For the Assembly every ratepayer has a vote, and also every male person of the age of twenty-one years, who has been resident for one year, and takes out an elector's right. The members of the Assembly are paid £300 a year each for their services, and this payment of members is universal throughout the colonies, except, as has been said, in Western Australia. The absence of a leisured class has made the practice almost a necessity. Yet it is worthy of remark that the "amateur," or unpaid, politicians of Western Australia are almost a by-word, at the moment, amongst their fellows, for what is held to be their excessive astuteness and tenacity in safeguarding the interests of their own colony. The amount of the payment varies in the different colonies; and it will, we may hope, be readjusted, or abolished, after Federation. Members of the Federal Parliament will be paid £400.

The Right Honourable Sir George Turner, who is Premier, has held office for over four years. It is a matter worthy of note that existing Ministries in all the colonies have been in possession of power for an unusually long time; almost all for over four years, some for over five. The average duration of Ministries in the past has been much shorter than this. In South Australia it was about ten months only; in Victoria about eighteen months. Whilst I was in Melbourne a Ministerial crisis arose, chiefly because the Premier lost his temper; but within twenty-four hours all was arranged, and peace reigned supreme once more. These longer-lived Ministries have been coincident with the period of depression, except in the case of Western Australia, where Sir John Forrest's extraordinary tenure of power, which he has held ever since the colony obtained self-government, is perhaps chiefly due to the fact that no one has come forward to replace him. Elsewhere, political differences have been for the time laid aside, in order that Ministries which have instituted a steady course of retrenchment should have a fair opportunity to carry out their reforms. A policy of retrenchment is, however, one of which democracies soon

VICTORIA

tire; and already what is termed a bold progressive policy has been forced upon the Victorian Government. A loan of two and a half millions has been authorised, one million of which is for expenditure in railway construction and other public works, and the remainder for the conversion of a loan of one and a half millions, falling due in 1899. Sir George Turner is of a retiring disposition, hating all the public appearances necessary in connection with his position. He is a very hard worker, a great master of detail, and a plain, straightforward, lucid speaker, making no pretentions to the name of orator. In politics, like Mr Reid, the late Sir Henry Parkes, or, for that matter, most successful Australian Premiers, he may be termed an opportunist, having no definite or far-reaching views, but being quick to discern and follow the movements of public opinion. Many of his friends have stated that, if he followed his own judgment, he would not advocate a return to a free expenditure upon public works; and, indeed, most of his past utterances belie his present action. But if he had not proposed such a policy, some one else would have done so; and he bows to the public will. When I ventured to remark to a Victorian politician that possibly it would have been more honest had the Government had the courage of their opinions, I was told, and I am bound to admit, with some justification, that people who lived in glass houses should not throw stones. It seems likely, in view of the eclipse of Mr Reid, that Sir George Turner will be the first Premier of the Commonwealth.

In Victoria the policy of Protection has been carried to as great an extreme as it has reached in any part of the world. Sir Graham Berry, formerly Premier for several years, more recently Agent-General in England, and afterwards Speaker of the Legislative Assembly, built his

D

reputation upon the advocacy of Protection. So far was this policy carried that "ad valorem" duties of from 50 to 60 per cent were placed upon many articles, whilst the fixed duties often reached as high as 150 to 200 per cent. This created a reaction, and some of the duties have been modified in recent years; but still they are higher than in any Australian colony. The promises held out when the policy was introduced have not been carried out, and the bright hopes entertained have not been fulfilled. Victoria is a colony of such great natural resources that it was bound to progress in spite of its Protectionist tariff rather than because of it. Sir Graham Berry promised thirty years ago that he would make the colony a paradise for the working man. If it is so, then the working man does not realise his privileges, for nowhere in Australia is there greater discontent; whilst the problem of what to do with the unemployed is always present. It is a theme of constant discussion in Parliament, and the renewal of a borrowing policy is mainly justified on the plea that work must be found for the workless. There is an Anti-Sweating League in Melbourne, which is mainly composed of members of the Protectionist Association, and the deliverances of the same men in their different capacities are strikingly inconsistent. On the one hand they claim that Victoria owes almost everything it possesses to the Protectionist policy, which has been a brilliant success. On the other hand they present reports of misery and destitution amongst factory workers, of unconscionably long hours and wretchedly poor pay, which could not be exceeded in heart-rending detail in the thickly populated lands of Europe.

Victoria has one of the most severe Factories Acts which have ever been enacted. Boards are appointed to fix rates of remuneration in various trades, such as furniture, boot and shoe-making, clothing, and white work. No one is permitted to work outside a factory without receiving a permit from the chief inspector. The competition of the alien races is most severely restrained. One Chinaman working at the furniture trade is by law a factory, and is treated, and inspected, as such. The effect of all this legislation has been to make the condition of the slow, the aged, or the unhealthy workman worse than ever, the tendency being to drive all factories to employ only the best hands. It does not pay them to find room for the slow at piecework, and factories are not allowed to give the work out except under stringent conditions. When a minimum weekly or daily wage is fixed, as it is in some cases, only those who are well worth that wage are employed, and inferior or slow workmen have been driven out of work altogether, in spite of their piteous appeals to be allowed to earn what they can, and in spite of the reluctance of humane employers to refuse work to such cases. So great was the cruelty in many instances that the Chief Secretary has been obliged to break his own law, or to wink at its evasions. But the cry is for still more legislation, and just before the last session closed a Bill was introduced which provided that, where the door of any shop was found to be open after the closing hours fixed by law, the occupier should be deemed to be selling after hours, and be required to prove a negative to avoid a fine. At this proposal the Assembly revolted, and it was struck out; for it was pointed out that in hundreds of cases in the metropolis the front door of the shops is the only safe entry, after nightfall, to the dwelling attached. The dominion of the petty inspector is rapidly extending and becoming more burdensome. Whenever he finds a difficulty in obtaining a conviction, he asks for an amendment of the law; but fortunately there is a point at which the common sense of the community revolts, as in the instance given.

The reason Protection has obtained such sway in Victoria is that it secured the adherence of the working classes, being at the outset advocated by Liberal politicians: thus it came to be regarded as the Liberal policy. In New South Wales the reverse happened. And there the working men are clamorous in their defence of their favourite doctrine of Free-trade. Nothing is more surprising, to the traveller, than to hear the working men of Melbourne "boo-hoo" whenever Free-trade is mentioned, and to hear the same class of men in Sydney cheer it lustily. The truth is that in Australia the question has never become one of principle, but has been considered rather, as, after all, perhaps, it ought to be, as a matter, for the balance of local and immediate expediencies. Both parties are gratified by the arrangement come to for the Federal Commonwealth: which provides for Protection against the outside world, and for Inter-Colonial Free-trade.

A law which has been found to work well in Victoria is that which enables the Government credit to be made use of to provide money at a cheap rate for settlers who have security to offer. Commissioners are appointed to administer the Act; they make advances up to two-thirds of the value of freeholds at 3 per cent., with a small amount for a sinking fund added, the repayments being spread over a long series of years. The system has been in operation for several years, and hundreds of thousands of pounds have been thus advanced; whilst the default has been so small as not to be worth mentioning, though the colony has been passing through a period of prolonged drought. The working of the Act is strictly guarded from political interference.

VICTORIA

Large areas of the best lands of the colony were bought up in the early days and formed into great grazing stations. Natural causes are gradually operating to break up these large estates. Fathers die, and, as there is no entail, the land is divided amongst their sons ; while some owners are tempted into disastrous speculations in great sheep stations in the far north of the continent, and are obliged to sell to meet their engagements. It is thought, however, that the process of disintegration is too slow, and provision has been made in a Land Bill just passed to allow the Government to make purchases of land where the owner is willing, and then to lease or sell it on long terms in small farms to persons who will put it to a profitable use. A similar practice obtains, as we shall see, in New Zealand, Queensland, and elsewhere. It was proposed to give the power of compulsory purchase, but this was fiercely combatted in the Lower House, and rejected by an overwhelming majority in the Council. The Legislative Council of Victoria is probably the most powerful institution in the Australian colonies. The weight and local influence of its members makes it impregnable to the assaults of the demagogue : and not on this occasion only has it been able to save private rights from unnecessary spoliation. At the same time, there is no doubt that the future, in Victoria, is with the small holding. The real founder of Victoria, Mr Henty, was also its first agriculturist : whose plough is preserved in Melbourne as a sacred relic to this day. But the pastoralist, naturally, had the first innings ; and the day of mining and its attendant commerce followed. Agriculture has been progressing less and less slowly during the last quarter of a century : but it may be said to be still only in its initial stage ; a fact which no one appreciates more clearly than Mr Taverner, the energetic

Minister of Agriculture. Measuring about 420 miles from east to west, by 250 from north to south, with an area, roughly, of 88,000 sq. miles, Victoria is the smallest colony on the continent, its area being about equal to that of Great Britain. One thirty-fourth part of Australia, it contains one-third of her inhabitants; and has a density of population equal to thirteen and a half souls to the sq. mile as against four and a quarter in New South Wales, and one in the colonies as a whole. Of a total of 1,170,000 souls, (65 per cent. of whom are native-born Australians, a mere 215,000 being British, and 85,000 Irish), 458,000 are settled in Greater Melbourne : leaving for the country districts but little more than 700,000, of whom half are females. 350,000 males, then, had, in 1898, 3,240,000 acres under cultivation of some sort, as cultivation is understood in Australia, out of a total territory of 88,000 sq. miles ; turning out in agricultural produce the equivalent of five millions sterling, and in pastoral (to leave mining for the present out of the account) seven and a half millions. It will be profitable to turn aside for a moment to consider the history of the Henties. In Horsefield's *History of Sussex*, it is written :—" In the year 1796, Thomas Henty, Esq., purchased the demesne lands in this parish (West Tarring), consisting of 281 acres. . . . The breed of merino sheep has been brought by Mr Henty to great perfection, and from his flock many have been sent to New South Wales." Mr Henty, we have it on good authority, took first prize wherever he exhibited his sheep in England, till at last he became an exhibitor merely for honour, being barred from taking prizes, on account of the immense superiority of his sheep over those of any other flock in Great Britain. His flock, which was formed with pure merinoes from that kept by H.M. George III., was sent out in part to

Western Australia; where James Henty took up a location of 1500 acres in 1829. But the early months of settlement on the Swan were full of wet, misery, and blundering; scab, and discouragement. The merinoes, which were in charge of Mr Henty's sons, did not thrive on the salt-bush of Fremantle. They were shipped to Tasmania in the *Cornwallis*, where they were joined by Mr Henty himself with the rest of the flock. Dissatisfied with Western Australia; finding both Colonies full of scab; and unable, again, to obtain certain lands he had been promised in Tasmania, Mr Henty sailed in 1834 for Portland Bay, on the Australian main, in what was then an unknown land, where he was free from neighbours, disease, and Government interference. And this was the real foundation of Victoria; though Batman sailed also from Tasmania next year in the schooner *Rebecca*, ascended and named the Yarra, and tried to buy the site of Melbourne for thirty tomahawks, some trousers, and 100 lbs. of flour. It was Henty's merinoes, bred on the pastures of the Western District, that stamped Port Phillip wool, as the most valuable wool in the world, with a primacy which it still retains; though MacArthur's sheep from the Cape, connected, by the way, with that same flock of George III.'s, had reached New South Wales in 1797. The great flats and rolling downs of Colac and Camperdown were marked out and occupied by the Robertsons and other allied families, mostly of Tasmanian extraction; and Victoria was a land of flocks and herds for many a day to come. Henty, indeed, tried agriculture, as his plough is there to testify: but the Henties tried everything,—many things which are now forgotten included,—such as whaling, which they carried on with success from Portland as well as in Western Australia. Even the gold rush, which gave a market to the graziers, rather discouraged agriculture, until the decay of mining, in the period of transition from alluvial to reefing, before the value of the deep levels was established, threw some of the miners back upon the cultivation of the soil. The separation of the colony from New South Wales was obtained by great efforts. It was held that, being a remote district, it was neglected. So keen did the feeling become that the electors of Port Phillip District, as Victoria was then called, refused to send an actual representative to the Sydney Parliament, and elected Earl Grey, who was then Secretary of State for the Colonies, as their member. This drew pointed attention to the grievances of the settlers, and the Privy Council decreed the separation of the present colony from the parent stem, the river Murray becoming the boundary. It is alleged that it was owing to a mistake of a clerk in the office of the Secretary of State for the Colonies in writing " Murray " instead of " Murrumbidgee "—(perhaps he found the former easier to spell) —that the Murrumbidgee was not made the boundary, that being the original intention. This would have given Victoria a large additional extent of fertile land ; and she was left with a hankering for extensions even so lately as the 'eighties, when there was still talk of the Debateable Land on the South Australian boundary, and a vague notion of annexing the Riverina was a constant source of alarm to New South Wales. However, at the time, so delighted were the colonists with their success, that Separation Day was proclaimed a public holiday : and it was continually observed as such until a few years ago, when it seemed so inconsistent with the desire for federation to be still celebrating separation that the day was taken out of the list of public holidays.

It was the discovery of gold in 1851 which sent the

VICTORIA

colony forward by leaps and bounds, attracting population from all parts of the world. I cannot retell that old story, but let it be stated that from that time to the present over 63,000,000 ounces of gold have been produced in the colony, of the value of £250,000,000, and gold production is still going on at the rate of 800,000 ounces a year. Bendigo is the main gold-producing centre, after Ballarat; having a record of some fifty odd millions sterling. It has been frequently alleged that Lord Salisbury was once a digger on the Bendigo goldfield, and it is undoubtedly a fact that he visited the colony in the height of the gold fever. Some few years ago a colonist wrote to the Prime Minister on the subject, and received a reply stating that Lord Robert Cecil certainly visited the colony, and that he journeyed to the goldfield, and stayed there as a guest of a Government officer. But his residence, unfortunately for the tradition, was for a few days only; and he could have seen little of the practical side of mining. Bendigo is a most important provincial centre, having a population, as we have seen, of about 40,000. The deepest gold mine in the world is in this district; Mr Lansell, a wealthy and public-spirited mine owner, having sunk a shaft to a depth of 3350 feet, practically two-thirds of a mile, and at that great depth the mine is still auriferous. There are eleven other mines in Bendigo which have been sunk over 2400 feet—five of them are down to the 3000 feet level and over; and mining will probably be possible at 4000 feet, so far as the heat of the rock is concerned. There are many other private mine owners in Victoria, though Mr Lansell is by far the most successful and best known. The industry, so far, has been carried on, fortunately for the colony, as is the case with Queensland mining, almost entirely with locally-provided capital. The Victorian bred manager is perhaps rather given to the rule-of-thumb, and has been supplemented or superseded, in the great mines of Western Australia, by engineers of American experience and training, and by mining chemists from Germany. But, both for prospecting for reefs, and for " following the gold " in the earlier stages of a mine's development, it is probable that Victoria is the true home of mining knowledge in the English-speaking world. Cornish and Welsh labour, for reasons which are notorious amongst practical men, requires careful supervision.

Nearly one-third of the world's annual production of gold is raised in the Australasian colonies, and amongst these Victoria is not yet tired of claiming the premier position. The real fact is that Western Australia is easily first, and must remain so, in all human likelihood, for many years to come; while, though the Victorian yield for 1897 was 812,000 ounces (say £3,250,000) as against Queensland's 807,000, the Queensland figures for 1898 overpassed that limit by 100,000 ounces, and left Victoria hopelessly behind. The enthusiasm for gold dredging, which the speculators of Melbourne have caught from New Zealand, is not likely appreciably to swell the gold returns, as many of the claims pegged out are distinctly wild-cat.

It must not be supposed from anything I have said that Victoria has not established manufactures. On the contrary, she has only lately recovered from a craze which was leading her to sacrifice everything to the attempt to acclimatise them. There are in the colony 50,000 people engaged in manufactures: though it is true that New South Wales, the Free-trade Colony, has just about the same number, and that there is a larger proportion of females working in factories in Victoria

VICTORIA

than in New South Wales. Woollen mills, tanneries, potteries, agricultural implement works, coach factories, and many more works are very successful in their productions.

The point is, however, that it is not to its manufactures but to its productions that Victoria must look for its future prosperity. There are 300,000 workers in the natural industries, which, from the nature of the case, cannot be protected, for they depend for their success now, or must ultimately do so, on ability to compete in the markets of the world. Wheat, wool and gold are the staple productions at present. The dairying industry has been very profitably developed. Its great rise is due to the system of co-operative production. Factories are established in which the dairymen are shareholders, and butter of first-class quality is produced at an economical rate. A few years ago there was no export of this product to England. Now they are sending over £1,000,000 worth a year. The visit of the delegates of the Manchester Co-operative Association a year or two ago was very highly appreciated in the colonies. What the practical results of it have been I am unable to say ; but the spirit of Englishmen who evinced a desire to trade with their own kinsmen was warmly recognised, and personally the delegates were very popular. The butter produced from the sunny fields and sweet herbage of Australia should be superior to that of stall-fed cattle. At any rate, this industry is rapidly growing, and it has been very useful in showing how a large population may be settled on some of the great areas previously given over to sheep and cattle.

Fruit can be grown in abundance all over Victoria. There are 40,000 acres of orchards in the colony, and the export of apples to England is a large and growing one. Great care is now being taken to ascertain the best varieties for export, and to grow them. There are apple orchards in Victoria of 200 acres in extent. Packing, which is the chief difficulty to the British fruit-grower, seems to give trouble also in Australia. We are not so neat-handed as the Americans. 27,000 acres are down in vines, and about 23,000 acres are bearing, the produce being over 2,000,000 gallons per annum. A great deal is being done in this trade, also, by co-operation, through wineries, or wine factories. But the future all over Australia lies, probably, for perfection, with light wines, and, for those who prefer rough methods of production, with grape brandy. Growers should remember the history of Marsala, and of the Cape wines. A permanent wine trade in England is only to be secured from the top. The famous, or notorious, settlement of Mildura, on the Murray, carried out at first on too expensive a scale, has, so far as production is concerned, shown wonderful results. But, placed too far from a market, and requiring a large original outlay from the settlers, it has proved a disappointment to many. The Government has come to the assistance of the settlers, and advanced £40,000 for the purpose of putting the irrigation works in order. A railway to the settlement has also been authorised by Parliament, and will be constructed within a year or two. One of the greatest obstacles to progress will then be overcome, for, depending on river communication as they do now, the orchards are shut out from their markets for four months in the year, just when their produce is ready; for the Murray is not navigable all the year round.

The colony is fifty-six million acres in extent. Twenty-three million acres have been alienated to private owners; and of the 30,000,000 acres available for settlement,

VICTORIA 61

11,500,000 are in the mallee scrub. The wheat of Victoria, like that of South Australia, is the best in the world; and it is very cheaply harvested. But the available Crown lands are mainly taken up, and the only means now of obtaining the fee-simple of Government land is by taking up a 1000 acre agricultural and grazing block, and selecting 320 acres for freehold out of it. This is only possible to the successful applicant to whom a land board awards the right of leasing these blocks, the applicants on every occasion being many more than there is land to go round for. The rise in the price of land which may be expected to follow in Victoria on the alienation of the last available blocks will probably hasten the rush for the soil in the other colonies. Western Australia, owing to her peculiar conditions of settlement and to the patchy nature of her lands, is already, for practical purposes, almost in the same stage as Victoria in this respect. The latter colony has been a large exporter of wheat to the United Kingdom this season, having shipped over 2,000,000 bags during the first thirty-one weeks of the year. The average yield, for nearly a decade, has not exceeded 8 bushels; but agricultural authorities have advised the farmers to adopt better mechanical means, a more rational system of manure, and a more careful selection of seed, assuring them that if they only increase their yield by 2 bushels to the acre they will increase the wealth of the colony by £400,000 a year.

What I have said as to education in South Australia applies also to Victoria, where the system is similarly free, secular, and compulsory. The masses are well educated in their way, and there are no illiterates to speak of. On the other hand, sound learning is scarcely indigenous. The University of Melbourne is a fine institution, and its degrees high rank in the teaching world. It is perhaps, however, only natural that the more likely students, who have ideas of scholarship rather above the pass, or professional, standard, should come home to breathe the atmosphere of Europe.

CHAPTER IV

TASMANIA

TASMANIA, the Garden Island, is as large as Scotland : and considerably more sleepy than the Channel Islands. Like the rest of Australia, it was at one time a sort of dependency of Java, having been discovered, and named Van Diemen's Land, by Tasman in 1642. It was taken possession of as a British colony in the first years of this century, shortly after Dr Bass had discovered that it had ceased (since the tertiary period, approximately speaking) to form a part of Continental Australia. It is still marked in the old charts, specimens of which, printed on pottery ware, are still to be bought in the china shops of Kensington, as the southern extremity of the mainland ; though the error has been corrected, probably, in maps of more recent issue. This mistake, however, together with the fact, already referred to, that the north shore of South Australia faces New Guinea, is possibly responsible for the extraordinarily confused state of the British mind in respect of Australian geography. The name of the colony was subsequently changed to Tasmania, in order to encourage a discreet oblivion of a chapter of history about which, even now, the less said the better, except that it is fully set forth in Marcus Clarke's "For the Term of His Natural Life." And since that time Tasmania has settled down to the production of potatoes, contentment, and jam. The guide-books call the island the Sanatorium of the South. That, of course, is the alliterative sort of thing guide-books usually give way to; but Tasmania really has a most delightful climate, which Sir Edward Braddon very justly describes, after dinner, as balmy, and which is as much its characteristic boast as is his Harbour to the Sydney man. The island is about twelve hours by steamer from Victoria: and for many years it has been known to jaded Melbourne folk as a holiday resort; to Federal Conventions (in the days when politicians did not take Federation very seriously) as a place for a picnic; and to Her Majesty's Australian squadron, which commonly passes the summer at anchor in the Derwent, as possessing one of the pleasantest capitals in Australia. Babies never die in Tasmania, or nine out of ten of them survive the first year of life. Yet 21 per cent. of the total deaths are of infants under one year, and 34 per cent. of old men: —nearly 11 per cent., indeed, of the deaths are of persons between 80 and 100 years of age. The young men, perhaps, have rather a tendency to drift away to a more stirring environment, though even here, as universally throughout Australia, there are more men than women. There are, it is true, on the other hand, more widows than widowers, and more unmarried females than married; which perhaps only makes it the more extraordinary that there should be, according to the Registrar-General, 22,000 married men, to a beggarly 21,000 of married women. But statistics will prove anything. It is more important to observe that, though there are, no doubt, openings for domestic servants, Tasmania is scarcely the place for the immigrant. There is, to begin with, no nominated assisted immigration. There is very little Crown land at once available for profitable settlement. The population is only about 146,000, of whom a bare 73,000 are over 21; and includes only 40,000 males over 21. This handful owns a heritage of 26,000 square

TASMANIA 65

miles, out of the Australian total of three millions; whereof they have alienated some four and three-quarters million acres, and still hold twelve million acres in reserve. In 1897 they had under cultivation 500,000 acres, and they broke up new land in that year to the extent of 9000 acres. Yet the bush is so luxuriant, markets so small, and communications so difficult, that the newcomer will usually find it better, on reflection, to buy an existing farm, of which there are plenty for sale, rather than to tackle the virgin forest. The real inwardness of Tasmanian life is clear from a few figures. There are upwards of 60,000 breadwinners in the colony, of whom some 5500 are employers of labour : and in the whole community there are a bare 28,000 habitations, of which near two thousand are slab, bark, or mud huts, tents, or dwellings with canvas roofs, 8000 are of brick or stone, and the balance are either wood, corrugated iron, or lath and plaster shanties. The colony owns 30,000 horses, 157,000 cattle, one and a half million sheep, and 43,000 pigs. Its exports are nearly £300,000 of pastoral produce, nearly £400,000 of agricultural produce, and nearly a million sterling of mineral produce, or an average of about £10 per head, as against imports of £8 ; figures which compare favourably enough, in Australian finance, with a taxation of £2, 18s., and a public debt of £48 per head. And of the sum of inhabitants, 115,000 are Australian born (107,000 of them born in the colony), as against 21,000 British, 5000 Irish, and 1000 Asiatics. All of which simply means that Tasmania is an old and quiet settlement, colonised many years ago, and troubled with no recent influx of people ; where mining, however, is prosperous and advancing ; where wages are rather lower, at times, than in the other colonies ; where plenty of cleared agricultural land may be rented at from 8s. to

E

15s. per acre; and from whence potatoes, plums, and red currants are sent to Victoria, apples to Covent Garden, and fruit pulp all over the world.

It has been, perhaps, unfortunate for the little island that Victoria is so near. Her most busy times, and periods of expanding trade, have twice been associated with an actual depletion of both capital and population; once in the years after 1835, when the first settlement of Victoria by colonists from Tasmania took place (for not only was Melbourne planted by Batman and Fawkner, but Portland, the first town in Victoria, was founded, as we have seen, by Henty, and the best stations of the Western District were taken up by Tasmanian squatters), and secondly in 1853, when another emigration to Port Phillip was stimulated by the gold discoveries. The last expansion of trade, in 1885, unlike the two former, is marked by a growth, still continuing, in capital and population, due to the increasing output of copper, gold, silver, and tin; all of which, in the order named, are contributing to the colony's prosperity. But there has been no rush. Few enough Tasmanians were on "the long trail" when Coolgardie broke out in 1893 and 1894: and few of the migratory crowd which made Coolgardie have, now that their day is over, been able to reconcile themselves to the calm atmosphere of Tasmania. You may find them in the Transvaal, in Pekin, or at Singapore, but not at Zeehan or Mount Lyall. Which, perhaps, may be all the better for Tasmania; whose progress, for the rest, though sure, is likely to be less slow in the future, especially after Federation. The opening of the great markets of Melbourne and Sydney to her fruit and vegetables will make a great deal of difference to the island colony. Under the Crown Lands Act of 1890 first-class agricultural waste lands of the Crown may be

TASMANIA

selected, in blocks of not less than 15 nor more than 320 acres, at £1 per acre cash, or 26s. 8d. spread over fourteen years. By an Amendment Act of 1893, the smaller settlers (on 15 to 50 acres), if actual occupants, pay nothing for the first three years; and by another Act, of 1894, provision is made, as in Queensland and other colonies, for co-operative settlement. The long period of purchase under these Acts is intended to help the industrious individual who has little or no capital to secure himself a home on the land. But the newcomer from England, either with or without capital, will find it necessary to acquire his colonial experience before committing himself to the expenditure of either work or money in any particular locality; and, in the course of so acquiring it, will probably come across more immediately remunerative means of employing his energy than in a struggle with the primitive bush. At the same time, it should not be forgotten that the methods of clearing heavy scrub have very much altered since fifty years ago. The pioneer insisted on expending from £6 to £15 per acre, and an infinity of trouble and time, in grubbing and clearing his land for the plough during the first year. Not only are there now stump-jumping ploughs, and the "devil," the American machine which draws trees from the ground like teeth; but experience has proved that the best methods are the cheaper ones of ring-barking the large trees and burning off the scrub, while first crops of fodder, or even of potatoes or grain, are taken off the land years before it is completely cleared. The average return for a crop of potatoes may vary from £5 to £20 per acre, and the first cost of scrubbing the land out from 8s. to 25s. per acre.

The following samples of properties advertised for sale in a recent issue of a local property register will serve to show the range of values, and to illustrate what has been said :—

FRANKLIN.—Twenty acres, all cleared, and two acres planted with apple trees. Cottage of five rooms, etc. £55.

FORCETT.—Farm of seventy-five acres, twenty-one acres under cultivation. Cottage of two rooms. Price, £140.

HASTINGS. — Fifty-one acres, one-and-a-half acres in orchard, two acres cleared for planting, ten acres cleared and fit for running cattle. W.B. Cottage, four rooms, cowshed, etc. Price, £130.

DROMEDARY.—Farm of fifty acres, about twelve acres under cultivation, one acre in orchard, house of five rooms, and outbuildings, etc. Plenty of water. Price, £150. Terms.

GOULD'S COUNTRY, EAST COAST.—Farm of eighty-one acres, about seventy acres cleared and in grass, cottage of six rooms, barn, stable, and cowsheds, etc., orchard of three acres. Price, £200.

CLAREMONT.—Sixty-three acres, twenty-one acres have been under cultivation. W.B. cottage of four rooms and kitchen, barns, piggeries, cowshed, stable, and stock-yard; orchard of one acre just coming into full bearing, an excellent stream of fresh water. Farm implements, furniture, carpenters' tools, carts, drays, harness, etc. Price, £325.

HUON ROAD, 6½ miles from town.—Fifteen acres, six acres cleared and partly grassed, raspberry and currant beds, potato paddock, etc. New cottage of four rooms, stable, hut, etc. Price, £370.

WEST DAVENPORT.—Good cottage of four rooms, and usual outhouses, fowlhouse, piggeries etc. Fruit and

vegetable garden in full bearing. The whole comprises ten acres of good chocolate soil. Price, £525.
SPRING BAY, EAST COAST OF TASMANIA.—" Louisville Estate": comprises eight hundred and forty-two acres of good land, part in small vineyard, fine orchard and flower garden. The house contains eight large rooms, servants' rooms, etc., stables, coach-house, cow-shed, and a splendid supply of water. A jetty also belongs to the property, at which local vessels can berth, and the Swansea and Hobart coach passes the gate. Price, £3000. And so on.

New South Wales has her unrivalled back country, her outlook on the Pacific, and the rather doubtful benefit of the Federal Territory, which is to be within her borderline. Queensland has her herds and flocks, her Mount Morgans and her frozen meat: Melbourne her Bendigo and Ballarat; the land-boom, and the bank-smashes, to look back upon; the butter-factories and wineries which are retrieving the past; and the wealth of the Western District, where the sons of the squatters play polo, and draw rents, when they can get them, from their onion-farms. South Australia sits content with her wheat and wine, her piety, politics, and gambling share-brokers. Even Western Australia has at least Kalgoorlie and the jarrah trade. Tasmania has been looked on mainly as a health resort, with her quays often covered with a glut of fruit, and with no more exciting question to debate than whether her capital should be called Hobart, Hobart Town, or Hobarton. But all this may be changed by the growth of the mineral output, and by the stimulus of the Federal markets: and it is highly probable that more than nine thousand acres of new land may be broken up annually for many years to come. Federation has been, all along, mainly a commercial question for Tasmania.

Chapter V

NEW SOUTH WALES

IT has been said with some point that the tourist should only approach the capital of New South Wales by sea; the entrance, through a narrow gateway, flanked on either side by towering cliffs, on one of which stands the lighthouse, visible at night thirty miles away, being very striking. The inner headlands are crowned with batteries planned in the days when artillery had a less effective range than now; and, as a consequence, the defect in the defences (a defect common to those of several of the New Zealand cities) is that a battleship with heavy guns, lying outside the entrance, could pitch shells into the city without any risk of a return fire. This is not the case with the rival city, Melbourne, whose main defences are many miles distant from the capital.

Sydney harbour opens out in all its beauty as the steamer comes through the "Heads"; and though in other parts of Australia the phrase "our harbour," as applied to Sydney, has become a joke, it is, indeed, a most wonderful sight, with its labyrinth of bays and channels. One might live in Sydney a lifetime, and then not quite know every arm and nook of Port Jackson. Everywhere the red cliffs rise straight from the water, and even in midwinter these headlands are decked with white and red heaths, dwarfed banksias, hakeas, and other shrubs with rich waxen flowers. In steaming up an arm of the harbour in one of the fast excursion launches—which look like miniature Mississippi steamers—it often seems as though one were rushing directly into a cliff, when suddenly a little opening is seen to one side, and another inlet opens out for miles. Each of these inlets is in a way a reproduction of the main harbour ; and for boating, or fishing, the waters of Hacking River, George's River, Botany Bay, Narrabeen Lake, Hawkesbury River, and Lake Macquarie, offer further and unlimited facilities. It is easy to see why the professional scullers of New South Wales are ahead of our Britons. A great sculler is a natural product, as it were, of a large expanse of suitable water. Hanlon, the founder of modern sculling, lived in his father's hotel on a small island at Toronto. Beach and Searle never " trudged unwillingly to school." They flashed down the Parramatta in wager-boats.

As the mail steamer glided to the inner anchorage known as Circular Quay, I got a glimpse of a group of men-of-war—the largest of them the *Royal Arthur*, the flagship of the Australian station—lying in Farm Cove, with the lovely Botanical Gardens, in the ponds of which bloom the pink and purple water-lilies of the tropics, partly encircling them between two headlands of mown lawns—a crescent of green turf. Sydney is the headquarters of our strength in the South Pacific. And besides being the capital of the greatest of the colonies, she is the true metropolis and rendezvous of those pathless seas ; the Queen city of that strange half-squalid, half-romantic Empire of the Islands. In her purlieus you may find, beside the lean squatter of the Riverina, the rustic selector from Twofold Bay, or the stunted cockney-looking larrikin of Wooloomooloo, a curious element from the corners and forgotten by-ways of a half-known world ;—traders, *bêche-de-mer* fishers, pearlers, blackbirders, whalers, beachcombers, missionaries, savants, and the heterogeneous rascaldom of the Pacific. Viewed in comparison with the other provincial centres, she is at once more rudimentally national and less obtrusively Australian; the inevitable capital, wherever the Federal centre may be, of the continent.

It is a 567 mile run from Melbourne to Sydney by sea, and about the same distance by rail. The boundary of the two colonies, crossed at Albury, is the Murray, which we crossed also on the journey from Adelaide. It is the only river of importance in Australia, and, except in very dry seasons, is navigable for about 1,200 miles of its length. In the busy season the scene on the river is interesting. The wool clip of stations in the far interior has been brought down the Darling, the Murrumbidgee, and other tributaries of the Murray in huge shallow barges. These are towed by steamers up the river to Echuca; a great part of the New South Wales clip thus finding an outlet through the rival city, Melbourne.

The war of hostile railway tariffs between the two colonies has resulted in New South Wales pushing her railways into the far west to divert this traffic; a legitimate move as between rival communities, but one of the developments of inter-colonial competition which must end with the federation of the colonies.

Riverina, the largest province of New South Wales, is geographically part of Victoria; which colony, having failed to include them in her boundaries, apparently finds it the next best thing to repel her profitable neighbours and their trade as much as possible by taxing their cattle at the border.

There is a break of gauge where the railway systems of the two colonies meet at Albury, which not only converts the ordinary traveller into a keen Federationist, by vexing him with a superfluous change of trains in the middle of his journey, but would be a source of trouble and

NEW SOUTH WALES 73

dangerous delay in the movement of troops in case of an invasion.

Returning, however, to Sydney; the first view from the sea front shows a city built largely in red and yellow sandstone, upon rolling coastal ridges, with little level ground anywhere. Some of the older buildings almost overhang the sea, as one often notices in some of the Mediterranean towns; though, apart from Sydney, this is not a characteristic of Australian ports. The city itself is something of an old-world jumble, dug out of its own cellars; the streets being narrow and irregular, unlike those of Melbourne, which the pioneer surveyors (who came from Sydney and profited by its mistakes) planned broad, stately, and in chess-board fashion, at the start. Sydney is said to have been laid out on the lines of the cattle-tracks made by the first imported cows, who wandered about the infant settlement. In leading thoroughfares, such as George and Pitt Streets, the crush of hansom cabs and omnibuses is exceptional, for an Australian city. The heart of the city is not cut up with tram lines, however, as in Melbourne; for the steam-motor cars pass along a single route, and almost at the limits of the city branch off to the different suburbs. The tram system, controlled by the Government, is really a railway system in miniature; and though it gives the advantage of fast travelling to the outer suburbs of Sydney, it has nothing else in its favour, being unsightly and dirty. It is soon, I hear, to be superseded in favour of an over-head electric system. For some years after the introduction of the motor trams, the number of accidents in the city streets was alarming; but either the drivers have become more clever or the population more cautious, for of late years accidents have been rare.

In one respect,—in an attempt, at all events, to live

rationally and to adapt themselves to the climate, the Sydney folk set an example to the rest of Australia, where the conservative tendencies of the Anglo-Saxon race are in many things amusingly manifest. In Melbourne, particularly, men seem to have given up all attempt to follow the abrupt changes of their climate; and top-hats and heavy frock-coats are common in Collins' Street in weather when "whites" and solar topees should be the only wear. But, speaking generally, the majority of Australians follow English customs in dress and methods of living, totally oblivious of the fact that our customs developed, through many ages, in a comparatively cold country. Beef, mutton, bottled beer, and boiled potatoes, with whisky between meals, cannot be the ideal diet for a hot country; and the blazing plum-pudding is as much a Christmas institution in Australia as in England, though very few of their days, at that season, are favoured with a temperature of less than 100 degrees in the shade.

All the conditions tempt to outdoor life, and in Sydney a great many of the residents, especially young men, establish camps round the picturesque bays of the harbour and live there in tents through the summer. This period in Sydney has the moist and clammy peculiarities of the tropics, but is not subject to the same remarkable changes as in Melbourne, where during my visit there was, on one occasion, within less than forty-eight hours a drop in temperature of over 60 degrees. This is why the Melbourne man despairingly adheres to the traditional stove-pipe hat; while in Sydney there is more of an effort to make the habiliments suit the clime.

One cannot look upon Sydney to-day, then, without feeling quite sure that in trade and social importance she has become the capital of Australia, a position once unquestionably held by its great rival, Melbourne. In the earlier

NEW SOUTH WALES 75

days the inflow of outside capital for Australian development was mainly through Melbourne, then the headquarters of all the great wool firms and pastoral agencies. But when Victoria built a protective wall about itself, much of its outside capital was diverted to Sydney, which has grown steadily at the expense of the sister city, and become infected with that American bustle which was once the characteristic of Melbourne only.

But even now, in New South Wales, there is something left still of the true colonial simplicity, which you will scarcely find near Melbourne. In Tasmania, for example, when the girls are of a fair age, the mistress of a house will often do without a servant, and, with her daughters, take the household duties on her own shoulders. One may be engaged, again, in manual labour, and yet not cut off from society. It is possible to meet in the morning a man dressed like a navvy, working on his farm or in his orchard, and to see him again in the evening in his dress clothes, and not concerned for his roughened hands. I have seen, in one of the colonies, a lady whose husband occupies the highest position in local politics, and is largely indebted to her tact and popularity for his long lease of power, doing some of the family washing on her back verandah, while her guests of the afternoon drank tea with her, thirsty and unashamed. That was due to a mistake as to her "at-home" day, and the washing was mainly lace and such matters; but she did not put the tub away. The Private Secretary to a Governor, in another colony, has been known to spend his affable summer three miles out of town in a small tent on the banks of the river, riding in to his work on a bicycle. Perhaps it is partly, in some way, a result of her sympathy with this sort of colonial realism, that not only in business, but in art and literature also, Sydney has gone completely ahead of her rival: though it is singular that, while the latter city has become the home of budding art and literature in Australia, Melbourne has retained her prominence in music. Thus both Melba and Ada Crossley are Victorian born. And when Miss Amy Castles, the young Victorian soprano, whose singing has created a furore in Australia, sailed for England, in September last, to complete her musical education before appearing regularly in public, her admirers enthusiastically responded to the appeal to provide her with funds for this purpose, and the concerts she gave realized between £3000 and £4000. But Sydney is unquestionably the centre of Australian intellectual life, and during the last few years has enriched the prose and poetry of Australia by a succession of notable volumes, though there is yet, perhaps, a tendency to dwell upon station life and customs as giving the only typical Australian colour, overlooking much that is characteristic, and will yield matter for treatment in the literature of the future. Sydney artists establish camps by the water side, and study all the fleeting impressions of the sunlit harbour; so that it is not surprising to find them, almost to a man, disciples of the French and Impressionist schools in art. Not even a single volume of verse published in Sydney, however, dwells upon the beauties of the harbour beside which the poets live. As an illustration of the difference in the intellectual calibre of the two cities, it is worth noting that while Ethel Turner and Louise Mack—two charming young Sydney writers, who have made child life a special study—are known to every one in their own city, and much honoured, scarcely any one in Melbourne is aware that Ada Cambridge, a lady with an established reputation in fiction, has been for years resident there. And it is most remarkable to

NEW SOUTH WALES 77

observe the difference between the two capitals in respect of their press. Although the *Argus* has a respectable past, and Victoria is governed, in a sense, by Mr Syme and the *Age*, yet the Sydney *Bulletin* is the only Australian paper with anything of a national outlook, and with an inter-colonial circulation. It is the only paper, moreover, which tolerates original work; for the Melbourne press, though often vulgar, is consistently philistine, and never has a deeper respect for the conventionalities than when it is outraging them. Now the Australian artist, in his original work, has a tendency to become very strong meat. And the *Bulletin* is in thorough sympathy on this point, and on others, with the Australian artist. Hence, though a blatently disloyal rag, of blasphemous tendencies and American antecedents (and a prey, moreover, to many absurdly incompatible radical fads), the *Bulletin*, which produced, by the way, Phil May and Louis Becke, is read and passed on in the remotest camps of the Bush; gives a perceptible tinge to the mind of the average Australian; and has had a great deal to do, through its influence in New South Wales, with the success of Federation.

Architecturally, the city of Sydney has not many striking features; though it is well equipped with business buildings and offices. In its public buildings it falls considerably behind Melbourne. Its Houses of Parliament are a block of ruins, and until the site of the federal capital is definitely fixed it is unlikely that they will be rebuilt. For years there has been an agitation for new buildings, and a too ambitious scheme for the expenditure of half a million. An alternative, and later, scheme, to spend half that sum, has also been rejected by the Committee of Public Works, the authority of which has to be secured before any expenditure can take place on public works in New South Wales. The truth is that most of the Australian colonies have spent far too much on 'talking-shops' and public buildings generally: a fact which they will begin to appreciate when all their leading statesmen, and the main part of their revenues, have gone to the Federal city—whatever its name is to be.

Government House, where Lord Hampden, son of the late Speaker of the House of Commons, has recently been succeeded by Lord Beauchamp, is a picturesque Elizabethan building, with a magnificent outlook, and beautiful grounds, stretching down to the water side. When, on a summer night, the gardens are lit up for some vice-regal fete, and one sees beneath, on the one hand, the illuminated hulls of the near ships in Farm Cove, and on the other the scores of little passenger launches rushing away from Circular Quay to the marine suburbs, the spectacle is satisfactorily brilliant, and has something of Venetian colour in it. The best of the public buildings in Sydney is the Chief Secretary's office, the exterior of which is decorated with statuary. The Town Hall is not merely the finest in Australia, but one of the largest in the world. It has a magnificent vestibule, and includes amongst its equipments one of the largest organs ever built. The Corporation of Sydney, though fortunate in its home, is not otherwise quite a happy family, and its affairs of late years have become so entangled that there is some talk of an inquiry by a Royal Commission.

The General Post-office is a very fine building, once disfigured by grotesque carvings, which were the laughing-stock of Australia. They were an attempt, in the style of Mr Kruger's stone "topper," to apply up-to-date art to the representation of every-day Post-office business.

NEW SOUTH WALES 79

But the sculptor overlooked the fact that fashion in dress changes amazingly fast, and the well-dressed people of to-day become caricatures a few years hence. The Walt Whitman of democratic statuary, the would-be revolutionist of brown-stone art, had the mortification of seeing his egregious figures removed. It is perhaps a pity that some old-world statues cannot follow them. Sydney University is a fine building in the Gothic style. In one respect, at least, this is the progressive city of Australia. The National Art Gallery, the Public Library, and the museums are open on Sunday afternoons; and are then largely visited, notably by visitors from other parts of Australia, who may have their working days fully occupied with business.

The pastoral interest is the support of New South Wales to a greater extent even than of the other colonies. But the drought of the last few years, coming upon the heels of a strike of shearers and other bush-workers, has given the wool-grower a severe shaking. The flocks of the colony have shrunk from 66,000,000 to about 46,000,000, representing a loss of about 20,000,000 sheep. If to this is added the loss of natural increase, the shrinkage amounts to 50,000,000; enough, that is, to equip a considerable colony. In addition there has been a loss of nearly 300,000 horses and 150,000 cattle. That the colony has been able to survive these terrific blows is a striking proof of energy and resource. The entire substance of Job, it will be remembered, amounted to no more than 12,000 beasts, sheep, cattle, camels, and she-asses included; which were increased at his latter end, after his bad times, to 25,000. And yet this man was the greatest of all the sons of the east. Translated into money, the Colony has suffered a loss, due to mere inadequate rainfall, of from £12,000,000 to £20,000,000 sterling.

One of the results of these four years of drought was that Mr Reid, the late Premier, who had for several years past claimed a surplus, admitted, in November last, a deficiency in the revenue of £248,000. In the face of the heavy losses by drought, the colony can claim to have done very little in water conservation or irrigation as compared with Victoria, where, however, the money devoted to irrigation projects has, in many cases, been shamefully squandered.

In the western, and more arid, portion of New South Wales the stock carrying capacity of the country has, in many districts, been increased by the fine flow of water from artesian bores, which, as in Queensland, have changed the whole face of nature, and literally caused the wilderness to blossom as the rose; but, owing to the fact that in summer time even the largest rivers of the interior are nothing more than a chain of water holes, it is probably impossible to carry out large irrigation schemes in New South Wales, as the cost of storage would be too great; and, moreover, the loss by evaporation from Australian tanks sometimes amounts to more than six feet a year.

Following upon a period of falsely inflated land-values in Australia, we notice everywhere a tendency to promote legitimate land settlement. In New South Wales this is being effected by throwing open for settlement land formerly held under lease by squatters. In the southern districts there has been a great rush for this land, and in a few years settlement will, in consequence, have become much denser throughout the province of the Riverina. This movement, which is strictly parallel to and co-incident with the settlement of the Darling Downs in Queensland, and the operation of the *Land for Settlement Act* in New Zealand, may be compared also with the settlement of the mallee in Victoria. It has

NEW SOUTH WALES 81

not led, so far, to any perceptible immigration from Great Britain.

Another interesting development in land cultivation, which is perhaps more common on the Riverina than in Victoria, is the growing of wheat and other produce on the shares principle—the squatter providing the land and seed and the agriculturalist the plant and labour. This approximation to the *metayer* system has very great possibilities, being capable of extensive application in many parts of Australia, from the rich potato and onion soils of Colac to the sugar lands of tropical Queensland.

The system of co-operation is to be carried still further in the shipping of wheat to London. These developments, together with the increase of the export trade in frozen meat and other products, are giving the variety which the farmer requires, and he no longer has all his eggs in the one basket. The best will never be got from the frozen meat trade, however, until a higher standard is sought for in the quality. It is estimated that during the year 1897, for example, quite forty-five per cent. of the bulk shipped was defective in quality. Irregularity of supply is another source of weakness, and several efforts to secure united action, and so found a better system of supply, have failed. A few figures as to the pastoral and agricultural industries of New South Wales may be of interest. The area of land under wheat is extending rapidly; for whereas in 1895-6 there were 596,684 acres under wheat, this year there are 1,000,000 acres, though the crops, owing to dry weather, will be lighter than usual. As the land policy—under leasehold—is exceptionally liberal to the State tenants, the area of land under occupation should increase largely year by year. The latest agricultural returns for the colony show that 1,820,209 acres were under crop in 1898, giving the remarkable increase (on the 798,966

F

acres of 1889) of over a million acres in nine years; while nearly 100,000 people are engaged in farm work, and over 30,000 in pastoral pursuits. The last wheat harvest in New South Wales yielded ten and a half million bushels, averaging ten and a half bushels to the acre; and before the expiry of many years the colony will be a large exporter of wheat. Along the rich flats of the northern rivers maize is largely grown, about 212,000 acres of the best land of the colony being devoted to it. Although the wines of New South Wales had a reputation many years ago, they have failed to keep progress with those of Victoria. In New South Wales a larger area of land is given up to oranges than to vines, and the orange groves of the Parramatta are, in the season, one of the interesting sights to a visitor. About 40,000 acres are under orchards; but here, too, recent developments in New South Wales have not at all equalled those of Victoria and South Australia. Sugar growing is one of the great industries of Northern New South Wales, where there are over 30,000 acres under cane, beet being at present only an experimental crop. The sugar growers have of late figured largely in the politics of New South Wales, and have even had their influence upon Federation. It was necessary to their existence that a duty should be placed upon imported sugar; but when, in furtherance of his Free-trade policy, Mr Reid, the Premier, swept away duties to the extent of £1,000,000, the sugar growers of Richmond, Tweed, and Clarence Rivers seemed likely to suffer, in common with other producers. Mr Reid, however, yielding to judiciously applied pressure, decided to retain the duty at £3 per ton; and he received his reward. For when, some time subsequently, his position was endangered by a vote of censure moved by the Federal party under Mr Barton, the sugar members,

NEW SOUTH WALES 83

to a man, voted with, and for the moment saved, the Ministry. A few years back the sugar growers of New South Wales declared that, unlike their Queensland competitors in the business, they could make the industry a success without the help of coloured labour; but that principle is being slowly abandoned, and black labour is largely employed. It is a question, however, by no means settled in the minds of the planters themselves whether, with expensive machinery to maintain, white labour is not in the long run the cheaper. Under the Commonwealth it is very probable that, both in New South Wales and in Queensland, they will either have to settle the question in the affirmative or—abandon the industry.

New South Wales is the colony of wide acres; the total area of land alienated up to the end of 1896 being nearly 46,000,000 acres, while 126,000,000 acres are under lease, and about 25,000,000 remain in possession of the State; the total area of the colony being nearly 200,000,000 acres. The returns as to live stock grazing on New South Wales pastures are interesting—viz., 490,000 horses, 2,050,000 cattle, and about 50,000,000 sheep; though the recent drought, as we have seen, has affected these figures to an extent which it is hard to estimate with exactness. The total wool clip of 1896, the latest for which official figures are obtainable, was 255,000,000 lbs.— an increase of about 16,000,000 lbs. on the previous year. Amongst woolgrowers there has for some time past been a keen controversy as to the merits of the Vermont or American types of sheep, crossed with the Australian merino, as against the old Australian type; and the flock owners of New South Wales have taken the lead in advocacy of the American cross. The co-operative methods of dairying which proved so successful in Victoria have been largely adopted also in New South Wales, especially in those districts where the rainfall is sufficient to give heavy crops of lucerne and maize as green fodder.

The first discoveries of gold in Australia were made by Hargreaves in New South Wales. But Victoria, Queensland, and Western Australia, each in their turn, have left her behind in the development of gold mining, and the golden fleece is still the colony's best friend. Of late, however, many Southern miners have found their way into New South Wales fields. In 1898 the total yield of gold was 341,700 ounces, valued at £1,250,000. The August gold returns for 1899 show that the output of New South Wales for the month amounted to 46,300 ounces, being an increase of 30,700 ounces as compared with August 1898. The output during the preceding eight months amounted to 295,700 ounces, being an increase of 98,200 ounces as compared with the corresponding period of last year. The silver output was worth about £1,800,000. The famous Broken Hill silver mines contribute the bulk of this, but, though territorially they belong to New South Wales, the whole of their business is done with Adelaide and Melbourne. About 7000 square miles of New South Wales give indications of copper, the biggest yield being from the Great Cobar Mine, viz., 2650 tons, valued at over £100,000. The copper output for the colony showed an increase in 1896 of about £60,000 worth as compared with the previous year, and still more recently great progress has accompanied the rise in the price of the metal. The great coal mines of Australia are those of the Newcastle, Wollongong, and Bulli coastal districts, within easy reach of Sydney. They supply not only the whole of Australia, but, to some extent, California and Eastern Asia. During the year 1896 the coal output was 3,909,517 tons, valued at £1,125,280. An important

NEW SOUTH WALES 85

coal seam was struck in boring under Sydney Harbour, and a project (not yet brought to completion) is to drive beneath the harbour; when the ships could be loaded, it is contended, from the dump. There have also been important discoveries of diamonds and opals, the former being chiefly found on the concession of a lucky British company, which has so far shown no desire to come into collision with the De Beers ring; while the latter, like the Queensland opals, though mined in great quantities, and sometimes surpassing in fire and colour the opals of Hungary itself, do not appear to find much favour with the trade. The case of Australian sapphires and emeralds is much the same. But it is whispered that some consignments of antipodean stones, otherwise unsaleable, have been shipped home by astute dealers *viâ* Rangoon or elsewhere; and have then been accepted in Bond Street without question, on their supposed Asiatic merits.

To close finally with figures, the population of New South Wales at the last census of 1891 was 1,132,234. But it has gained largely since then, its manhood not having been drained to the same extent as that of the other two colonies by the gold discoveries in West Australia. Its population is now estimated to be 1,323,460.

The colony has a large and ever increasing system of State-owned railways. About 2700 miles are in existence, the total capital cost of which is 40 millions. The railways are under the management of Commissioners, who are able to pay working expenses and interest and show a small profit; which is the ideal condition for State-owned railways. A system of cheap pioneer lines, communicating with the remote pastoral districts of the colony, has been commenced, but it has yet to be ascertained whether these light lines will not eventually swallow up more in repairs than it would have cost to construct a substantial road in the first instance.

The politics of New South Wales are at present slightly confused, owing to the introduction of the Federal question, which has obliterated the line (formerly clearly drawn) between the Free-trade and the Protectionist camps. During the Federal fight the Free-trade party suffered slightly; and the Labour party are now generally masters of the situation, holding the balance of power. Formerly, Mr Reid, as leader of the Free-traders, had little difficulty in carrying the Labour party with him; but for some little time before his recent fall from power they not infrequently carried him with them. They have practically determined that the fiscal policy of the colony for the time being shall neither be one of absolute Protection nor one of Free-trade; but that revenue shall be drawn to the utmost extent possible from property, leaving the working classes free from taxation, except on such items as tobacco and alcohol.

With all its advantages of area, varied climate, and extensive resources, there can be little doubt but that New South Wales has a future second to that of no other colony of the Australian group; and the position her public men have been able to take in connection with Federation is simply an assertion of the fact that she knows and feels her future greatness. In addition to her vast grazing areas, the productiveness of which in wool and meat is being yearly increased by the establishment of artificial pastures and the improvement in water supplies, she has on her southern coast the same rich pastures and temperate climate which have done so much for the dairying industries in Victoria. In her northern provinces, in addition to magnificent forests of both hard and soft woods, there are tropical conditions of climate

NEW SOUTH WALES 87

and soil which give further variety to the vegetable products of the colony, and allow free play, under the most favourable conditions, to the various new cultures which are every year being introduced with success.

While avoiding the unprofitable extremes of climate, therefore, New South Wales has all the intermediate zones—and in them all those conditions which are the elements of future greatness. No other colony of the group has, to my mind, so fine an outlook.

CHAPTER VI

QUEENSLAND

FROM Sydney to Brisbane is a short run of a little over 700 miles. The mail train leaves Sydney at 6.15 P.M., and in the course of the evening reaches Newcastle, the great coal centre of the Southern Hemisphere, whence, by-the-by, a cargo of coals (for smelting purposes) was actually sent to Newcastle, England, in 1883: a case of γλαῦκ' εἰς 'Αθήνας which has not affected the proverb. We crossed the border at about noon next day, and for several hours steamed steadily through one of the finest stretches of agricultural land in the world—the Darling Downs—arriving at Brisbane, after mounting the hills of the Main Range, east of Toowoomba, at 10.45, P.M. The Darling Downs are only as yet known to the outside world as the home of the squatter. Discovered in 1827, by Allan Cunningham, the explorer and botanist, who penetrated inland from the poorer granite country of the coast to the head waters of the Condamine, it was settled by the early pastoralists in 1840 and the succeeding years. They took possession, under a liberal tenure, of the entire Downs country from Warwick to Toowoomba; an expanse, measuring about 70 miles by 30, of beautifully undulating and well-watered plain, surrounded by mountainous country, the detrition from which has filled it with a strong black alluvial deposit, compared by Americans who have seen it to the characteristic black soil of their own prairies. The district as a whole comprises about four million acres of magnificent agricultural country, or a territory equal to Illinois and Missouri ; and will be the home, as an enthusiastic Yankee professor of agriculture, imported to take charge of the Agricultural College at Gatton, lately wrote to his friend at Chicago, "of millions of people, and that, too, in the near future." For the present it is the great cattle and sheep ranch of the colony, carrying in 1897 about 3,000,000 sheep and 200,000 cattle. But the Acts of 1884 and 1886, which covered the redemption of great portions of the lands occupied by the squatters as their leases expired, were followed by the Agricultural Lands Purchase Act of 1894, under which many of their freehold estates in the neighbourhood, ranging from 10,000 to 150,000 acres, have been acquired by the Government for re-sale. The operation of this Act is fast transforming the territory into a great wheat, maize, and lucerne country, which is also of growing importance in dairying and fruit-culture ; and, as the colony advances, will become a centre of mixed farming, in which large quantities of wheat, oats, potatoes, and malting barley will be produced, as well as butter, cheese, bacon, and fruit for exportation. Nothing could be more prosperous or more fertile than the countryside as seen from the train ; and the Darling Downs, when emigration to Queensland re-commences, should repeat the history of Manitoba. Brisbane is a prosperous city of about 100,000 souls, and in some ways one of the most attractive settlements in Australia. The public buildings are, as usual, handsome ; the hotels are perhaps better managed than is common further south ; and the standard of comfort generally, as of the commissariat in particular, is distinctly high. There is an open air restaurant or kiosk in the public gardens, where a better lunch or breakfast is served on tables set out on the grass, in the shade of the trees overlooking the water, than it would be easy to obtain elsewhere in the colonies. The city is about 12 miles from the sea, facing an abrupt curve in the river, and is subject to most disastrous floods, one of which, some years ago, 'piled up' a gun-boat of Her Majesty's Navy in the Botanical Gardens, high and dry in a secure position, from which it was only rescued by the opportune though unprecedented arrival of a second flood. Brisbane has two theatres, an opera-house, an excellent service of electric tramways, and not so many mosquitoes as Perth. The colony as a whole, with an area of 668,000 square miles, stretching over 18 degrees of latitude, from New South Wales to within 11 degrees of the equator, had, at the last census, less than half-a-million of people. Her exports for 1898 amounted to £22 per head of population (as against £19 for 1897), one of the highest averages known [see Appendix F]; the altogether exceptional case of Western Australia being of course left out of account. The raw produce of her flocks and herds—wool, tallow, hides, and meat—came to £5,770,000—five and three-quarter millions sterling straight from the grass, leaving agriculture and mining out of the question. No wonder Sir Henry Norman, the late Governor, said the other day, "Humanly speaking, very little seems to be wanting for the progress of Queensland but good Government, and enterprise and industry on the part of the people." The country is divided into three sections by three lines of railway which stretch inland westward from the coast; so that, though it is possible to go north to Rockhampton by train, it is more convenient to avoid changing and go by boat. After Rockhampton there is no alternative, for Queensland has not attempted to centre her whole resources by converging lines of traffic upon her capital, but has rested content with a long series of

QUEENSLAND

flourishing ports up the coast. [See Return, Appendix, F.] Each line serves its own back-country, with vast pastoral and other resources, and each has its subsidiary system of goldfields besides. On the 27th parallel the railway runs from Brisbane in towards South Australia and the country of the Barcoo and Cooper's Creek, with Gympie and Maryborough on the way to the north. On the 23rd parallel we have the central line, running west from Rockhampton to Longreach and the Barcaldine district, with Mount Morgan near the coast. And on the 20th parallel the Northern Railway (also east to west) connects Townsville with Hughenden, and serves Charters Towers. Beyond these, again to the north, come the ports of Cairns and Cooktown, with their back-country stretching across to the Gulf; and the scattered and neglected mineral wealth of the Palmer and the Hodgkinson Fields, as well as Chillagoe. And what these things mean it is worth while to consider. Mount Morgan, for example, a few years ago, was one of several low hills included in the selection of a farmer named Gordon, who had found it easier to secure the freehold of his property than to make it return him a profitable living. Two wandering prospectors, named Morgan, who were his guests for a night, examined the Mount, which he suspected might contain copper, at his request; found indications of gold; and acquired his farm at the price of £1 an acre, which he thought himself lucky to get. The Morgans sold a half interest in the mine for £2000, to secure machinery; and almost at once became millionaires. With a nominal capital of one million, the mine has distributed, from its handsome block of offices on the river-front at Rockhampton, nearly five million pounds in dividends, and continues to return over £300,000 per annum (£30,000 a month in 1898). The output from June 1898 to May 1899 was 166,078 ounces from 204,502 tons, and the dividend for the six months ending May 1899, £175,000. A thousand miners find steady employment, and a town flourishes at the foot of the Mount. It was a hill of gold, and apparently only needs quarrying. The accepted theory is that it was a geyser, or thermal spring, of the Tertiary period; though the bed of mundic which is now being worked is said, by practical men who know Kalgoorlie, to bear many points of resemblance to the great decomposed formations of Western Australia, which may yet turn out to have their overlooked parallels in many parts of the world. Charters Towers, the premier field of the colony, was prospected in 1872. Stubley, a blacksmith, one of its pioneers, became member for his district; returned, after losing one fortune, to look for another, and died a pauper by the wayside. There are 20,000 inhabitants at Charters Towers; £13,000 weekly is distributed in wages to the miners, and fourteen millions sterling have been won since 1872. The figures for Gympie give eight millions since 1867. The once famous Palmer goldfield, during the first four and a half years of its working, gave the phenomenal yield of 839,000 ounces of gold. The field has since been almost deserted, but there are still many rich reefs which only require capital for their development. The Hodgkinson has been half tested, and deserted. " Had it stayed undiscovered until now," says Mr Jack, the Government geologist, " there would have been no half-hearted working of the mines. The agents of capitalists are running all over the world looking for mines such as have been abandoned on the Hodgkinson by the score." The treasures of Chillagoe, in copper, silver, lead, lime,

QUEENSLAND 93

and iron, have been but feebly guessed at as yet. In Rhodesia a four foot reef averaging 10 dwts. of gold per ton is, according to Mr Knight of the *Times*, a marvellous claim. There are sixty-eight proclaimed goldfields in Queensland, 95 per cent. of the output from which is from reefs. And reefing returns, according to the official statistics of the colony, about £300 per head for each miner actually engaged in obtaining the metal. The nominal capital of the gold mining industry of Australasia is about ninety-seven millions, of which at least seventy-six millions is British money. The nominal capital of Queensland gold mines is about six millions, of which at least three-fifths is held by Queenslanders; and which, with a bare million sterling invested in machinery, yielded dividends amounting to half a million in 1898. Queensland gold mining is a home industry, maintained by local money, which is the reason of its slow development (for local capital is not unlimited, and local men have their hands full), and the reason, also, of its good management and small waste of money; while the fact that the best mine in the Malay countries, a well-known property near Singapore, is owned in Brisbane, is one of those exceptions which sustain the rule. The gold yield for 1897 was 807,926 ounces; for 1898, 918,106; an increase of 110,180 ounces, or, say, £440,000.

The most conspicuous industry of the colony, to the traveller along the coast, is the export trade in chilled meat; and it is curious to notice that on the map attached to the handbook of the Australasian United Steam Navigation Company, apart from the names of towns, and routes of railways and steamers, nothing is marked but the sites of freezing works, boiling-down works, preserving works, and chilled meat stores. The annual cast, from about twenty million sheep and six million cattle, is about 700,000 cattle and three million sheep. The export of live cattle has been tried, and found expensive and risky; but, between freezing and tinning, and allowing for the demand from other colonies, as from New South Wales after the late drought, it is not, on reflection, strange, though the figures are large, if the number of cattle utilised has sometimes exceeded the available cast, and the export of sheep has left the colony with no great surplusage. A demand is springing up from countries so far apart as Austria, Natal and the Philippines. Receiving stores are being erected at Singapore and Colombo; the Japanese are acquiring a taste for meat; South Africa is thinking of Australian supplies to make up for the deficiency due to the rinderpest; and the American troops in Manilla are supplied with fresh Queensland beef in preference to the malarious flesh of the water-buffalo.

The vast territory of this colony, extending as it does for 1300 miles from north to south and 900 miles from east to west, with a coast line of 2,500 miles, of necessity includes great varieties of soil and climate. Upon the whole, especially towards the south, its physical features correspond roughly to those of New South Wales; the dividing range which separates the eastern from the western waters following the coast at a distance of from 100 to 300 miles inland. Although large herds of cattle are depastured on the eastward side of the range, the great stations of Queensland, both for cattle and sheep, lie on the cretaceous formation of the broad and slightly elevated inland plateau. The cattle from inland are easily distinguished at the meat works by their larger carcases; and vast flocks of sheep graze on the saline pastures of the interior, the squatter not infrequently numbering his sheep by the hundred thousand, while the grazing farmer, pursuing the same industry on a smaller scale, contents himself with a flock of ten or twenty thousand. Apart from tick, the only enemy has been drought; and this has been overcome by the discovery, denounced as a physical impossibility by all the geologists until it became an accomplished fact, that the whole of these uplands, occupying the bed of an old sea which joined the Gulf of Carpentaria to the Australian Bight and separated the continent into two islands, form a great artesian area, whose inexhaustible subterranean reservoirs are supplied from sources as yet unknown, but which are held by many to be the great mountain heights of New Guinea. Over three hundred successful bores have been put down to tap these stores, five of which were down two years ago below the 4000 ft. level, and one below 5000 ft.; four or five of which have an output of 4,000,000 gallons a piece daily; and the total flow from which is approximately 200,000,000 gallons in the twenty-four hours; so that country which a few years since it was dangerous to occupy, is now traversed for miles by the lines of rushes which follow the overflowing waters as they meander for miles over the downs, led in channels formed by huge ploughs made for the purpose. The water issues from the bores under great pressure, and usually at a temperature of from 100 to 140 degrees. The last season when disaster from drought overtook the stockmasters was in the year 1883-4, when many wealthy squatters were ruined. The sugar industry, which was originally opened up, many years ago, by Melbourne enterprise and capital, has had its vicissitudes, connected with the Kanaka, or "black-birding" trade, upon which it chiefly depends for labour. At present about £5,000,000 is invested in the business, which has been found extremely profitable to the small cane-growers as well as to the big companies; but its future will depend to some extent on the attitude adopted towards it by the Federal Commonwealth, as well as on the abolition of bounties by the nations of the European continent. The proposal that the United Kingdom should take off the duties on tea, coffee, and cocoa, and levy a like amount on beet sugar, has not unnaturally found support in Queensland. And it has been pointed out that, when sugar was put on the free list, it was produced entirely by British colonists, while tea was the product of a foreign country: exactly the reverse of present conditions. Coffee planting has not yet become a staple industry, though it has been found that in the scrub lands of northern Queensland an investment of £1000 on 20 acres will give a return of £400 per annum after the fourth year. The world's demand exceeds 500,000 tons, worth £40,000,000 sterling; but Liberian coffee, which is the variety mostly grown in Queensland and the Pacific, as well as in the Malay Peninsula and Borneo, has not yet recommended itself to the British or American palate, or at least has not overcome the prejudices of the middleman. A project is afoot at Singapore, amongst the planters of the Far East, to take some common action, as was done by the Ceylon tea-planters, to bring their wares before the consumer. Java or Malay coffee has merits of its own; and certainly an enforcement of the Adulteration Act should result in a great falling off in the sale of alleged coffee extracts, and would vastly alter the quality of the brew sold at our coffee stalls. The United States have not the same objections as ourselves to adulteration; yet even there the burnt beans which are served out to troops and civilians alike might be abandoned in favour of the real article. After all, the first coffee

QUEENSLAND

drunk in Europe came from Java. And, while real coffee is originally as cheap as its substitutes, there is surely no reason why the working man or even the ordinary householder should be forced to drink nameless and pernicious abominations. In this matter, as in many others, the interests of tropical Queensland, if not altogether sacrificed to the prejudices, or principles, of the Labour Party in the new Commonwealth, will be found coincident with those of her northern neighbours in the British Empire. Upon the whole, it is not surprising that Queensland Government statisticians, in computing the wealth of the community, should take credit for their crown lands at 7s. 6d. per acre. The wealth per head of the United Kingdom is given by Mulhall at £247, and of the United States at £210. That of Queensland works out at £281 : or, if the Crown assets, including land, and deducting the public debt, be distributed as *per capita* wealth, at the extraordinary figure of £615.

A few more data may be excused, as throwing some light on the prospects of possible emigrants from the old country. The population of Queensland was 472,000 at the last census, of whom 264,000 were males, and 86,000 children under 15. The regular defence force numbered 2000, giving a total, with volunteers and rifle clubs, of 4500, or, with all reserves, of 129,000 men liable to military service under such conditions as would obtain in England if the Ballot Act were enforced. The actual expenditure in these matters, taking into account the gunboat on the river, the contribution to the Federal squadron, and that towards the Federal battery on Thursday Island, amounts to 3s. per head. The population is as to about 52 per cent. native-born Australian (45 per cent. native-born Queenslander), 25 per cent. British, 11 per cent. Irish, and 5 per cent. Asiatic and Kanaka. Over

G

200,000 State-aided emigrants landed between 1861 and 1896. The revival in British farming, which dates from the last named year, has been followed by a decline in the departures from the old country for the United States; but those for Canada and Australia have remained stationary, while those for South Africa, owing to matters of recent history, have gone up 40 per cent. Queensland, though she doubled her population in the five years preceding 1886, has increased much more slowly since then. But she has been the first of the Australian colonies to recur to the system of encouraging immigration, setting an example which has quite recently been followed by New Zealand : and assistance towards the cost of passages, second and third class, may now be granted, through the Agent-General, to the families of small capitalists, farmers, market-gardeners, dairymen, etc. The policy of "bursting up the big estates," urged by the Radicals of Victoria in the 'eighties, has been followed by Queensland after a more peaceable fashion in the Acts of 1884, 1886, and 1894, already referred to. Grazing farms of 20,000 acres and under are granted on the resumed lands upon leases of 30 years. Practically, the only outlay required for "improvements" is for a 6-wire fence, costing, say, £30 per mile. Good young ewes may fetch from 6s. to 9s. "off shears," *i.e.* without wool. But the cautious flock-master will probably, at the start, purchase 5000 aged ewes at about 2s. 6d., taking the chances, in good seasons, of getting a couple of lambings off them. The resumptions also include lands which are open to the new-comer in farms of 1280 acres or less, on a 50 years' lease, but which are easily converted into freehold at about £1 per acre. To one of these he is allowed to add a grazing homestead of not over 2560 acres, on lease, at ¾d. per acre, and a homestead selection, freehold, of 160 acres, on

QUEENSLAND 99

easy terms of residence and improvement. Further, cooperative settlements are arranged, with freeholds of 160 acres, where special facilities are given for State schools, etc. : and these are particularly suited to families, as each member can have his holding, and yet some can remain free from time to time, during the early period of struggle, to contribute to the common stock by wages earned elsewhere. To come back to the Darling Downs, —which, it will be remembered, were discovered in 1827, and leased by squatters in 1840,—the squatters' country, which had become freehold, was opened up by the railway constructed by Messrs Peto & Brassey in 1867. The land became of agricultural value, as was proved by the small holdings acquired here and there by selectors. But private owners could not afford to extend the terms of payment for the land sold over 20 years. Parliament therefore sanctioned repurchase; for resale on 20 years' terms, or £7, 12s. 10d. per annum for each £100 ; being £5 interest and £2, 12s. 10d. for redemption, or £152, 16s. 8d. in the end, unless the purchaser shall elect to clear off the debt sooner. The payments, of course, with the exception of the first instalment, come out of the land itself; which, besides, keeps its owner and his family in comfort during the process. A typical case of a farm of 323 acres, thus secured in 1896, gave nearly 200 acres under cultivation by the end of 1897—100 of them under wheat, and the remainder in oats, potatoes, onions, peas, beans, pumpkins, and maize. All this was done with a double-furrow plough, while fencing, wells, dwelling-house, dairy, milking-shed, and yards were in course of construction. The cottage stands in an orchard of three acres ; and, with twenty cows and a score or so of pigs, there is very little difficulty in meeting the Government instalments. Close by is the steading of a farmer of another sort, who came to Queensland from Essex forty years ago, to work on a station at 15s. a week. He contrived to take up a selection, which has grown into his present fine property; some of which has been cropped for thirty-four years continuously with wheat, without manure, and some of which again, under lucerne, is valued at £50 the acre.

There are drawbacks, of course, to unmitigated agriculture; faults inherent, apparently, to a population of small farmers, unrelieved by the civilising, or supervising, influence of a landlord or larger landed class. It is often remarked by Australians that, while their upper classes of pasturalists or commercial men, and successful men generally, are largely Scotch, the colonial Irish, when not policemen, publicans, or professional politicians, are generally small and rather thriftless and disorderly selectors.

In Queensland, as we have seen, there is a large element of Irishmen (11 per cent., as against some 3 per cent. in Tasmania), who have shown a certain tendency to congregate in particular country sides, to which their inherited ideas in some measure give the prevailing tone. The Gatton murders, for example—perhaps the most horrid crime of this century—struck terror, in the early part of this year, into the rural population of the northern end of the Darling Downs district, not so very far from Brisbane itself. And in their investigation of the Gatton murders the police were baffled by a conspiracy of half-cowed and half-sympathetic country-folk, which almost seems to have imposed itself on the very relatives of the unfortunate victims. The state of society near Gatton has points in common with that obtaining in the purely agricultural parts of Gippsland, in Victoria; a district where the squatter has been improved out of existence, and where, consequently, the young bloods among the selectors, who

QUEENSLAND 101

find time heavy on their hands and seek to kill it by indulgence in petty agricultural crime, are insufficiently checked by a magistracy drawn from the storekeepers with whom they deal. The Gatton tragedy, again, drew attention, by some of its attendant circumstances, to another danger affecting the isolated homesteads of the bush—the prevalence of crimes against the female person. This is a matter seldom spoken of in the colonies, though it is at the bottom of the universal prejudice against Indian and Syrian hawkers. It finds its natural parallel in the putting away—seldom discovered and still more seldom brought home to the murderer—of the solitary "hatter," or of the prospector by his mate.

The leaflet published by the Agent-General for Queensland is interesting, and shows, in the very incoherency of its punctuation and grammar, a strong desire to attract immigrants.

"More People Wanted for Queensland," it is headed; "Free Passages for Farm Labourers and Single Women (Domestic Servants). Assistance towards actual Money Cost of Passage is now granted by the Agent-General of this British Colony to Farmers, Dairymen, Market Gardeners, Orchardists, etc., and their Families, where (*sic*) they may obtain Freehold Homes in a Sunny Land!

"The Queensland Government is now granting free passages to farm labourers. Single men must be between the ages of 17 and 35—married men under 45. Must be ploughmen, shepherds, and generally competent farm labourers or servants. Single women (domestic servants) must be between the ages of 17 and 35 and of good character. An application form must be filled up and signed.

"Each applicant must be approved by the Agent-General, and when approved for a passage will be required to pay £1 for a ship kit. This becomes the property of the passenger. Persons obtaining one of these free passages will be sent to the Colony by splendid mail steamships as ordinary 3rd class passengers. Nothing to pay back at any time. The great demand for farm and female labour being the cause of this absolute gift by the colonists of Queensland to a few hard-working British people.

"The demand is kept up by the *Farm Labourers* of to-day becoming the *Farmers* of to-morrow, and in their turn wanting to hire men. And in the case of *Single Women* through a large proportion leaving their situations to *get married*.

"Wages are high, land cheap, provisions abundant. Life is better and brighter and more hopeful for the wage-earner than in England.

" The chance has come to some of these by this offer of a free passage !

" Cheap land under Queensland Government Land Act :—

"*Agricultural Homesteads* :—The area to be selected varies with the quality of the land, from 160, 320, to 640 acres, at 2s. 6d. per acre, payment extending over 10 years.

"*Agricultural Farms* :—Areas up to 1280 acres at 10s. per acre upward, payment extending over 20 years.

" *Grazing Selections* :—Farms and homesteads, in areas up 20,000 acres, on 14, 21, and 28 years' lease, at annual rent of ½d. per acre upward.

" Plough your own acres !   Own your own farm !

" There are upwards of 400,000,000 (four hundred million) acres of unsold land in Queensland. Hundreds of thousands of acres are open to selection and purchase at 2s. 6d. per acre, in all parts of the colony.

" Capital necessary ?   Yes, if you have it ; come and

QUEENSLAND

buy Government Land and improve it ; or buy with care improved farms in the market. Queensland has more railways in proportion to population than England. More constantly being made, and with the rapid development and progress taking place, every acre bought now will increase in value year by year.

" If you have no capital, do not hesitate, but come where hard work and perseverance will soon create it !

" A settler in Queensland, after a year or two's experience, can work for wages on adjoining farms or plantations to his own, and take contracts for supplying timber or cartage. It will thus be seen that a working farm man in Queensland actually *requires no capital* to start on a small Government selection. The first 12 months may be safely passed in a tent (the climate is so mild), while at odd times a house is being built.

" In 1897, the total quantity of land under cultivation was only 386,259 acres, of this area—

59,875 acres of Wheat yielded 1,009,293 Bushels, equal to 16·86 Bushels to the acre.

65,432 acres of Sugar yielded 97,917 Tons, equal to 1·50 Tons to the acre.

2077 acres of Barley yielded 49,840 Bushels, equal to 24·00 Bushels to the acre.

1834 acres of Oats yielded 31,496 Bushels, equal to 17·17 Bushels to the acre.

109,721 acres of Maize yielded 2,803,172 Bushels, equal to 25·25 Bushels to the acre.

8197 acres of English Potatoes yielded 18,520 Tons, equal to 2·26 Tons to the acre.

391 acres of Arrowroot yielded 2888 Tons, equal to 7·31 Tons to the acre.

311 acres of Coffee yielded 81,614 lbs., equal to 262·42 lbs. to the acre.

2196 acres of Oranges yielded 1,628,167 dozen, equal to 741·43 dozen to the acre.

" But more farmers are wanted to grow crops, especially wheat and barley, for which there is a market on the spot, Queensland not producing half enough for own consumption!

" Population, Total, 500,000 people, about half as many as in Liverpool—one English town. The people are mainly British. English character, English laws, customs, money, weights and measures. 160 acres freehold can be purchased at 2s. 6d. an acre payable in yearly instalments of 6d. an acre each year for five years. Single farm servants get £35 to £50, married couples up to £75 a year and all found; female domestic servants from £20 to £75 a year with board and lodging. Nothing to pay back. Persons obtaining a Free Passage are entirely free on arrival. Nothing to work out. Free to work at what they please, where they please, and for whom they please; twelve month's trial, and of (*sic*) residence in Queensland being the only condition. Government Homes at all ports of landing on the other side until hired, board and lodging in them being free of any expense. Free passes up the railways to New Arrivals. Cheapest Australian Colony to Reach. A full paid 3rd class passage by Mail Steamer can be obtained for £13, 13s. (including ship kit). Only vessels of the very highest class are engaged by the Government to carry their passengers. It is the safest and pleasantest voyage in the world."

Truly an energetic pamphlet!—which is, quite seriously, worth reading throughout. The charms of the voyage would be hard to exaggerate, since the route is

QUEENSLAND 105

through the sheltered seas of Java and New Guinea, and southwards within the Great Barrier Reef. But it is unkind of Mr Taverner, the Victorian Minister of Agriculture, to remark, in a book on his colony (which does *not* go in for free or for assisted immigration) that " Free land is generally worthless, and is only obtainable in inaccessible or badly-governed countries, where it can be of little value to the settler." There are distant portions of some of the Australian colonies, he remarks, where land is nominally much cheaper than in Victoria ; but, when its inaccessibility and distance from market are taken into account, it is really dearer. Purchase money is paid once for all, but distance from market means paying annually a heavy tax in the shape of carriage, which would represent the annual interest upon an immense sum of money. The intending emigrant would be wise always to ask for a candid opinion of the country he meditates going to from the representative of a rival community. When agents-general fall out, the honest emigrant comes by some sidelights on the situation. After all, few men who are moderately successful in England will wish, or should be encouraged, to leave the comforts of civilization for the chances of the Bush. A woman who is not sure of getting a husband at home is perhaps in a different case.

As to the public finance, the latest Treasury returns show that the revenue of the colony, during the three months ending September 30, 1899, amounted to £1,253,000, as compared with £1,121,000 during the same period of last year. The expenditure was £653,000 as compared with £565,000.

Chapter VII

NEW ZEALAND

ONE'S first impressions of New Zealand, or Maori-land, are distinctly favourable. Seen from the coast, it is a more pleasant land than Australia; though, even after passing through Australia, the traveller from the old country, still measuring all things in his heart by our ancient and time-stained buildings, and by the bright verdure of our country districts, will find something strange, almost menacing, as of a transitory civilisation still struggling with unconquered nature, in the numerous wooden buildings and the darker green of the Bush. But, after all, New Zealand being subject to occasional shocks of earthquake, wooden buildings are perhaps safer than those of brick and stone. Besides which, quarries are few and far between. *Enfin*, it is not the fashion yet to build great houses before the land is tamed. It is much the same with the landowners as with the miners of the country, one of whom lately voiced his contempt for a Russian gold dredger he had seen, fitted with carpeted saloons, cosy cabins, and the electric light. "In this country," he said, "we spend our surpluses, not on carpets, but in the construction of more dredges." It is the true spirit of the Anglo-Saxon: especially when (as in the Australasian colonies) he is not possessed of much capital. However, most of the principal places of business and warehouses in the chief towns are now being erected in brick, and on entering the port of Wellington one sees a goodly array of warehouses and public buildings.

Wellington is rapidly becoming the distributing centre of the whole of the colony of New Zealand, of which it became the seat of government in 1865. Here Parliament holds its sittings; to Wellington, also, most of the principal banks and places of business are transferring their headquarters; and the numerous lines of steamers which make it their chief port of call testify to its being regarded as the capital of New Zealand. Situated on a narrow strip of land, lying at the base of a range of high hills, it may easily be imagined that it is not an ideal site for a city. But its geographical position in Cook Strait, which traverses the centre of the colony and is provided with a magnificent harbour, demanded that here the capital should be; and, with the disregard of personal convenience which is such a characteristic of colonial life, here it has been built. To make up for the want of flat land, large areas of the harbour have been reclaimed; and even comparatively young colonists can remember when the waters of Port Nicholson washed over what are now the principal streets in the business portion of the city.

Auckland, the former capital, "The Queen of the North," far surpasses Wellington in beauty, and somewhat in size, while her harbour is a yachtman's paradise. The climate, however, is warmer and more humid than that of Wellington; and her geographical position, isolated from the other centres, is also against her. Auckland is the port of arrival and departure for the San Francisco mail boats; though Wellington, where the wharf appliances are of a very high order of excellence, is the port of arrival and departure of the Canadian, or All-British line. Christchurch, on the east coast of the Middle Island, the capital of Canterbury Province, was originally a Church of England settlement, and presents more of the characteristics of an English town than any other place in the colony. The district is wholly flat, and is liable to be swept by fierce north-west winds. Further south is Dunedin, the capital of Otago, originally a Scotch settlement, but rendered cosmopolitan at the time of the gold discoveries. Dunedin is essentially hilly and picturesque. The business part is situated on level land near the harbour, and the residences occupy the sloping hills which rise on the west side of the city.

New Zealand is first a pastoral, secondly an agricultural, and thirdly a mining country. Ten million acres are laid down with sown grasses, and in the Middle Island a large area is covered with native grasses, all useful for grazing purposes. This great extent of pasture has made the colony a leading producer of wool and meat; democratic agrarian legislation is encouraging agriculture (though New Zealand, like West Australia, still imports wheat); and the yield of gold has been over fifty-four millions sterling in value to the present time. The first authenticated visitor to the islands was that doughty navigator Tasman, who sailed from Java in a cock-boat in August 1642; visited Mauritius; discovered and named Van Diemen's Land; and sighted New Zealand (which was apparently already marked on the Dutch charts) in December. Captain Cook, not having access to the Dutch charts, any more than Columbus had known of the Viking charts in the Vatican, was obliged to rediscover New Zealand for us, one hundred and twenty-seven years after Tasman; and he was followed by the French, as usual two months too late. The missionaries landed in 1814; colonisation companies followed; an expedition, under Colonel Wakefield (there is always a Wakefield), was despatched from London in 1839; and annexation by the Crown followed in 1840. The Middle Island is the size of England and Wales; the North Island is half as big again as Scotland; and for practical purposes there is no South Island at all.

"Nearly all the public works of New Zealand," says the official guide, "are in the hands of the Government of the colony, and in the early days they simply kept pace with the spread of settlement. In 1870, however, a great impetus was given to the progress of the whole country by the inauguration of the 'Public Works and Immigration Policy,' which provided for carrying out works in advance of settlement. Railways, roads, and water-races were constructed, and immigration was conducted on a large scale. As a consequence, the population increased from 267,000 in 1871 to 501,000 in 1881." This is the discreet (or official) way of saying that Sir Julius Vogel adopted, as Sir John Forrest has adopted in Western Australia, a bold policy of borrowing British money, with the difference that Vogel was provident enough to help to meet the interest, by introducing population to lighten (by sharing) the burden. However, the policy was pushed too far; and the country suffered from a terrible reaction, from which it has only lately recovered. The inhabitants of the colony now number nearly 750,000. But they seldom mention the name of the man who doubled their resources, and their population, in ten years: preferring to point to the steady perseverance (for which they are undoubtedly entitled to admiration) with which they set themselves to work, as did the Victorians after their disasters, to redeem their credit by increasing their output.

To the newcomer, in the summer time, the climate appears to be warmer than in England, especially as you go north. The air is not relaxing, and hot winds, such as are so often met with in Australia, are infrequent. In winter, snow and frost are met with in the higher country, and in the southern portion of the Middle Island. In the North Island, except on the ranges, snow is seldom seen, and the frosts are of a very mild nature compared with those of even the warmer parts of England. Their place is taken by cold southerly winds, generally accompanied by heavy falls of rain and sleet. As to the scenery, it is equal to that found in any part of the world. For grandeur and majesty it would be difficult to surpass the Southern Alps, or the West Coast Sounds and the lake districts in the Middle Island, which are very properly called by the guide-books "a scenic wonderland." In the North Island is the Wanganui river, similarly called the New Zealand Rhine. This is traversed for the greater part of its length by well-appointed, flat-bottomed paddle steamers, starting at frequent intervals from the thriving and beautifully laid-out town of Wanganui, which is within about eight hours train journey from Wellington. A journey up this river is simply delightful, fresh pictures meeting you at every turn, while the glimpses one gets of the Maori in his native home give an added charm to the trip. But the real wonderland of New Zealand is Roturua and the adjoining district. Forests of extraordinary luxuriance and beauty clothe the mountains and border the extensive plateaux, and hot lakes, boiling geysers, and thermal springs are met with everywhere; in fact, hundreds of hot springs exist within the district, besides numerous mud volcanoes, fumaroles, and solfataras. The mineral waters and baths are highly esteemed in the treatment of various diseases, and at Roturua the Government has established a well-equipped sanatorium, which is in charge of a highly-qualified medical man. The famous Pink and White Terraces, and the Lake of Roto-

NEW ZEALAND 111

mahana, were blown up in 1886 ; but the district, whose natural facilities for cooking are applied by the Maories to their potatoes as well as by the invalid to his lumbago, has been proclaimed a National Park.

Society, of course, radiates from Government House, Wellington, where resides his Excellency the Governor, the Earl of Ranfurly, K.C.M.G. New Zealand has of late years been particularly fortunate in its Governors. Lord Glasgow, who preceded the Earl of Ranfurly, was esteemed by all classes of society for his kindly and unassuming manner, and his genial yet dignified bearing. It was no easy task to follow such an one in the Governorship of the colony. But the Earl of Ranfurly is already displaying qualities which cannot fail to make him popular ; and his hospitality is of the most generous description.

Next in importance to the Governor is the Premier, the Right Hon. R. J. Seddon, LL.D., P.C. (to give him his full title ; " Digger Dick " he used to be called in his gold-mining days on the West Coast) : a man who forced his way to the front rank of New Zealand politics by sheer strength of brain and will, and has for years retained his position by the exercise of the same valuable qualities. Tall, upright, of portly habit, with a commanding presence, Mr Seddon knows exactly what he wants, and generally manages to get it. (It is a thing worth observing, that most successful colonial statesmen are portly, and most of them are also bluff.) As a politician, he stands head and shoulders above all his Ministers, while his tactics are the dismay of the Opposition. " Unscrupulous " his political enemies call him ; but for all that they admire his strength of will and ability as a party leader, and the untiring energy he displays in the prosecution of his plans. Next to him comes the Minister of Lands, the Hon. John

M'Kenzie, a big, and (also) bluff, outspoken, hot-headed Scotchman, fierce in the political battle, and always ready for the fray; but having the reputation of straightforwardness and honesty in his endeavour to settle the people on the land. He is not so strong physically as a Minister requires to be in New Zealand, and there is some talk of his retiring early in the New Year. The Hon. A. J. Cadman is Minister of Mines and Railways—an arduous billet in a country where nearly all the railways are owned by the Government, and where the Minister is expected to show a surplus of revenue over expenditure at the end of every year. Mr Cadman is quiet, self-contained, and methodical, but a good departmental man, and an indefatigable worker. The Minister for Public Works is the Hon. W. Hall-Jones. He was a builder and contractor before he was chosen a member of the Ministry some three or four year ago, and hails from Kent, England. He devotes himself assiduously to running his department, and also to supervising matters relating to the Customs and Marine, in all of which he succeeds remarkably well. The Minister of Defence and Justice is the Hon. T. Thompson. He has charge of the Police Department, among others; and there is some talk of his being forced to resign, in consequence of the inquiries of a Royal Commission into the state of the police force of the colony, which is under direct Government control. The Hon. W. C. Walker is the Minister of Education, with a seat in the Upper House. Last of all comes the Hon. James Carroll, member of the Executive as representing the native race. "Jima Kara," as he is called by the Maoris, is a half-caste—a well educated, genial, good-tempered sort of being, on whom care sits lightly, and who goes through life as if ministerial responsibility was a thing of naught. He is excellent

NEW ZEALAND   113

company—can sing a good song or tell a good "yarn"
in the most approved style, and is much in request at
social functions. When his natural indolence is for the
time overcome, he can speak with telling effect: in fact,
he is one of the orators of the House of Representatives:
and there are few empty benches when "Jimmy" is
opening the floodgates of his eloquence. The Opposition
in Parliament is led by Captain Russell, a wealthy
squatter from Hawke's Bay, one of the richest districts
in the colony. Tall, and still retaining a decided military
bearing, he is courteous and kindly in his demeanour.
There are seventy-four members of the popular Chamber,
the House of Representatives, four of them being Maoris.
Each of the white members represents about 10,000
constituents: and all but one of the natives require the
assistance of an interpreter when addressing the House.
As a rule they only speak on matters directly affecting
the native race. The nominated Chamber is known as
the Legislative Council. Unlike members of the powerful Upper Houses of Victoria and Western Australia, who
are elected on a wide property basis, Members of the
Legislative Council here hold their seats, as in Queensland,
under writ of summons from the Governor, and are very
cavalierly treated, on occasion, by the Representative
Assembly. Two members of the Council are aboriginal
native chiefs. Formerly members were appointed by the
Government of the day for life: the term now is seven years,
though Councillors may be re-appointed. Female suffrage,
as in South Australia, has made but little difference in
politics. Of the 319,000 adults of both sexes in the
colony, the extraordinary proportion of 96 per cent. are
on the rolls, of whom 76 per cent. voted at the last
general election. It is a remarkable fact that 197,000
men, almost the full number of adult males in the colony,

are on the electoral rolls. New Zealand is the most perfect and in some ways the most prosperous democracy in the world.

For a young country, New Zealand is fairly well supplied with railways, although an agitation is on foot to raise a large loan for the purpose of completing, more expeditiously than can be done otherwise, the main trunk lines through the centre of the two islands. Travelling by rail is somewhat more expensive than in England, and the trains run at a lesser speed, especially in some parts of the North Island, where the gradients are steep and the curves sharp. The country, however, is well served by its railways, which, with three unimportant exceptions, are owned by the Government and under the control of a Department, at the head of which is the Minister of Railways, who is beset with numberless applications for new lines in all parts of the country. Coastal communication is chiefly maintained by the Union Shipping Company of New Zealand, which also provides a fine fleet of fast steamers for communication with the Australian Colonies. But there are few good harbours in the North Island, and navigation has been shown by a series of wrecks, comparable only to the successive disasters which spoiled the route by the north of Queensland to Europe for the saloon passenger traffic, to be highly dangerous.

In a colony like New Zealand, chiefly devoted to pasture and agriculture, the system under which the lands of the colony are administered is a matter of supreme importance. The distinguishing feature of the present land system of the colony is State-ownership of the soil with a perpetual tenancy for the occupier—in fact, a considerable portion of the Crown lands is disposed of for terms of 999 years. Settlers may, however, take up land for cash, or on lease with a purchasing clause, or on lease in perpetuity, at a rental of 4 per cent. on the capital value. A system that is daily growing in favour is known as the "Improved Farm Settlements" plan, which may be briefly explained as follows :—In order to find work for the unemployed, considerable areas of bush-covered Crown lands have been set aside, and small contracts, for clearing, burning the bush, and sowing it with grass, have been let. The land is then sub-divided into small farms, and let on lease in perpetuity, at a figure sufficient to cover the cost of clearing, etc., together with a fair rental of the land. The size of holdings averages 100 acres. By the Land for Settlement Act, too, the Government has the power to compel owners of large blocks of land to sell them to the Crown; and these properties are, when acquired, sub-divided into small farms not more than 320 acres in extent. The Government is also yearly purchasing large areas of native reserves; and it will thus be seen that there is no lack of land on which persons, even with small means, may settle and make a home for themselves. Further, by an Act passed in 1894, the Government was empowered to borrow money for the purpose of lending it to farmers on the security of a first mortgage on their land, the amount being payable by instalments; and there are not wanting signs that the operation of the Act has resulted in a great deal of relief being afforded to struggling settlers. Most of this agrarian legislation, it will be seen, has its parallels in Queensland, Victoria, and New South Wales, though these colonies, for the most part, have been able to improve upon New Zealand precedents. Western Australia, characteristically, contented itself with starting a State Agricultural Bank, which appears to have used up its available capital mostly in loans to wealthy absentees.

Closely associated with the colony's land system is the

dairy industry, which has made marvellous strides within the last few years, and has developed into one of the settled industries of the colony. It is under the special care of the Minister for Lands, himself a farmer, and during his term of office the Government have been at great pains to assist in its development. Dairy experts have been introduced to the colony, their business being to instruct the farmers and factory owners in all the most approved methods of butter and cheese manufacture; and graders are employed examining all butter and cheese for export, and branding each packet with its proper quality. The export of butter and cheese from the colony for the year 1898 amounted to nearly £540,000, as against £211,801 for 1889—a big stride to make in ten years.

The frozen meat industry is also a very large factor in the prosperity of the colony, and the freezing works are in full work during the greater part of the year in almost every part of the country. The protracted drought in Australia has reduced the number of sheep depastured by many millions. New Zealand escaped with a loss of only a few hundreds of thousands, and still has 19,210,702 to her credit. The prodigious advance which the frozen meat export trade of this colony has made since its establishment seventeen years ago may be gauged by the fact that whereas in 1882 1,707,328 lbs. were exported, in 1898 there were 159,223,720 lbs., and during the first half of this year 106,008,848 lbs. The value of all the exports in 1898 was £10,500,000; the value of New Zealand produce exported, £10,325,000, being at the rate of £13, 17s. 9d. per head of population, as against £13, 6s. for the previous year.

Gold to the value of £53,372,634 had been obtained in New Zealand prior to December 31st, 1897, and the

NEW ZEALAND 117

value of the gold obtained during 1897 was £980,204; during 1898, £1,080,691, an increase of £100,500. There are extensive coal mines, but little has been done towards working the other minerals in the colony. The wool clip for 1898 was 154,000,000 lbs., worth about £4,700,000, showing an increase of 65 per cent. in eleven years. There were 19,500,000 sheep in the colony in 1898, as against 15,000,000 in 1888, the growth being chiefly in the small flocks, which number 12,886 of under 500 as against 6,579 in 1888, while those of 20,000 and upwards have decreased. This is because the small owners are better able to cope with the rabbit difficulty than the large runholders.

The total declared value of the imports in 1898 amounted to £8,230,600, as compared with £8,055,223 in 1897, and £7,137,320 in 1896. The excess of exports over imports, excluding specie, was nearly £2,250,000.

The cost of living in the colony is estimated at about £35, 6s. 1d. per head of the population. But the average rate of wages is distinctly higher than in Great Britain, and the average income of the New Zealander is £37, as against £29 for the Briton and £32 in the United States. Bread is 1½d. per lb., beef 3¾d., mutton 3d.; while agricultural labourers get about 15s. weekly, with board, and artizans about 10s. daily, without. There is £19 per head deposited in the banks, and the estimated private wealth of £201,000,000 works out at £271 to the individual, in 1898: to which must be added the public wealth, of about £45,000,000.

Manufactories and works show a satisfactory increase over the previous years.

Generally speaking, the Revenue duties are not protective. Clothing and boots are, however, subject to a heavy tax, as both the clothing and boot-making industries are being developed. An agitation is now on foot to take the duties off the necessaries of life. Under the Assessment Act of 1891, there is an ordinary land tax on the actual value of land, an owner being allowed to deduct any amount owing by him secured by a registered mortgage. The value of all improvements is exempted: besides which, an exemption of £500 is allowed when the balance, after making the above deductions, does not exceed £1,500. Above that a smaller exemption is made, which ceases when the balance amounts to £2,500. Mortgages are subject to the land tax. There is also a graduated land tax, which commences when the unimproved value is £5,000, the present value of all improvements, but not mortgages, being deducted. Twenty per cent. additional tax is levied in the case of persons who have been absent from the colony for three years or more. Income-tax is levied on all incomes above £300; and a deduction of £300 is made from taxable incomes. Companies are not allowed the £300 exemption, and pay a higher tax than individuals. Seventy-five per cent. of the colony's revenue is raised by the Customs and Excise duties.

A noteworthy feature of the Government which now holds, and has held for eight years, the reins of power in New Zealand is the several Acts passed for the benefit of the working classes. The whole body of legislation known in New Zealand as the "Labour Laws" has been collected and published by the Department of Labour, in a pamphlet which contains in its preface the following passage:—

"The labour laws have been passed in the effort to regulate certain conditions affecting employer and employed. Their scope embraces many difficult positions into which the exigencies of modern industrial life have

NEW ZEALAND

forced those engaged in trades and handicrafts. The general tendency of these laws is to ameliorate the position of the worker by preventing social oppression through undue influences, or through unsatisfactory conditions of sanitation. It will undoubtedly be found that, with the advance of time, these laws are capable of improvement and amendment; but they have already done much to make the lives of operatives of fuller and more healthy growth, and their aim is to prevent the installation of abuses before such abuses attain formidable dimensions."

The laws referred to comprise the appended statutes and regulations made under various Acts :—

"The Conspiracy Law Amendment Act, 1894."

"The Contractors' and Workmen's Lien Act, 1892."

"The Employers' Liability Act, 1882," with amendments of 1891 and 1892.

"The Factories Act, 1894," and Amendment Act, 1896.

"The Industrial Conciliation and Arbitration Act, 1894," with amendments, 1895, 1896, and 1898.

Labour in Coal-mines: Extract from "The Coal-mines Act, 1891."

Labour in Coal-mines: Regulations for the management and administration of funds and moneys under section 69 of "The Coal-mines Act, 1891."

"The Master and Apprentice Act, 1865." Master and Apprentice: Extract from "The Criminal Code Act, 1893," sections 150 and 213.

"The Mining Act, 1898."

"The Servants' Registry Offices Act, 1895."

"The Shearer's Accommodation Act, 1898."

"The Shipping and Seamen's Act, 1877," with Amendment Acts of 1885, 1890, 1894, 1895, and 1896.

"The Shops and Shop-assistants Act, 1894," with Amendment Acts of 1895 and 1896.

"The Sunday Labour in Mines Prevention Act, 1897."
"The Trade Union Act, 1878," and Amendment Act, 1896.
"The Truck Act, 1891."
"The Wages Attachment Act, 1895."
"The Workmen's Wages Act, 1893."

Chief among these is the Conciliation and Arbitration Act, which provides for the settlement of all trade disputes before Boards of Conciliation in the first place, and Courts of Arbitration, whose awards can be enforced in the same manner as an award of the Supreme Court.

Societies consisting of five or more employers, or of seven or more workers, may be registered and become subject to the jurisdiction of the Board and Court appointed by the Act. Any such society may bring a disputed case before the Board of Conciliation appointed for the district, and, if the Board fails to effect a settlement, the dispute may be referred to the Court of Arbitration. The amount, however, for which such an award may be enforced against an association is limited to £500.

The manner in which the Act has operated may generally be regarded as satisfactory; and, although its existence has undoubtedly tended to bring into prominence a number of disputes about small matters which would otherwise probably never have been mentioned, on the other hand, it must be admitted that it has succeeded in finding a settlement for more than one cause of disagreement between employers and employed which, but for it, would have resulted in strikes and lock-outs. Some difficulty has lately arisen in regard to the Conciliation Board at Wellington. One of the members was away from the colony, another laid aside by illness, and yet another absent on business. The consequent difficulty of getting a quorum to sit or adjudicate on certain trade disputes was rapidly coming to be felt as a grievance by the workmen concerned, when the unexpected arrival of the two absentees solved the problem. It is probable, however, that the Government will next session move to amend the law so as to provide for such contingencies.

"The Factories Act" is a consolidation of previous legislation, with some important additions. New Zealand has been divided into factory districts under the charge of a chief inspector and 163 local inspectors. As a "factory" or "work-room" includes any place in which two or more persons are engaged in working for hire or reward in any handicraft, there are few operatives who do not come within the scope of the Act. Children under fourteen years of age are not allowed to be employed, and the hours of labour, holidays, etc., of women and youths under sixteen are strictly regulated. Good ventilation, sanitary accommodation, and general cleanliness of buildings are points dwelt upon; while machinery has to be properly guarded, fire-escapes provided, and dangerous occupations especially classified. In order to assist the system of free general education which prevails in the colony, young persons are not allowed to work in factories till they have passed the fourth standard of the State schools, or an equivalent examination. To prevent the introduction of "sweating," articles made, or partly made, in private dwellings, or unregistered workshops, have to be labelled when offered for sale, so that goods so manufactured (often in unsanitary premises) may not be placed in the market in competition with work done in properly inspected factories. Any person removing such labels is liable to a heavy fine. The Factory Inspectors also exercise supervision over the sleeping accommodation provided for shearers in country districts.

As the sheep-runs and farms are widely scattered, sometimes in the rough and remote back-country, this part of the work of inspection is no easy task. A woman Inspector of Factories also gives her assistance to the duties of the department, travelling from place to place, and particularly looking into the condition of the operative women and girls.

The duration of the hours of business in shops is limited by " The Shops and Shop-Assistants Act," and " The Shops and Shop-Assistants Act Amendment Act." These provide for the closing of all shops in towns and boroughs for one afternoon half-holiday in each week. A few shops, such as those of chemists, fruiterers, eating-house keepers, etc., are exempted from the general closing, on account of their convenience to the public; but assistants in such establishments, in the bars of hotels, and in country stores, must have a half-holiday on some day of the week. Small shops carried on by Europeans without paid assistants are also exempt from closing on the general half-holiday, but must close on one afternoon in each week. The hours of work for women and young persons are defined ; sitting accommodation must be provided, and precautions as to the necessary time for meals, sanitary accommodation, etc., are enforced. The Act also enumerates the working-hours, holidays, etc., of clerks employed in banks, mercantile offices, etc.

" The Employers' Liability Act," added to and amended in 1891 and 1892, is designed to protect workmen from negligence on the part of employers, by defining under what circumstances compensation for injury or death may be recoverable. The Act covers all employments except that of domestic servants, and does not allow of any " contracting out " by agreement on the part of employer and employed. Another Act of this character has regard to the payment of workmen's wages, providing that if a workman shall demand payment of wages twenty-four hours or more after they are due, and the contractor does not pay such wages, the workman may legally attach all moneys due to the contractor from the employer until he is paid. "The Servants' Registry Office Act" regulates registry offices for domestic or farm servants, preventing friendless or uneducated people from becoming the prey of unscrupulous persons who formerly made a living out of fees by duping applicants for situations. The registry office keepers pay a licensing fee to the Government; must produce a certificate of good character when applying for a license; must keep books open to inspection; and are not allowed to keep lodging-houses for servants.

Combinations or associations of persons for regulating the relations between masters and masters, or masters and workmen, or workmen and workmen, are directed by the "Trade Union Act." The "Conspiracy Law Amendment Act" permits any combination of persons in furtherance of a trade dispute, provided that any act performed by such combination or society would not be unlawful if done by one person. "Such action," naïvely adds the Secretary to the Department of Labour, "must not include riot, sedition, or crime against the State"; a remark which somehow suggests that it may include riots or crimes against the employer. "The Wages Attachment Act" prevents wages below £2 a week being attached for debt; though it does not prevent any workman being sued for debt in the ordinary course.

The New Zealand democracy really, though no Australian would admit it, leads Australia; as will be acknowledged by any one who, after acquainting himself with the above body of law, will examine recent legislation in the other colonies. And it will be seen that the antipodean wages-man and his wife, given a free hand, lose no time in securing, through the action of their paid Parliamentary delegates, their economic position; while, with equal decision, they agree to leave the burden of taxation on the employer.

Last year the Legislature of New Zealand passed a statute entituled "The Divorce Act, 1898," which was assented to by Her Majesty in April 1899. The new Act places persons of either sex practically on an equality as regards petitions for dissolution of marriage; the same grounds, in substance, for a decree of divorce applying to man or woman.

Besides this important alteration of the law, the grounds for divorce are extended as under:—

1. Adultery, on either side.
2. Wilful desertion continuously during five years or more.
3. Habitual drunkenness on the part of husband, along with failing to support wife; or drunkenness and neglect, with unfitness to discharge household duties on the part of the wife.
4. Conviction, with sentence of imprisonment or penal servitude for seven years or upwards, for attempting to take life of petitioner.

An Act of similar tenor was passed in New South Wales several years ago, and one is now, or was lately, before the Legislature of Western Australia.

Finally, it will be interesting to consider the operation of a Local Option Poll.

Under "The Alcoholic Liquors Sale Control Act, 1893," each electoral district constituted for the election of a member of Parliament is a licensing district, and

NEW ZEALAND 125

Parliamentary electors are also electors under the Licensing Acts.

The licensing poll is taken at every General Election. The questions for the decision of the voters are—

1. Whether the number of licenses existing in the district shall *continue ?*
2. Whether the number shall *be reduced ?*
3. *Whether any licenses whatever shall be granted ?*

The voter may vote for one or two of these proposals, but no more.

The method of determining the result of the poll in each district is as follows :—

(1.) If the number of votes recorded in favour of the *continuance* of existing licenses is an absolute majority of all the voters whose votes were recorded, the proposal is carried, and the licenses continue until the next poll.

(2.) If the number of votes recorded in favour of a *reduction* of licenses is an absolute majority of the voters whose votes were recorded, the proposal is carried ; and the Licensing Committee then reduces publicans' licenses by not less than 5 per cent. or more than 25 per cent. of the total number.

(3.) If the number of votes recorded in favour of the proposal that *no license shall be granted* is not less than three-fifths of the voters whose votes were recorded, the proposal is carried ; and no licenses can be granted.

(4.) If none of the proposals respecting licenses are carried by the prescribed majority, the licenses continue as they are until next poll.

The result of a poll taken in December 1896, in sixty-two licensing districts, was that nearly 140,000 votes were cast in favour of proposal (1), the *continuance* of existing licenses; 94,500 for (2) *reduction*; and 98,300 for (3) *no license*. In fifty-two districts the majority was for *continuance*; in four a majority, but not the necessary three-fifths majority, voted for *prohibition*; and in the remaining six no proposal was carried. In this poll, it must be remembered, half the electors were women.

Education in New Zealand, as in the other colonies, is free (that is to say, it is provided for by annual vote by Parliament out of the Consolidated Fund); secular; and compulsory. The system is administered by a Government Department, through Education Boards, which in turn are served by school committees in charge of the sub-divisions of the various school districts. Technical education is yet comparatively in its infancy; but the urgent necessity for some proper and complete system of technical education is generally recognised, and there is every probability that the disadvantage under which New Zealand is labouring in this respect will be removed in the course of a very few years. There is a University of New Zealand; affiliated colleges being situated at Auckland, Wellington, Christchurch, and Dunedin. There are also schools for the instruction of native children, and the usual industrial schools under Government control.

The people of New Zealand may be generally regarded as sober and law-abiding. Serious crimes are rare, while drunkenness, which used to be so frequent among the old-time hands, in the days of the gold rushes, when money was plentiful, is becoming every day less frequent, especially among the younger members of the community.

While the New-Zealand-born formed at the last census 63 per cent. of the whole population of the colony, they contribute not more that 25 per cent. of the prisoners received in gaol. Of the New-Zealand-born population, however, a large number are under 15 years of age, a

NEW ZEALAND 127

period of life at which there are very few prisoners; another comparison, therefore, is necessary. It is found, then, that the New-Zealand-born over 15 years formed 44 per cent of the total population; but, as before stated, New-Zealanders constitute less than 25 per cent. of the total in their gaols.

The cities and the large towns are well kept, and usually up-to-date, although many of the small settlements in newly opened-up districts are still in a very primitive condition. The people are sociable and hospitable, fond of pleasure and all kinds of out-door sports, horse-racing being the form of amusement to which the greater number are addicted. Every little country settlement, as is the prevalent custom all over Australasia, has one or more race meetings every year, while meetings at which considerable money prizes are given are held several times a year at the principal centres of the colony. In cricket, New Zealand has yet much to learn; but at football her representatives have achieved a very large measure of success whenever they have travelled outside their own borders.

In regard to assisted emigration, it is now announced that the Agent-General is prepared to receive applications from intending settlers for passages at reduced fares, by the Shaw, Savill, and Albion Company's and the New Zealand Shipping Company's steamers.

Application forms and all particulars can be obtained from the Agent-General for New Zealand, 13 Victoria Street, London, S.W., and also from the agents in the United Kingom of the above companies.

It would be impossible to conclude without some reference to the Maoris, who held the country when it was first discovered, and who, unlike most savages to whom we have taken the blessings of civilisation, remain in possession of a very fair proportion of their inheritance to-day. They are said, by those amusing gentlemen who theorise about races, to be the remote descendants of the early inhabitants of India, who, driven from that peninsula by the Aryans, learned navigation in Java and Borneo, and, driven again from there by the Malays, sailed all over the Pacific, and very likely to Mexico and Peru. In any case, a section, either of these Polynesians or of some other persons of the same name, amalgamated with the indigenes of Fiji, and their progeny, becoming a species of Normans of the Pacific, conquered Samoa, Tahiti, the Sandwich Islands, and finally New Zealand, where they arrived in a fleet of canoes about the year 1350. These are the folk, now called Maories, whom Mr S. Percy Smith, F.R.G.S., an authority on the subject, describes as "daring voyagers, in comparison with whom the most noted European navigators of the Middle Ages were mere coasters. The Polynesian chronicles relate voyages extending from Fiji to Easter Island, from New Zealand to the Hawaii group, and even to the Antarctic regions. They were never equalled as voyagers until the sixteenth century, which saw such an extension of nautical enterprise, originating in Europe." When the colony was first occupied by Europeans, the Maoris were found to be a brave and warlike nation, fighting for the love of conflict, and practising cannibalism for want of butchers' meat. Real swine being introduced to their notice, they readily gave up "long pig;" and when the wars between the British and Maoris took place at a later date, they acquitted themselves like men, making a gallant stand, often-times with success, against their better armed and better equipped adversaries. Now, "*Nous avons changé tout cela.*" The Maori and the white man have, so to speak, coalesced, and live together in peace and amity. Gradually their

NEW ZEALAND

numbers are being thinned by disease, and, though slowly, they appear to be experiencing the inevitable fate of a weaker race coming into contact with a stronger one. Generally, the tribes hold land in common, on which they subsist; others hold large areas of land, and are comparatively wealthy; while others again, having sold their land, find it difficult to procure enough to live on. However, as they still have left them some 10,000,000 acres, valued at £3,000,000; and as they only number 40,000 souls (exclusive of 5000 half-castes of all sorts), it will be seen they are not without resources. And their representatives in the Legislature hold a record for stone-walling. For the rest, strong and active in body, and of undoubted ability, they make excellent farm hands; but their natural indolence is a decided disadvantage. They are good horsemen, are fond of racing, and dearly love to talk, some of their "huis" or meetings extending over several days. Generally law-abiding, they easily succumb to diseases brought on by intemperance and the insanitary conditions under which they live. Steps are being taken to provide them, where possible, with medical aid, and to instil in their minds some understanding of the laws of hygiene; and if this is done, there is every reason to hope that the decadence of the Maori may be arrested for very many years. But to anyone desirous of obtaining information about them, let me recommend a charming book, entitled "Old New Zealand, by a Pakeha Maori." It is most delightful reading, and full of details of Maori life.

It has for some time past been generally admitted by the leading technical journals that New Zealand leads the world in one department of mining—that of gold-dredging: a special and cryptic branch of the art, indeed, which is all but unknown, as yet, elsewhere.

"It will be observed from the returns published monthly in the *New Zealand Mines Record*," says that journal under date of May 1899, "that gold-dredging is one of the colony's most stable industries. It has gone on steadily increasing for many years past; and engineers, owners, and masters of dredges have been quietly perfecting their appliances to such an extent that it is generally acknowledged that in no other part of the world is this branch of mining so economically and scientifically carried on as it is in New Zealand. This has all been accomplished without booming, and shareholders have received substantial profits. There is danger just now of a solid industry being made a catspaw of by some of the company promoters, whose chief aim is the flotation of scrip, and those who are asked to go in for new enterprises should make full inquiry as to the probabilities of obtaining something like an adequate return on the capital they are asked to invest." "The consequences of booming," the editor goes on to remark, "are . . . fatal to those who get in too late." But how much temptation there is locally to boom may be, perhaps, vaguely gathered by the uninitiated from the annexed fragments, culled from the up-country press, which are informative enough in their way :—

"A report has been published in several papers that the Ranfurly dredge (Electric Company) last week obtained 1008 ounces. We are authoritatively informed that, although the dredge in question is getting very good returns, nothing has yet been obtained nearly as large as that quoted above. We are informed (on the best authority) that the record weekly yield for the Electric dredges stands at 647 ounces, which yield was obtained by the Electric No. 1 dredge nearly two years ago. This constitutes, we also imagine, the record for the river—in New Zealand, for that matter. It is admitted, however, that the Ranfurly dredge is very familiar with three-figures returns, and, when she reaches some proved ground a little ahead of where she is now working, it is expected that she will easily beat the above-mentioned record."—*Alexandra Herald.*

"Some of those individuals who were enterprising enough to peg out river claims on the Mataura recently have received offers from Dunedin and elsewhere of £50 and £70 for a quarter share in single claims. Faith in the Mataura for dredging purposes is not, evidently, confined to Gore alone. So intense has been the craze all over the district for pegging out claims that one local timber firm disposed of forty pounds' worth of pegs during this month. This sum represents about four thousand pegs. A little above Gore, on the north side, it is estimated that within a radius of a mile there are pegs on private property and river-banks sufficient to close-board a 200-acre paddock."—*Mataura Ensign.*

"What the return of 400 ounces 17 dwt. by the Magnetic really means may be understood from the following calculation:—Allowing 10 ounces 17 dwt. for the payment of expenses, which is ample, it means a clear profit of 390 ounces, or £1511, 5s., for one week's operations. On a capital of £7000 this gives a profit of $21\frac{1}{3}$ per cent. per week, or 1108 per cent. per annum. A dividend of 2s. per share was declared about ten days ago. The next monthly dividend, with returns like last week's, should be nearly equal to the paid-up capital of the company. This dredge has only been working about five months, has paid off nearly £3000 of debt, declared a 2s. dividend, and is still on the jugular."—*Cromwell Argus.*

What 'on the jugular' may mean it is hard for a home-keeping Briton to say. What should they know

of English who only England know? But it is clear
that a number of small local syndicates have been making
good money, and most of us would understand 1000
per cent. That it is understood locally is clear. It was
reported in September that since the beginning of the
year seventy-four companies, with capital aggregating
£600,000, have been formed. In Victoria, as we have
seen, the craze has caught on. The river banks are being
pegged there also, and dredges are being set to eat their
way through them into the worked-out alluvial flats, as
well as to tear up the river beds themselves. The
knowing mining "crowd" of Ballarat and Bendigo are
not ashamed to admit that for once they must learn
of another colony. They get their managers and (to
begin with) their machinery from New Zealand. And
that others besides Victorians are not above taking a
hint may be seen from the following, also taken from a
Maori-land paper of recent date. "Orders for three
dredges have been placed with (Messrs So and So) of
Dunedin, for Siberia. These dredges, which are to be
built from the designs of Mr (———), consulting engineer,
are to be of the type of the dredge near Cromwell, and
are to be delivered f.o.b. at Dunedin on the 1st August
next. The engines are to be made in England, and
the hulls are to be constructed of Siberian timber, which
grows plentifully in the vicinity of the river where the
dredges are to be placed. Mr Heine, a Russian gentleman, who lately made a tour of Central Otago with a
companion, and placed the order in this colony for
the dredges, stated to an interviewer that his claim ex-
tends a hundred miles along the course of the river in
Siberia, and that there are several dredges already at
work in that region, but of a very different type to those
in Central Otago, which require only two men at each

NEW ZEALAND

shift, while on the Siberian dredges there are about a dozen men on each shift." " Mr Heine, a Russian gentleman," is obviously a man of intelligence. But is there not, in the British Empire also, and as far, may be, from New Zealand as from Russia, " timber which grows plentifully in the vicinity of rivers " on which dredges might be placed? Have we not streams of our own, in Africa or in Canada, better than all the waters of Siberia? And have our concessionaires in China taken counsel of New Zealand managers?

Chapter VIII

OLD AGE PENSIONS IN PRACTICE

NEW Zealand has made the first practical effort to solve the problem of "Old Age Pensions," and the Act passed last session has become operative. As the principle of this notable law has been admitted in England, and most of its provisions are being adopted in the Bills which are under consideration in other Australian colonies, it deserves lengthy consideration. The preamble may be quoted.

"AN ACT to provide for Old-Age Pensions.
1st November 1891.

"WHEREAS it is equitable that deserving persons who during the prime of life have helped to bear the public burdens of the colony by payment of taxes, and to open up its resources by their labour and skill, should receive from the colony a pension in their old age :

"BE IT THEREFORE ENACTED by the General Assembly of New Zealand in Parliament assembled, and by the authority of the same, as follows :—"

What follows is mainly contained in the 7th clause, that, " subject to the provisions of this Act," every person of the full age of sixty-five years and upwards, being of our own blood and not guilty of any offence " dishonouring him in the public estimation " (a phrase, by the way, we seem to have heard, somewhere, before!), shall be entitled to a pension of £18 a year. The maximum

OLD AGE PENSIONS IN PRACTICE 135

amount of the pension is thus £18 : but for every complete £1 of income above £34 the pensioner has his pension reduced by £1, and a similar amount will be deducted for every complete £15 of the net capital value of all his accumulated property above £50. In making the calculation as to whether a person is entitled to a pension, and also as to the amount of the pension for the first year, the claimant's income for the past year is to be deemed his yearly income, and the same system of computation will be employed in fixing the rate of the pension in succeeding years. Further, in computing the income, deduction will be made of all income derived or received from accumulated property ; but the value of board and lodging received, up to £26 a year, will be included in the computation of the income. In the case of husband and wife, each will be credited with half the total of the income, but the rule will not apply when they are living apart pursuant to a decree, order, or deed of separation. During the passing of the measure through Parliament considerable discussion took place as to how the term "income" should be defined. Finally, the following definition was agreed upon, viz. : Any moneys, valuable consideration, or profits derived by any person for his own use or benefit in any year by any means or from any source. Personal earnings will be included, but not pensions paid under the Act, nor sick allowance, nor financial benefit from any registered friendly society. By accumulated property is meant all real and personal property owned by any person, to the extent of his beneficial estate or interest therein. From the capital value of such property will be deducted £50, and also all charges and encumbrances lawfully existing thereon, and the residue then remaining will be the net capital value of all his accumulated property.

To obtain the pension a good many conditions have to be fulfilled. First, a person must be sixty-five years of age or upwards. He must be residing in the colony when he establishes his claim, and must be able to show a continuous residence in the colony of twenty-five years immediately preceding the date on which he establishes his claim. Occasional absence will not be considered as interrupting the continual residence, providing that the terms of absence do not total two years. Some difficulty was experienced in making it possible for seamen to come in under the Act, as it was felt that, if special provision was not made in regard to them, they would, by the very nature of their occupation, be debarred from obtaining a pension. It was eventually enacted that the absence of seamen from the colony would not be considered (providing that they were serving at the time of their absence on board a vessel registered in and trading to the colony) if the claimant proved that during his absence his family or home was in the colony.

But that is not all. No pension is awarded to any person who, during the twelve years immediately prior to sending in his claim, has been imprisoned for four months, or on four occasions, for any offence punishable by imprisonment for twelve months or upwards, and "dishonouring him in the public estimation." No satisfactory explanation was given, in Wellington, of the meaning of the phrase "dishonouring him in the public estimation," except that it was said to be in the Danish Act. The Premier (Mr Seddon) was chaffed about it a good deal during the passing of the Bill; but he seemed to think it of great importance that it should be retained (like the old lady's blessed word "Mesopotamia"); and so it was retained. It is really, of course, as used by Mr Secretary Leyds as well as by Dr Seddon, a revival of the old Roman idea of "infamia."

Further, no one can get a pension who during the past twenty-five years has been imprisoned for a term of five years with or without hard labour for any offence "dishonouring him in the public estimation"; or (if a husband) has for a period of six months deserted his wife; or without just cause neglected to provide her with adequate means of maintenance; or neglected to maintain such of his children as were under fourteen years of age. If the applicant is a woman and a wife, she cannot succeed in her application if she has deserted her husband, or those of her children under fourteen years of age.

Applicants must also be of good moral character, and have been leading a sober and reputable life for the past five years; while their net yearly income must be less than £52, and the net capital value of their accumulated property must be not more than £270. Anyone directly or indirectly depriving himself of property or income with the object of entitling him to a pension will by that act be debarred from obtaining one.

Anyone desirous of obtaining a pension is required to fill in a pension claim, the truth of the contents of which he must affirm by statutory declaration. This claim will be forwarded to the deputy-registrar, and will eventually be investigated by the stipendiary magistrate. If necessary the claimant is required to attend to support his claim; but if the magistrate is satisfied that the documentary evidence in support of the claim is sufficient to establish it, or that the applicant's physical condition renders it inconvenient for him to attend, the applicant's personal attendance may be dispensed with.

Evidence given before the magistrate for or against the claim is on oath, and corroboration of the evidence of the claimant is required on all material points. In regard to the question of age, however, the magistrate is not obliged to require corroborative evidence if he is personally satisfied that the claimant is of the required age. Having heard the evidence, the magistrate may admit the pension claim as originally made; or he may modify it in accordance with the evidence called; or he may postpone it for further evidence, or reject it altogether. But, in rejecting it, he is required to specify in writing all the material points which he finds to be proved or disproved. The strict rules of evidence need not be observed in the inquiry, the magistrate being empowered to investigate and determine the matter by such means and in such manner as in equity and good conscience he thinks fit. The magistrate's decision will be held to be final and conclusive in respect of what he finds to be disproved in regard to the claim, but the claimant may at any other time produce fresh evidence on the points which have been found to be "simply unproved" or not sufficiently proved. So that the mere fact of a person failing sufficiently to prove certain points on the first occasion does not necessarily destroy for ever his chances of getting a pension. It is also provided that a claim may be sent in and investigated not more than two years before the date on which it is alleged it will be due, so that everything will be in readiness for the claimant to get his pension, if the claim is established, on the due date.

When the claim is established and the rate of pension fixed, the Stipendiary Magistrate will certify accordingly to the Deputy-Registrar, who will issue a pension certificate to the claimant; and a fresh pension certificate will be issued to him every year thereafter. The pension will be paid, in monthly instalments, at the money order office in the district in which the pensioner resides. The pensioner must personally apply for his pension, and produce his certificate, otherwise he will be unable to obtain the instalment and it will be forfeited; provision, of course, being made for cases in which the pensioner is physically incapable of making a personal appearance.

In cases where the pensioner is maintained in or relieved by any charitable institution, the reasonable cost of such maintenance or relief is payable out of the pension to the governing body of such institution; and any surplus remaining after defraying such cost is paid to the pensioner himself.

Instalments which fall due while the pensioner is in prison or an inmate of a lunatic asylum, or while he is absent from the colony, are absolutely forfeited.

A maximum penalty of six months is provided for any person who obtains, or attempts to obtain, a pension certificate to which he is not justly entitled, or a pension of a larger amount than he can legally claim, by means of any false statement or representation; or if he by any means obtains, or attempts to obtain, payment of any forfeited instalment of his pension, or aids or abets any person to so infringe the law. If a person is convicted of any such offence, the Court is empowered to cancel any pension certificate which is proved to have been wrongfully obtained, or to reduce to its proper amount any pension that has been proved to be too high, or to impose a penalty not exceeding twice the amount of any instalment, the payment of which has been wrongfully obtained. If the defendant in the case is a pensioner, the Court may direct the forfeiture of future instalments of his pension equal in amount to such penalty.

To satisfy the demands of the Prohibition party in the House of Representatives, it is provided that if any pensioner is convicted of drunkenness, or of any offence punishable by imprisonment for not less than one month, "and dishonouring him in the public estimation," then, in addition to any other penalty imposed, the Court has the discretion of forfeiting one or more of the pensioner's instalments falling due after the date of the conviction. Further, if the Court is of opinion that any pensioner mis-spends, wastes, or lessens his estate, or greatly injures his health, or endangers or interrupts the peace and happiness of his family, it may direct that the instalment may be paid to any clergyman, justice of the peace, or other reputable person for the pensioner's benefit. It may even go so far as to cancel the pension certificate. And it is bound to cancel the certificate if the pensioner is proved to be a habitual drunkard within the meaning of the Act. The certificate must also be cancelled if the pensioner is sentenced to imprisonment for twelve months or upwards for any offence " dishonouring him in the public estimation."

The pension is absolutely inalienable, whether by way of assignment, charge, execution, bankruptcy, or otherwise. The Act does not apply to aboriginal natives who are in receipt of aid from the Civil List, nor to aliens, nor to Chinese, nor other Asiatics, whether naturalised or not, and only to naturalised persons of other countries who have been naturalised for five years.

The Act, which applies, of course, to persons of both sexes, is admitted by the Premier to be merely a tentative measure, and appearances, before it was passed, pointed to the fact that considerable difficulty seemed likely to be experienced in putting it into active operation; that is, if any reasonable amount of care was to be exercised by those conducting inquiries into claims for pensions. A cursory glance at the qualifications necessary for a pension is sufficient to show that a considerable amount of extra

OLD AGE PENSIONS IN PRACTICE 141

work will devolve upon stipendiary magistrates ; who, in the more populous districts at any rate, have their hands so full that in more than one instance representations have been made as to the necessity of providing them with assistance. Would-be pensioners, too, must be put to a good deal of trouble to prove their claims, and in many cases will have to call evidence in support of their declarations from places far distant from those in which they at present reside. As to the question of age, the investigating magistrate is allowed to exercise his own power of observation ; but it will be by no means an easy or brief task for him to discover from applicants what amount of truth attaches to their statements that they are of sober and reputable habits, of good moral character, or that their income or the amount of their property is sufficiently small to entitle them to receive a pension. Naturally, the police will be called upon to speak as to their knowledge of the applicants, and in view of that contingency it is perhaps just as well that Parliament last session voted money for an increase in the numbers of the police force. In short, to prove what is required to be proved, each applicant is attended by a small army of witnesses, whose evidence needs to be carefully checked by the police authorities, and probably by those who are or have been concerned in the distribution of charitable aid. The official view of the matter appears to be that applicants, generally speaking, are not inclined to depart overmuch from the truth in the statements they make in support of their claims. The majority of the public, however, are inclined to be less charitable in their opinions.

Under the supplementary Regulations, 'the Deputy-Registrar is required to file all claims sent in, and to forward them to the stipendiary magistrate presiding at the court held at the place nearest to the residence of the claimant, who will be notified of the time and place at which he may attend to support his claim, forms for which are provided. The pension claim, bearing a minute of the magistrate's decision, is filed in the court, and a copy of the minute forwarded to the Deputy-Registrar, who is to enter its purport in the pension claim register. If the magistrate certifies that the pension is rightly claimed, an entry of the amount of the pension to be paid is entered in the register, and a pension certificate will at once be issued.

In order to facilitate the magistrate's investigation of pension claims, he is allowed to authorise the Deputy-Registrar, " or any other fit person," to inquire into the accuracy or otherwise of the matters of fact set forth in the claim; and for that purpose the person so appointed is allowed to have free access to the register of the Lands Transfer and Deeds Registration Office (for the purpose of searching title to land), the records of the Supreme Court (for the purpose of searching mortgages, etc.), and the District Valuation Roll (for the purpose of ascertaining the particulars and valuation of landed property), besides the property real and personal of the claimant, and all books, vouchers, etc., relating to his property or income. These inquiries are, where practicable, to be completed before the magistrate makes his investigation, and are to be reported to him either in writing or by way of evidence at the investigation. Discretion is given to the magistrate as to whether he will accept or reject such testimony; and he is also empowered to receive or accept or reject a statutory declaration made by any clergyman, justice of the peace, postmaster, " or other reputable person," on the subject of the claim. The magistrate, in fact, is given a very free hand; he is not bound by the strict rules of evidence, and may

OLD AGE PENSIONS IN PRACTICE 143

be guided by his own personal observation, or documentary evidence other than that already mentioned, or the sworn spoken evidence of any reputable person who deposes to what, from inquiries made by him, he believes to be true. Government officers and the police are instructed to assist claimants in the preparation and investigation of their pension claims.

In all this there is abundant evidence that several new offices will have to be created if the Act is to be administered with any degree of care ; while, on the other hand, it is equally certain that if every care is not exercised in the investigation of claims many undeserving people will be awarded pensions. At the same time, it must be remembered that, once a pension has been granted, any departure from the paths of virtue on the part of the recipient will probably be quickly noted, and the pensioner will be penalised to the extent of the whole or some part of his pension, according to the magnitude of his offence.

In introducing the measure to the House of Representatives, the Premier urged that it would result in a considerable saving in the cost of charitable aid. This was at the time disputed by the opponents of the scheme, but appears to be borne out by later developments. In the Benevolent Home at Wellington at the present time, there are no less than thirty-six inmates who are entitled to the full amount of the pension ; and the trustees of the Home deduct from the pension the reasonable cost of their maintenance. No figures have yet come to hand regarding similar institutions in other parts of the colony, but it may be safely assumed (and the assumption is borne out by people who are in a position to know) that the case of the Wellington Home is not an isolated one ; and the Charitable Aid Vote should show a considerable decrease next session. Altogether, it is computed that about 10,000 people in the colony may perhaps ultimately be found to be entitled to the pension, considering that it is granted to males and females alike. But it is not a matter to be settled in a day, and, judging by the results so far, 10,000 seems likely to be an overestimate.[1]

As to the effect of the Act on the Friendly Societies, it is expected to be very small. The majority of members of these societies over sixty-five years of age receive sufficient to preclude them from obtaining the pension.

A determined attempt was made during the passage of the measure through the Lower House to put the pension on a contributory basis, its opponents arguing that in the form in which it eventually passed it was neither more nor less than an extension of the present system of charitable aid. That, of course, would have prevented any immediate benefit being derived from the measure, and the proposed amendment was successfully resisted. Then considerable difficulty was experienced in coming to an agreement as to how the money should be provided. All sorts of suggestions were made. Some wanted the land tax increased, others proposed a tax on amusements; but all these were rejected as impracticable. The money, it was decided, should come out of the Consolidated Fund, that being considered the simplest way of dealing with the matter, more especially as of late years there has been a considerable surplus of revenue over expenditure, and there appears to be every probability that that surplus will be sufficient to provide the amount required without increasing the burden of taxation. The best account so far published of the way in which the experiment

[1] Actually 7500. See Appendix D.

is working was given some months ago in the Australian edition of the *Review of Reviews*. So far, 9015 claims had been registered, and only 2875 granted; and it is clear that the colony will easily bear the cost of the pension scheme out of its ordinary revenue, especially as Mr Seddon—always lucky in his finance—expects this year to have a surplus of £500,000. The task of deciding on applications for pensions greatly adds to the labours of the stipendiary magistrates of the colony, and not seldom tries their sensibilities. A procession of white-headed, semi-blind, tottering men and women passes before them—made up of applicants for a pension of £18 per year, or for some fraction of it. The magistrate has to inquire sternly into the moral character of the applicants; to ask some saintly old woman if she has ever been in gaol; to demand of some decent white-haired veteran how often he has been drunk, and whether he ever deserted his wife. The process of securing a pension, in brief, is a sort of secular and human version of the Day of Judgment. In some parts of New Zealand the daily papers draw a veil of kindly silence over the proceedings, and do not report the names of the applicants. The effect of the Bill, however, has been to bring to the surface all the poverty-smitten old age of the colony; all the human wrecks—friendless and penniless —who find themselves in need of charity. The feelings of compassion kindled by the spectacle certainly tell in favour of the scheme, and Mr Seddon, it is said, when the general election comes, will probably reap a political harvest from the Bill.

NOTE.—See Appendix D; and compare New South Wales proposals, Appendix E.

K

Chapter IX

THE NEW COMMONWEALTH

THE question of most interest to the English visitor to Australia at present is that of the proposed federation of the colonies. Founded at different times and under different circumstances, the colonies have no political bond of union other than the common one which binds them to the Motherland. When I was passing through the colonies there seemed to be every probability that the great work of bringing them together in a federal union was nearing completion. An inquiry into the origin of the movement; the difficulties that have beset and delayed it; and the means by which those difficulties have so far been overcome, and the hopes of the promoters of the movement raised, is one that I, who take an interest, like the rest of us, in political topics and in the development of the great British Empire, most naturally made. An epitome of the result of my inquiries will, I hope, prove of interest.

There are so many things which favour a federation of the Australian colonies that one wonders it was not accomplished long ago. The difficulties which have encumbered similar movements in other parts of the world are many of them quite absent from the Australian problem. The people to be united are of the same race and tongue. They are sprung from the same source, and enjoy the same free institutions. Geographically, they are all united, and the political lines which divide them are still merely abstractions set out on a map. They are all, with the

THE NEW COMMONWEALTH 147

exception of Tasmania and New Zealand, on the one continent; and they possess (more by good luck than good management) the whole of that continent, and are, therefore, not troubled by the presence of any foreign element.

The inducements to federation, again, are of course very great. One of the primary advantages to be derived is a common system of defence. At present each colony has its separate forces, and no force may act outside its own dominions; so that the troops could not be massed at any one point of danger under a single commander. Then there is the important consideration that an Australian Commonwealth will speak to the world with far greater weight than the whole of the colonies acting separately. It is also strongly felt by the colonists that the merely political divisions which exist might tend to grow more marked as time goes on; and that disputes between states of the same race are, like disputes in families, often embittered by the actual nearness of the parties to each other. There are some questions, such as the control of the few important rivers of Australia, which might in time lead to bloodshed, failing any other method of settlement. If one colony, for instance, absorbed so much of the waters of the rivers which flow through it as to interfere with the navigability of the lower portions, it might inflict great loss on its neighbours; a thing to which they could scarcely be expected tamely to submit. Then, again, there is a strong desire on the part of many to do away with the inter-colonial Customs duties, by which the products of one colony are heavily taxed on entering another.

For all these and other reasons Australian federation has been a matter of discussion in the colonies for many years past. It must be credited to Lord Grey that he had the foresight in 1850 to endeavour to pass an Australian Constitution Act through the British Parliament, empowering a voluntary union of any two or more colonies in a General Assembly, which should have power to legislate upon certain specified subjects, notably Customs taxation. But his proposal received so little support that it was withdrawn. Various steps were taken by the colonies themselves to draw closer together and pave the way for federation. One of the most practical of these was the holding of occasional conferences between leading members of the various Governments in order to discuss matters of common interest, and arrive at some uniform proposals to be submitted to the different Legislatures. Five or six such conferences were held; but, though the object was good, and they were carried out in perfect good faith, they accomplished little. It was found that very few of the arrangements ever got the force of law. Changes of Government were so frequent that there could be no continuous policy upon any subject; as the incoming Government was generally averse to the proposals of its predecessors. It was felt that something more was needed: and in 1883, spurred on by the claims of the French in the New Hebrides, which were then attracting a great deal of attention, a scheme for the creation of a Federal Council for Australasia was adopted at a conference in which all the colonies were represented; and the Imperial Parliament passed a measure permitting the formation of the Council.

The prime mover in this scheme was Mr James Service, the Premier of Victoria, a man of broad and statesmanlike views; to whose efforts it is mainly due that the New Hebrides are not now a French possession. Mr Service strenuously advocated the formation of the Federal Council, on the ground that it would lead the way to the establishment of a closer union, as its powers could be added to from

THE NEW COMMONWEALTH 149

time to time as the necessity arose. Mr Service is still living in Melbourne, but he has reached a very advanced age, and is in feeble health. During my stay in Victoria he resigned his position as a member of the Legislative Council, the only political office which he still held. Whatever ground there might have been for his hope that the Federal Council would grow into federation, it never had a chance of fulfilment; for the Premier of New South Wales, Sir Henry Parkes, after actually proposing the resolutions upon which the Council was founded, came to the conclusion that the body proposed to be created was too weak to be of any practical value, and he did not submit the Bill to his Parliament. With New South Wales standing out, any scheme for federating the Australian Colonies would be a failure. That Colony never was represented on the Federal Council, and, though the Council is in existence to-day, and has held eight sessions (in 1886, '88, '89, '91, '93, '95, '97, and '99) successively, at which matters of intercolonial import have been discussed, it certainly has held out no promise of supplying the place of a more complete federation. New South Wales, New Zealand, and South Australia at first declined to join. The last-named colony sent delegates to the session of '89. But the Federal Council is, and would in any case have remained, a purely deliberative body, without any funds at its disposal, or any power to put its resolutions into force. It can only recommend certain proposals for the adoption of the various Parliaments. At times, however, its united representations to the Home Government have had great weight, and have effected good in matters of Australasian interest.

Sir Henry Parkes, one of the most prominent and picturesque figures in Australian history, was the promoter of the next important movement towards federation. It was chiefly due to him that a National Australasian Convention, to which delegates were appointed by the Parliaments of each of the colonies, including New Zealand, met at Sydney in 1891. Sir Henry Parkes was appointed president, and on his motion resolutions were adopted affirming the following principles:—

"The powers and rights of existing colonies to remain intact, except as regards such powers as it might be necessary to hand over to the Federal Government."

"No alteration to be made in State boundaries without the consent of the Legislature of such State, as well as the Federal Parliament."

"Trade between the federated Colonies to be absolutely free."

"Power to impose Customs and Excise duties to rest with the Federal Government and Parliament."

"Military and naval forces to be under one command."

"The Federal Constitution to make provision to enable each State to make amendments in its Constitution, if necessary, for the purpose of federation."

"The Federal Parliament to consist of a Senate and a House of Representatives, the latter to possess the sole power of originating money Bills."

"A Federal Court of Appeal to be established; and an Executive, to consist of a Governor-General and such persons as might be appointed his advisers."

A draft Constitution Bill embodying these and other principles was adopted by the Convention. It was hoped by many that federation would almost immediately result. New Zealand, which is separated by four or five days' sail from Sydney, sent three delegates to the Convention, in place of the seven allotted to each Colony, and intimated that its immediate adhesion to any scheme of federation need not be expected, on account of its being cut off by

THE NEW COMMONWEALTH 151

such a waste of ocean from the other Colonies. But, apart from this, it was believed that federation of all the other colonies was now in sight. These hopes were doomed to disappointment. The Bill drafted with such formality was virtually still-born. By several of the Parliaments it was never considered at all. In Victoria it was passed, with considerable modifications, but met with much hostility.

The drawback to all the movements for federation up to this point was that they had no force of public opinion behind them, and they awakened no enthusiasm in the mass of the people. It was, in effect, necessary to wait for a few years, till the native-born Australians had, in two senses, attained their majority. During the 'eighties, this element of the population first perceptibly began to assert itself. The emigrants from the old country, the colonists, began to be outnumbered by their own progeny, the true colonials. And as these latter came to feel their strength (which they soon began to show, if only by an express preference for native-born politicians), the earlier provincial bitternesses, the result, in reality, of the rivalry amongst the pioneers of the infant settlements, seemed to them strangely unbusinesslike and out-of-date. The apathy of the public had been due to the natural inability of the Englishman or Scotsman who had settled in Melbourne or Adelaide (for example), to feel or think as an Australian. And it is largely due to the efforts of the Australian Natives' Association of Victoria that this apathy has, to some extent at least, been overcome. The Association, formed originally for mutual benefit purposes, and admitting Australian natives only to membership, was for some years looked at rather askance by the grey-beards. But it succeeded by sheer pertinacity, and by the force of the rising tide. It took up the cause of federation warmly, and advocated it with constancy and determination. It sent delegates to the other colonies, established branches, and worked up in the minds of the youth a desire that their native land should rise to the dignity of a nation. In its early years the association was viewed, as I have said, with some suspicion, on account of its supposed leanings towards a policy of separation from the motherland. It has now, however, removed all taint of such a suspicion from itself; for it is ultra-loyal, and has always laid it down that federation must be accomplished under the Crown. It was at a conference convened by the Australian Natives' Association, held at Corowa, a small town on the Murray, that the principle was first advocated on which the more recent effort for federation has been conducted. This was that the people must be directly interested in the movement, by themselves electing delegates to a convention, apart from the Parliaments.

It is at this point that Mr G. H. Reid, the then Premier of New South Wales, becomes a prominent figure in the federation movement: which, indeed, it will easily be seen, has throughout (until the uprising of the national sentiment to which I referred) been a favourite means of self-advertisement, or play-ground for the personal ambitions, of one politician after another. Mr Reid is the most astute of them all; and is, indeed, the one man with whom the Home Government will have to reckon in case of trouble over the proposed abolition of the appeal to the Privy Council. He was not a member of the Convention of 1891, and posed as a strong opponent of the measure drafted by that Convention. But it is a curious feature of Australian politics that everyone is in favour of federation—even its most determined opponents. It is always only to the particular form, time, or conditions of federation that ostensible objection is taken. Mr Reid's position, then,

THE NEW COMMONWEALTH 153

was simply that the movement was premature. He thought there was no occasion to hasten towards federation, and he thought also, at the moment, maybe, that New South Wales had more to lose than to gain by it. He is an ardent free-trader, as free-traders go in Australia ; and he saw that a federation accomplished between six or seven colonies, only one of which had adopted a free-trade policy, must almost inevitably be based on protectionist lines, so far at least as the outside world is concerned. However, he overcame his objections in this respect; and in 1895, on his suggestion, a conference of Premiers was held at Hobart, Tasmania. At this conference all the Australian colonies, with New Zealand as well as Tasmania, were represented. An enabling Bill was drafted for submission to the Parliaments, permitting the election (by the electors of each colony) of ten persons to a Convention to draw up a scheme of federation. This Bill was passed in all the colonies named except New Zealand and Queensland. It was not expected that New Zealand would come in ; but the defection of Queensland was a severe blow to the movement. The Parliament of that colony failed, after several attempts, to agree as to the basis of the representation of the colony.

Mr Reid made a special journey to Queensland to try to induce the colony to join, for New South Wales expected the support of its northern neighbour on some of the crucial matters to be decided by the Convention. There was a fear that Victoria might obtain the support of the Southern and Western colonies in a combination against New South Wales, and the mother-colony was reluctant to enter into a Convention without Queensland. As a matter of fact, it may be said that such fears were groundless. The delegates to the Convention found a natural cleavage according to their political convictions, but there was no attempt to combine colony against colony, or one group of colonies against another.

The delegates were elected by each colony, voting as one constituency. This plan enabled the predominant party in each colony to secure the whole of the representation, if the election were conducted upon party lines. Victoria was the only colony where this occurred, and all her delegates were elected by the Radical party. The relative strength of that party, as opposed to the Constitutional or Conservative party, was as six to four; but the minority got no representation at all. Such acknowledged political leaders as Sir Frederick Sargood, Sir Henry Wrixon, Mr Gillies, and Mr Murray Smith, were excluded in favour of much inferior men of the other political colour, and this weakened the Victorian delegation as compared with the other colonies. In the other colonies a fair representation of all parties was secured; Western Australia, however, as usual, taking her own line, and sending delegates appointed, not by the people, but by Sir John Forrest. In New South Wales strong feeling was roused against the candidature of Cardinal Moran, the Roman Catholic Primate of Australia. This incautious, though (to those best acquainted with Australia) highly significant step provoked a counter-combination, amongst the Protestants, which included the leading men of both political parties: and His Eminency was defeated.

The Convention met at Adelaide in March 1897, and Mr C. C. Kingston, the Premier of that colony, was elected president. An initial mistake was made in administering a snub to Mr Reid, and appointing Mr Edmund Barton, a delegate from the same colony, as leader of the Convention, to act as a Premier does in arranging and submitting business. Such an appointment was necessary, for there must be some recognised leader if confusion and endless debates upon points of procedure are to be avoided, but it would have been much more tactful to appoint Mr Reid. There was, on the part of a number of the delegates, a certain jealousy of him. He is a masterful man, and they feared that he might assert himself too prominently. Moreover, Mr Barton is a Protectionist, and this had some weight in an assembly largely Protectionist. The arrangement was privately come to before the Convention met, the ostensible reason being that Mr Barton was elected head of the poll in New South Wales, and that therefore a compliment was paid to the mother colony in selecting him. Mr Reid showed no resentment, but seconded, in graceful terms, the proposal that Mr Barton should be the leader. In other respects the appointment was an excellent one, for Mr Barton is a man of great ability and tact, and he led the Convention in a masterly manner. Still this matter, small as it may seem, is of importance to anyone who wishes to get a grasp of the federal movement. It was undoubtedly a slight to Mr Reid, the originator of the Convention, to pass him by and select a delegate from the colony he represented—and a man not at that time connected with politics—in his place. Such petty intercolonial and personal jealousies have had marked effect on the movement at various stages. The effect of this action was, as many think, to transform Mr Reid, the most powerful man in the most important colony of the group, from an ardent leader to a watchful critic. He took a leading part in the Convention, it is true; but the subsequent failure or, rather, delay of the movement may have had a direct relation to this primary mistake. In a word, Australia has paid for an affront to Mr Reid by waiting another year or so for the Commonwealth.

I have mentioned the inducements to federation and the facilities for its accomplishment, and I must now set out a few of the most important difficulties to be overcome, and show how they were met. The first of these is the question of State rights. The colonies differ widely in population, from New South Wales with her 1,346,240 inhabitants, and Victoria with 1,175,490, to Tasmania with 177,341, and Western Australia with 168,129. Yet Tasmania is as much a political entity as New South Wales, and had no intention of entering into a federation unless its position as a State was strictly conserved. Otherwise it would simply be absorbed, and become a province, and a minor province, of the larger States. On the other hand, how were the two large colonies, New South Wales and Victoria, to be convinced that Tasmania should have equal power in the federation as a State with either of them? Again, it was conceded on all hands that responsible government, the form of government to which British people are accustomed, must be continued. This means that the executive must be responsible to one House alone, and that House must hold the power of the purse. How this can be accomplished and yet the States House—the Senate—can remain a strong institution, capable of conserving the rights of the several communities as States;—this was the really great difficulty in the way of the Convention. There were some who boldly asserted that responsible government was quite inconsistent with federation ; that federation would kill responsible government, or responsible government would kill federation. On this question the Convention almost came to a deadlock. The representatives of the smaller States contended that if the Senate was to be a real protector of State rights it must have the power of amending as well as rejecting money Bills; and that its functions were entirely different from those of an ordinary Upper Chamber, which is merely a House of review, the representative of stability and deliberation, whose opposition

THE NEW COMMONWEALTH 157

is always to be set aside when the will of the people, clearly and unmistakably ascertained, is against it. What guarantee of the maintenance of State rights could there be if the Senate was thus to be always set aside, simply because a majority of the people of the Federation desired it? Ultimately a compromise was arrived at; several of the representatives of the smaller States giving way, against their own judgments—as they said—merely to save federation. The arrangement is that each colony shall be equally represented in the Senate; and that each House shall have equal power of originating Bills, with the exception of Bills appropriating revenue or imposing taxation, the right of originating which is reserved to the House of Representatives, the popular Chamber. The Senate will not have the power of amending these appropriation or taxation Bills, but it may return them to the House of Representatives, with a message suggesting the omission or amendment of any of their provisions; and the House of Representatives may deal as it pleases with such suggestions. This is the practice which obtains between the South Australian Houses, and it has been found to work well. There was bitter opposition to its adoption in the Commonwealth's Senate, on the part of both the smaller and larger States; so that it is probably the best practice possible. Some representatives of the latter contended that the power of suggestion is virtually the power of amendment. Some representatives of the smaller States maintained, on the contrary, that it gives away everything, for the House of Representatives may toss the suggestions aside and act as it pleases. However, as I have said, it was adopted as a compromise.

Allied to this difficulty was that of securing finality in regard to any legislation on which the two Houses may be opposed. It was contended by some delegates that under

the Commonwealth Bill a permanent disagreement could
not occur. The provisions of the suffrage were such that
the people could not disagree permanently with themselves;
for it had previously been provided that both Houses are
to be elected on the suffrage that prevails in each colony
for the election of the representatives of the popular Chamber
—that is, practically on the basis of manhood suffrage,
(or universal suffrage in the colonies which have adopted
it) with no property qualification for either electors or
representatives; every State to have six representatives
in the Senate or States House, and to be represented
according to population in the House of Representatives.
How then, it was asked, could the people of the Federation,
voting as States for the Senate, disagree with the people
of the Federation voting as different constituencies for the
election of their representatives in the Lower House?
However this might be, it was determined to insert some
provisions for the prevention of what are known as "deadlocks" between the two Houses. Here again there was
great difficulty, and danger of final disagreement. It was
proposed that the question in dispute should be decided
by the electors at a referendum. But this was strenuously
opposed by the representatives of the smaller States, as
tending simply to swamp them by force of numbers, and
give all power to the two large States. This, it was said,
was not federation, but amalgamation and absorption.
Finally, the following elaborate provision was arrived at.
In the case of Bills, other than appropriation or taxation
Bills, which have been twice passed by the House of Representatives, and twice rejected or shelved by the Senate,
the two Houses are to be simultaneously dissolved; and if,
after the election, they should still disagree, the members
of the two Houses will meet at a joint sitting, and the Bill
will become law if three-fifths of the members present, and

THE NEW COMMONWEALTH 159

voting at the joint sitting, vote for it. If less than that proportion vote for it, it will be rejected. In accordance with this arrangement, it is provided that the number of senators shall always be as nearly as possible half the number of representatives.

It had often been proclaimed by the political wiseacres that the protective system was the lion in the path of federation, for that no colony would consent to give up the Customs duties levied upon the goods of other colonies. There appeared, however, before the Convention met, a universal consensus of opinion amongst the people, guided still by the Australian Natives, that a federation must provide for the inter-colonial free-trade. And this point was conceded without dispute; the only question raised being as to how the colonies were to be compensated in their revenues for the loss of duties thus abolished. It was provided that within two years of the establishment of the Commonwealth a uniform Customs and Excise tariff shall be enacted; and that then trade between the colonies shall be absolutely free.

There was considerable difficulty over the question of the control of the rivers; for on this matter New South Wales, Victoria, and South Australia stood in a position of antagonism. The principal river system of Australia has its rise in New South Wales; and the Murrumbidgee joins the Murray, which is the northern boundary of Victoria, and which flows, in the latter part of its course, through South Australia. The last-named colony wished to provide that the navigability of the rivers should be the first consideration in the federation, fearing that New South Wales might in the future adopt some extensive system of irrigation, which would deprive the rivers of a considerable portion of their waters, and interfere with the navigation of the Murray. After a long discussion it was decided that the right to a "reasonable" use of the waters of a river for the purpose of irrigation or conservation shall be preserved to the people of the colony through which it flows. The interpretation of the word "reasonable" is left to the High Court of the Commonwealth, in case of dispute.

Another question, the importance attached to which people in England will find, at first, some difficulty in understanding, was the site of the federal capital. I have before alluded to the rivalries and jealousies existing between different colonies. Nowhere has this rivalry been so manifest as between Sydney and Melbourne. So strong is it, even now, on the part of Sydney residents more especially, that if the Convention had decided that the federal capital was to be fixed in Melbourne, New South Wales would not have consented to enter into the federation. On the other hand, Melbourne residents would be very reluctant to see Sydney chosen, as it is considered that great importance would be given to the rival city if the residence of the Governor-General was fixed in that capital, and the Houses of Parliament held their sitting there.

It was resolved to leave this matter to the Federal Parliament to settle; but a proviso was added, on the motion of Sir George Turner, the Premier of Victoria, that the site of the federal city must be federal territory. This was designed to prevent either Melbourne or Sydney becoming the capital, for neither place, of course, could afford to excise a large proportion of valuable city property from its possessions, and hand it over to the Commonwealth.

The taking over of the public debts and the railways was strongly advocated by some, but there were so many difficulties in the way that it was felt that federation

THE NEW COMMONWEALTH 161

would be unduly postponed if it was not accomplished till these matters could be adjusted. Power was, however, given to the Federation to take these over, with the consent of the States.

The financial problems involved in federation proved to be most intricate, and no satisfactory solution was arrived at. It was provided that, immediately on the establishment of the Commonwealth, the Federal Government shall assume the administration of the departments of Customs and Excise; and at subsequent dates to be arranged it shall take over from the States posts and telegraphs, naval and military defence, lighthouses, lightships, beacons, buoys, and quarantine. Other matters of government may be given over, but only on federal legislation. The transfer of these services would leave the States with a large deficiency in their revenues, and it was therefore provided that for the first five years all the surplus raised by the Commonwealth, after paying for federal services, shall be returned to the States in the proportion contributed by them. In the meantime accounts are to be kept, with the help of which the Federal Parliament may arrive at an equitable method of distribution at the end of that term. Special concessions were made to Western Australia, which derives nearly all its revenue from Custom duties, most of which are levied on goods coming from the other colonies. If these duties were to be abolished without any compensatory arrangement, Western Australian finances would be hopelessly disarranged. It will be allowed, therefore, gradually to diminish its Customs tariff during a period of five years. Just at the close of the Convention, a provision was added, on the motion of Sir Edward Braddon, the Premier of Tasmania, that three-fourths of the revenue derived by the Commonwealth from

L

Customs duties must be returned to the States. This
clause, which, it will be perceived, might make it
necessary, in order to secure enough revenue for Federal
purposes, to impose a crushing weight of taxation on the
States, was quickly assailed by the *Bulletin* as the
"Braddon blot."

These were the most important points of difficulty,
and the arrangements arrived at in respect to them.
But it is necessary to mention one or two other matters
in order that a clear understanding of the present position
may be gained. The judicial power of the Commonwealth is to be vested in a High Court of Australia, which
is to hear appeals from the Supreme Courts of the States,
and from the inter-States Commission. This interference with the common-law right of all British subjects
to appeal to the Privy Council, *i.e.* to their Sovereign,
would be by way of depriving the Australian of his
citizenship in the Empire. It was bitterly opposed by a
large section of the community, especially amongst those
lawyers whose opinion should carry most weight; a peti-
tion against it was presented to the Convention by the
Australian National League; and it will probably be
disallowed by the Imperial Parliament. It is a pity
that a source of possible friction was not avoided by a
hint, which might easily have been given by the Colonial
Office, to Mr Reid and the other Premiers. But I
have dealt more fully with this matter in a subsequent
chapter.

The inter-States Commission is a body to be appointed
for the proper administration of the federal laws relating
to trade and commerce between the States of the
Commonwealth. It will have jurisdiction, for instance,
over the question of railway rates. There has been
great rivalry on the borders between the different rail-

THE NEW COMMONWEALTH 163

way systems, specially low rates being charged to attract trade from one colony to another. This has proved to be a most difficult matter to settle. I need only mention further that the Commonwealth has no powers except those specially delegated to it, all other matters resting in the control of the States; that the name "Commonwealth" was chosen, after much discussion, as being preferable to "Federation"; and that the members of each House are to be paid £400 a year each for their services.

The Federal Constitution can only be amended by an absolute majority of the members of each House of the Federal Parliament. The amendment is then to be submitted to the people by means of the referendum, and has to be accepted by a majority of the people of the Commonwealth, as well as by a majority of the States, before it becomes law. These precautions are held to be necessary, in the interests of the smaller States more especially. For if the Constitution were subject to any ready method of amendment, any provisions they might make at the outset for their preservation as States might be swept away by subsequent legislation.

The results that I have summarised were arrived at after three meetings of the Convention. Between the first and the second meeting the draft Bill was submitted to the various Parliaments, and many amendments were made. These were taken into consideration at a meeting in Sydney, which adjourned to Melbourne before it could finish its sittings. I have given the final results, attained after the Convention, all adjournments included, had sat for about a year, from March 1897 to March 17, 1898.

The next step was the submission of the Constitution Bill to the people, as provided in the Enabling Acts.

Popular interest in the subject was kept alive by the press (which is a potent factor in political matters in Australia), and by public discussion. The advocate of the Bill worked hard, but there was in each colony a strong party of opposition. A tax of 30s. per head is levied on all cattle coming into the colony of Victoria, and it was gravely contended, on behalf of the grazing interest, that the abolition of this stock tax would reduce the value of land in Victoria by no less than £37,500,000. In New South Wales Mr Barton and a large party made splendid efforts to induce the people to accept the Bill, but Mr Reid's attitude was peculiar. For a long time he refrained from expressing his opinion. Then he made a speech in the Sydney Town Hall, so carefully balanced in praise and blame, that till the last sentence no one knew what course he proposed to recommend. He finally said that though he would vote for the Bill himself, he could not recommend others to do so, but would leave them to the exercise of their own judgment. He had, however, previously declared that if the Bill was accepted as it stood, he thought the federal capital would be certainly fixed in Melbourne, and had raised other strong objections.

The draft of the Enabling Bill, agreed to by the Premiers at Hobart, provided that in New South Wales the Commonwealth Bill should not pass unless 60,000 electors voted for it, in Victoria 50,000, and in the other Colonies in proportion. The Bill was at first passed in that shape in New South Wales, but subsequently, with the consent of Mr Reid, the minimum for New South Wales was raised to 80,000.

On June 3, 1898, a vote was taken in Victoria, New South Wales, South Australia, and Tasmania, on the Draft Commonwealth Bill, as passed by the Federal Convention in March, 1898. The voting was as follows:

Victoria	96,600 for Federation	21,200 against it.
New South Wales	71,472 ,,	65,954 ,,
South Australia	35,317 ,,	17,173 ,,
Tasmania	10,709 ,,	2,532 ,,
Total	214,038 ,,	106,859 ,,

Majority for the Bill 107,179. The Bill was carried in Victoria, South Australia, and Tasmania; but was lost in New South Wales, as the statutory number in favour (80,000) was not reached.

The Bill was not submitted to the people in Western Australia, as the Enabling Act of that Colony provided that Western Australia should only join a federation of which New South Wales formed a part. The three other Colonies, which had affirmed the Bill, might have proceeded to form a federation; but this was never even proposed, so general was the conviction that the Commonwealth was inevitable, and that, weary as everyone was by this time of the prolonged discussion, the matter must now be seen through once and for all.

The constituencies of New South Wales now became the battle-ground of federation, for a general election took place not long after the federal poll was taken. Mr Barton entered the lists in favour of the Bill, and opposed the Premier in his own constituency. No candidate declared against federation itself, but only against the particular form proposed. Mr Reid proposed in vague terms certain amendments, and invited the Premiers of the other Colonies to meet him to consider them. Sir George Turner replied by asking what amendments were proposed; but the Premiers of South Australia and Tasmania declined to go behind the vote of the people, and discuss amendments in a Bill which they had sanctioned by large majorities. Mr Barton was defeated, after a close contest, by the Premier, but the result of the elections as a whole was that Mr Reid's majority was reduced from one of over twenty members to four only. A considerable majority of the electors voted for those candidates who supported the Bill. Mr Barton was subsequently elected for another constituency.

After the election, Mr Reid submitted and passed through the Assembly of New South Wales the following amendments to the Bill :—

1. "That if equal representation of the Colonies in the Senate be insisted on, the provision for a three-fifths majority at the joint sitting of both Houses be removed, and a simple majority decide, or that the provision for a joint sitting be replaced by a provision for a national referendum." Mr Reid contended before the electors that the three-fifths majority provision would enable a minority to defy the majority.

2. "That what is known as the Braddon clause (three-quarters of the revenue from Customs to be given back to the States) be removed.

3. "That provision be made in the Bill for the establishment of the federal capital in such place within the boundaries of New South Wales as the Federal Parliament may determine.

4. "That better provision should be made against the alteration of the boundaries of a State without its own consent.

5. "That the use of inland rivers for the purpose of water conservation and irrigation should be more clearly safeguarded.

6. "That there should be a uniform practice in respect to money Bills, and that all money Bills should be treated as Taxation Bills.

7. "That the mode of appeal from the Supreme Courts

THE NEW COMMONWEALTH 167

of the State should be made uniform, namely, that the appeal should be either to the Privy Council or to the High Court, but not indiscriminately to either." And, lastly, a demand was made for a more thorough consideration of the financial clauses; the evil to be avoided, if possible, being "excessive burdens of taxation, a prolonged system of book-keeping, uncertainty as to the amount of the surplus to be divided, and uncertainty as to the method of distributing it among the States."

The other Premiers, after some difficulty, were induced to meet Mr Reid, and to take his proposals into consideration. And a final compromise was arrived at, the chief points in which were that deadlocks should be dealt with by a simple majority of both Houses at a joint sitting; that the operation of the Braddon clause should be limited to ten years; that the appeal to the Privy Council should be disallowed, in all matters affecting Federal or State rights, and, in private matters, should be restricted, if necessary, by Federal Legislation; and that the Federal Capital should be in New South Wales, at some point not less than 100 miles distant from Sydney. The Governor-General and the Parliament of the Commonwealth will use Melbourne as the temporary capital pending the selection (and construction) of the place of their banishment. And it is generally hoped in Australia that the land-values of this antipodean Washington (the name of which, by the way, remains to be invented) will go a long way towards lightening the burthen of taxation.

The amended Bill was again submitted to the popular vote in June and July of this year (1899), with the result that Victoria, South Australia, and Tasmania have reaffirmed, with additional emphasis, their former decision. New South Wales this time accepted it with a sufficient majority: thus leaving only two colonies (for New Zealand

is definitely outside the Commonwealth) to be consulted.
Queensland came in early in September, after a lively
campaign, which was carried on throughout the colony:
in which the anti-Federalists of Sydney and the whole of
Australia showed themselves anxious to spare neither
pains nor money over their last stand. Every use was
made of the Queensland Separation movement, which had
smouldered, with a gradually increasing intensity, for the
last thirty years, or, indeed, since the foundation of the
colony in 1859. The Separatists desired the sub-division
of Queensland into three autonomous States; believing
that their vast stretch of coast cannot be administered fairly
from Brisbane, which is in the extreme south-east corner of
the colony. Now, clause 123 of the Commonwealth Bill
forbids the Federal Parliament to sub-divide a State without the consent of the State's Parliament; and moreover,
Federation would abolish the right of appeal in such
matters (expressly reserved, as it happens, in the existing constitutions of both Queensland and Western Australia) to the Imperial Government. Again, the Southern
Colonies would in any case have objected to Queensland
being represented in the Federal Senate as three States,
with eighteen Senators instead of six. While, therefore,
many of the farmers and manufacturers of the south were
opposed to federation because it involves inter-colonial
free-trade; and the planters were of course against it by
reason of their fear of the Australian working-man and his
inevitable Asiatic Exclusion Bill; the Northern and Central
voters objected to it because it would make their dream of
separation for ever impossible; and, finally, the whole South,
as such, professed itself resolute to resist any attempt to
meddle with Clause 123. The Asiatic question was, and
is, particularly serious. Some form of coloured labour is
probably essential to the prosperity of the far North. Yet

THE NEW COMMONWEALTH 169

the Australian democracy, and more especially the native-born Australians, who are, as has been seen, the very soul of the federal movement, are resolute not to allow any part of Australia to be over-run, as it easily might be, by swarms of such Chinese, Japanese, Cingalese, Javanese, Malays, and Kanakas, as have already secured a foot-hold in Queensland. The danger is far from being imaginary. Japanese women fill the brothels of the colony; Japanese men employ white labour in the pearl fisheries and on sugar plantations; white unfortunates are used as prostitutes by the Kanakas; Thursday Island is Asiatic; and the existence of a "secret protocol" between the Brisbane Government and that of the Mikado is apparently not denied. There were, it must be confessed, all the materials for a very pretty quarrel over these matters, taken as a whole. And yet, as seems to have been all along the expectation of those who know Australia most intimately, the one dominant desire for union carried the day, though, it is true, by a very bare majority; and even these final and most serious obstacles were somehow adjusted.

The case of Western Australia has been left to the last, because her case is singular. She is, in the first place, not essential, at all events at present, to the formation of the Commonwealth; and, in the second place, after having obviously waited to see if the recusancy of Queensland, or some other accident, might not give her a much desired excuse for not entering the Union, she is now showing her heartfelt reluctance (or rather that of her governing class) to pass under the central control. The history of this colony, as we have seen, has been entirely separate from that of the rest of Australia. Her population—the older section of it—has lived apart; and she is in a different stage of political and economic development. Her agriculturalists are anxious to keep their home market, which the producers of the rest of the continent are equally anxious to exploit; and her statesmen wish her to have time peaceably to assimilate her new-comers, and (probably) to attempt new loans. She fears neglect and mismanagement; though no mismanagement of the gold-fields, it is true, could be worse than that which has allowed the whole of the dividend-paying mines to drift into European ownership, while the wage-earning population are left mostly without homes, and must remit half their incomes to their families on "the other side." Finally, under the Commonwealth, South Australia could refuse to permit a trans-continental railway, which it has now become Western Australia's chief ambition to construct. British Columbia, under similar circumstances, made the Canadian Pacific Railway the price of her adhesion to the Dominion. The Government, and the party of the old settlers, with the exception of their leader, Sir John Forrest, who is bound by his pledges to the Convention, are undisguisedly hostile to federation, and here is a rough statement of its "advantages" by a Radical and Outlander member of the Legislative Assembly ;—

"The advantages of Federation :—New South Wales gets the federal capital, the biggest political power, the control of all the inland navigation of Australia, and the abolition of all border duties for her sheep and cattle. Victoria gets the temporary capital, the second political pull, and a free market for all her over-glutted manufactures. South Australia gets the sole right of building a trans-continental railway, or of refusing the same right to any other State. Queensland keeps her black labour, and has a huge protected market for her sugar, bananas, coffee, and other tropical produce. Tasmania gets the free run of Australasia for her fruits and jams. Western Australia gets the right to extra-tax herself for five years, and to lose £330,000 a year. No wonder George Reid reckons it a good bargain!" (*Cf.* Appendix C.)

The odds seem, on the face of it, to be against federation in Western Australia. Yet here, again, after all, opposition may melt away. The Premier is not in a hurry to go to the referendum. Mr Reid, shortly before his fall, thought it worth while to send him a rather blustering telegram, reminding him of his pledges, and threatening him and his with every penalty which can be visited on the back-slider. (Somehow telegrams do not make altogether for diplomacy.) But the Bill, which has suffered drastic amendment from the Select Committee of the two Houses in Perth, must be submitted, in the end, to the people. And then, it is to be remembered that, whatever may be the course taken by the older population, the majority of the adult males of the colony are new-comers from "the other side"; who care little for the agriculture of their latest home, but a great deal for a cheap breakfast-table; who owe it to the management of Perth that they have mostly, till this referendum, been without a vote, and are likely to use their new power against their late masters; finally, who will refuse to be influenced by fiscal considerations, because the Australian working-man, in the plenitude of his power, as we have seen, always refuses to tax himself.

The obstacles to a perfectly complete federation of Australia are thus worst, perhaps, in the final lap. But in Western Australia, as was the case in Queensland, the conflict of local animosities and interests is so confused that men are as likely as not at any moment to turn, in sheer weariness and bewilderment, to the simple panacea of the Commonwealth. For Australia as a whole, federation, in the end, is now not only inevitable, but desirable, as the only hope of permanent security against the foreigner, and the very beginning of a national life. And the Empire has nothing to lose, but everything to gain by it. No cut-and-dried scheme of Imperial Federation will be brought forward by the discreet statesman who remembers how near we seemed to it in the years before the revolt of our American colonies, and how perilous a matter, among Anglo-Saxons, is taxation without representation. But Australia is our depôt and main strength on that side of the world, whither the battle of world-interests is now shifting. Too much stress must not be laid by the enthusiast on the offers, which are for the moment fashionable, of colonial contingents for our ever-recurring wars. They are sometimes merely symptoms of a desire to combine a sort of authorised filibustering with the benefits of a camp of instruction; the outcome as well of the natural desire of officers and men for adventure and experience, as of a willingness of the colonial authorities to wash the spears of the young men of their embryonic armies at the expense, in the main, of the British tax-payer. Australia cannot afford to go seriously to war until she is obliged; though it is far from impossible that the stress of war, when it does come, may be productive of good, in the shape of renewed moral earnestness and the heightening of the national ideals. Yet in the meanwhile, on the other hand, it would be base, as well as unwise, to under-estimate the friendliness, the confidence, the racial loyalty, of which such spontaneous offers must necessarily be the outcome. And it is as well to remember that, even as things are, the forces locally raised by our colonial possessions generally almost equal our own Militia, which may yet again some day become our more specially British Army, when, if ever, the Imperial Army, as such, is re-organised to serve the requirements of an organised Empire: while, to look only to the immediate future, the Australian Commonwealth, in particular, which will take over the fortifications of

THE NEW COMMONWEALTH 173

Thursday Island and King George's Sound, must fortify also Hobart and Port Darwin; will organise its forces to protect its provincial capitals from the raids, with which they have repeatedly been threatened, of marauding European powers; and will probably maintain a field army capable of dealing with an invasion, for instance, of Mongolian sepoys. [See Appendix A.] The existing Federal Squadron, of five third class cruisers and two gunboats, will probably be increased; the formation of a Federal Naval Reserve is being considered; in a word, the newest nation in the Greater English Commonwealth is not to be, even at the outset, without its complement of national armed strength: which is always so much the better for us. The whole process is one of inevitable, because organic, growth: the formation of true political organisms. The Canadian Dominion and the Australian Commonwealth will be followed, as Lord Grey hoped to have seen, by a South African Union, and after that— But that is as far, perhaps, as we shall look (if we are wise) for the present. In the meantime, the Commonwealth Bill will be submitted to the British Parliament before long, and it will be for us to see that our colonial fellow-subjects are not legislated out of their Imperial citizenship. The constitutional link between the nation and the colonies is through the person of the Queen in Council. The Privy Council, which administered our first plantations, and which, so recently as Earl Grey's time, was held to be the proper authority to settle the then proposed constitutions of Australia and the Cape, is, for many reasons, more likely than Parliament itself to become the centre round which the ultimate organisation of the Imperial Commonwealth may crystallise. The judicial prerogative of Her Majesty is, as Mills puts it (apart from our control over the foreign relations of the colonies), the one yet unquestioned element of our Imperial power. And it is, for that matter, in a very experimental democracy, a great safeguard and convenience, as the Legislative Council of New South Wales and others have discovered, to the propertied Australian. But this is a matter which demands separate treatment.

CHAPTER X

A POINT IN THE COMMONWEALTH BILL

THERE are only three bonds by which our present Empire is held together; (1) our hegemony in matters of foreign policy; (2) the legislative veto; and (3) the judicial prerogative of the Crown.

The first is a vague power, depending on abundant good management as well as goodwill from all parties concerned. How valueless it is bound to become in cases where the spontaneous friendliness born of racial solidarity is lacking, may be seen in the cases of the Transvaal and the Orange Free State; both of which (not to enter upon any discussion about that precious word suzerainty) we claim to hold under our hegemony; a claim which they as frankly repudiate. Canada has accepted the necessary drawbacks of her position as a secondary state with a loyalty past all praise. The sagacity and statesmanship of her leaders has led them to postpone the interests of the Dominion to those of the Empire, as freely as though the organic union of our world-state were an accomplished fact, instead of an ideal which they have done much towards realising. And their lofty subordination, their politic unselfishness, has won them an established and honoured place in the councils of the Empire. But it will be seen that the position needs regularising. Colonies are not all, nor always, so wisely administered as Canada. Australia, in the past, has often shown a quite pardonable restlessness, in face of the irritating, though comparatively unimportant, foreign complications which have been forced on her attention. New Caledonia, the New Hebrides, New Guinea, have each in turn been used by the bolder sort of colonial politician as an excuse to force the hand of a supposedly neglectful Colonial Office. Armed vessels have been sent from New Zealand on missions which the Imperial Government has been forced to disavow. The Chinese and Japanese questions are, perhaps naturally, considered in our colonies with sole reference to local predilections and convenience, and with no regard to the exigencies of British diplomacy. The arbitrary exclusion by Natal, for example, and Western Australia, of the Queen-Empress's Indian subjects, some of them wearing war-medals on their breasts; or by New Zealand of Austrian immigrants; are not, perhaps, great matters at present. But there are coming questions in the Pacific which, when the Australian Dominion makes her voice heard, will not be small matters at all. Meanwhile, the position, in regard to our half-veiled, half-acknowledged, ascendency is that it is asserted from time to time, as occasion demands and as circumstances may permit, by the Colonial Office, through the Governors; and is generally, perhaps, understood to be based upon a latent claim of the British Parliament, as such, to supremacy; a claim which is unconstitutional in itself, and the only historical basis of which derives from the days of the great Whig encroachment. Government without representation is foreign to the spirit of the constitution. The less Parliament interferes with India and the Colonies, the better it will be for the Colonies, for India, and for the Empire. The Crown conducts our foreign policy through its advisers of the Privy Council, who possess the confidence of Parliament. Sir John Macdonald understood the theoretical position when, in shaping a Canadian Privy Council, he foreshadowed a Kingdom of Canada; for in the three great secondary dominions of Canada, Australia, and South Africa, each with its legislature, and each with its Council advisory of the King-Emperor, while the original or British Privy Council (supplemented, as it has already begun to be, from the colonies) "animates the whole," we see the real future constitution of self-governing Anglo-Saxondom, the real British Empire to which India and the other dependencies should be attached.

The second bond of union, the legislative veto, is useful as securing, amongst other things, some degree of legislative uniformity within the Empire. This power is not threatened by the new Commonwealth Bill, which proposes, on the contrary, substantially to strengthen it. But it is purely negative, both in its nature and influence, and can of course form no foundation of empire.

The third, the judicial prerogative of the Crown, is the very central of those crimson threads of which a recent school of Imperial Federation Leaguers was so fond of talking. Tod calls it one of the most stable safeguards, as well as one of the most beneficial acts, of the sovereign power. The appellate jurisdiction of the Queen in Council is retained primarily for the good of the colonies, and not for that of the mother country. Nothing is more necessary, particularly in the Australian colonies, than to secure the rights and property of the individual citizen, in a young, hasty, and democratic community, against the bureaucratic enthusiasms of departmental tyranny. It is not infrequently useful, for reasons more generally understood at home, to change the venue. The standard of legal training, again, is not always at its highest in the most remote parts of the Empire, and the field from which judges are picked is necessarily less extensive than at home. But more serious is the tendency of colonial executives, in communities where the authority of the common law, and the dignity and independence of the Bench, have not yet had much time to become established in the public mind, to try to subordinate the judiciary to themselves. What the legislature has established as the law, it is argued, the legislature can interpret. The legislature is supreme, as the representative of the people; and the legislature, which, for the purpose, means the Government, knows the intention with which particular laws were passed. Hence a quite frequent (though, to the English mind, all but incredible) recourse to retrospective legislation; and, especially in the smaller colonies, a parallel and growing tendency to obstruct or prevent Petitions of Right. Nor is this subordination of the Courts to the Executive confined to the more corrupt communities, though its most flagrant and most complete manifestation has been in the most corrupt of all, the Transvaal. It is quite compatible with the purest and most disinterested zeal for democracy or for the immediate public good; and may be the fruit, at times, of nothing worse nor more uncommon than narrow views and an ignorance of law. The Commonwealth Bill provides for the establishment of a Federal High Court of Australia, to hear and determine (1) all cases of dispute between the Federated States, or all cases in which State rights are concerned; and (2) private cases, except such as the subsequent legislation of the Federal Parliament shall permit to be taken to the Privy Council. In Canada, the Act of 1875, which was drafted by Sir John Macdonald in 1869, gave the Supreme Court final and conclusive jurisdiction, "*saving any right which Her Majesty may be pleased to exert by virtue of her royal prerogative.*" These last words, it has since been held, leave untouched the prerogative to allow an appeal, and the correlative right of every subject of the realm to make one. Consequently appeals from Canada, as from all other parts of the Empire, to the Privy

Council are of frequent occurrence, and of the utmost convenience. Three new judges, from Canada, the Cape, and Australia respectively, have been added to the Judicial Committee of the Privy Council within the last three years, and sit regularly for the hearing of colonial cases. And the Judicial Committee of the Privy Council is empowered (again to quote Tod) to consider " any matters whatsoever the Crown shall think fit to refer to it."

As to opinion at the Antipodes, there is good reason to suppose that the majority of Australians themselves are opposed to the serious encroachment on the royal prerogative threatened by the Bill. Not only has it been a commonplace of the large, and in some colonies influential, anti-Federal party to denounce the whole institution of the new High Court as a source of oppression and expense—an argument which is still freely employed in Western Australia—but the more intelligent property-holding classes are perhaps generally opposed to it, or at all events to its substitution for the Privy Council as a final Court of Appeal. The Legislative Council of New South Wales, as we have seen, has already expressed itself strongly on this point; and has been followed in its course of protest by various other representative bodies. The insertion, by Parliament, of some such clause in the Bill as that which preserved the constitutional position in the case of Canada is, therefore, it would seem, likely to be at least not unpopular in Australia; while, having regard to Imperial interests, it is vitally essential.

APPENDIX A

DEFENCE

THE AUSTRALIAN SQUADRON, MAINTAINED BY AUSTRALASIA, FOR PROTECTION OF FLOATING TRADE IN AUSTRALASIAN WATERS.

[N.B.—*Exclusive of H.M. Ships of the British Navy on the Australian Station.*]

Boomerang, twin screw torpedo gunboat, first class, 2 guns, 735 tons, i.h.p. 2,500 n.d. (in reserve).

Karrakatta, twin screw torpedo gunboat, first class, 2 guns, 735 tons, i.h.p. 2,500 n.d. Lieut. and Commander, Richard M. Harbord.

Katoomba, twin screw cruiser, third class, 8 guns, 2,575 tons, i.h.p. 4,000 n.d. Captain, Herbert W. S. Gibson.

Mildura, twin screw cruiser, third class, 8 guns, 2,575 tons, i.h.p. 4,000 n.d. Captain, Henry Leah.

Ringarooma, twin screw cruiser, third class, guns, 2,575 tons, i.h.p. 4,000 n.d. (in reserve).

Tauranga, twin screw cruiser, third class, 8 guns, 2,575 tons, i.h.p. 4,000 n.d. Captain, W. L. H. Browne.

Wallaroo, twin screw cruiser, third class, 8 guns, 2,575 tons, i.h.p. 4,000 n.d. Captain, George N. A. Pollard.

MEMORANDUM OF AGREEMENT BETWEEN GREAT BRITAIN AND AUSTRALIAN COLONIES.

1. There shall be a force of sea-going ships of war to be provided, equipped, manned, and maintained at joint cost. 2. Officers and men to be changed triennially. 3. The vessels to be

under the control of the Commander-in-Chief on the Australian Station, and are not to be taken from Australian waters without the consent of the Colonies. 4. *By reason of the new agreement, no reduction is to take place in the Imperial Squadron on the Station.* 5. The vessels shall consist of five fast cruisers and two torpedo gunboats; of these, three cruisers and one gunboat are to be always kept in commission, and the remainder in reserve. 6. (*a*) The first cost of vessels is to be paid out of Imperial Funds. (*b*) The Colonies are to pay the Imperial Government interest at 5 per cent. on the prime cost, such interest not to exceed £35,000. (*c*) The annual charge for maintenance is to be borne by the Colonies, but this is not to exceed £91,000. 7. Imperial Government to replace any vessels lost. 8. Agreement to last for ten years. 9. In time of peace two vessels of the Squadron to be in New Zealand waters.

NOTE.—This agreement was extended by the Premiers in Conference at Melbourne early this year (1899) until after Federation, when the matter will of course be dealt with by the Commonwealth.

COLONIAL SHIPS OF WAR FOR HARBOUR DEFENCE, ETC.

VICTORIA.

Cerberus, double screw, iron armour-plated turret ship, 4 18-ton M.L. guns, 4 Nordenfeldts, 3,480 tons, 1,660 h.p.

Nelson, training ship, 22 guns, 1 Gatling, 2,730 tons, 500 h.p. Commander, R. M. Collins.

Albert, steel gunboat, 4 guns, 2 Nordenfeldts, 350 tons, 400 h.p.

Also, 3 armed steamers, carrying 6 guns, 2 Gatlings, and 4 Nordenfeldts; 3 torpedo boats, and 3 torpedo launches, carrying 14 Whitehead torpedoes, 2 Hotchkiss guns, 1 Nordenfeldt, and fitted with spar torpedoes.

SOUTH AUSTRALIA.

Protector, cruiser, 6 guns, 920 tons, 1,641 h.p.

QUEENSLAND.

Gayundah, double screw steel ship, 2 guns, 360 tons, 400 h.p.
Otter, steel gunboat, 1 gun, 220 tons, 460 h.p.
Paluma, double screw iron ship, 2 guns, 450 tons, 400 h.p.

NEW SOUTH WALES.

Two small torpedo boats.

TASMANIA.

One torpedo boat.

NEW ZEALAND.

Eight torpedo boats.

TOTAL MARINE FORCES OF AUSTRALASIA.

2437 men (of whom 1004 New Zealand).

MILITARY FORCES

1,484 *paid*.
10,984 *partly paid*.
13,043 *unpaid*.

Total, 25,511 men. Of whom 4,000 are artillery, 700 engineers, 1,000 cavalry, 2,800 mounted rifles (the real national arm), and nearly 16,000 infantry. Twenty thousand men could be mobilised in Queensland, New South Wales, Victoria, or South Australia. There were 700,000 men of the soldier's age (20-40) in Australasia in 1891.

The 6 colonies expend altogether about half a million annually (say 2s. 9d. a head of the population) on defence, and have sunk a total of about 2½ millions sterling in defence works.

APPENDIX B
GAUGES OF AUSTRALIAN RAILWAYS

Victoria, 5ft. 3in.; South Australia, 5ft. 3in. and 3ft. 6in.; New South Wales, 4ft. 8½in., except Moama to Deniliquin (connecting with Victorian line), 5ft. 3in.; Queensland, 3ft. 6in.; Western Australia, 3ft. 6in.; Tasmania, 3ft. 6in.; New Zealand, 4ft. 8½in. and 3ft. 6in. In England and Scotland the gauge is 4ft. 8½in.; in Ireland, 5ft. 3in.; in India, 5ft. 6in.

APPENDIX C
AUSTRALIAN FEDERATION

On the occasion of the presentation of the address by both Houses of Parliament of Victoria to the Queen, praying that the draft Bill to constitute a Commonwealth of Australia be passed into law by the Imperial Parliament, Lord Brassey spoke as follows: "Departing from formal precedent, I shall venture on this historic occasion to say a few words not officially inspired, but which will, perhaps, the better give utterance to the feelings of the hour. The address which you ask me in your name to transmit, marks a turning point in your national history. It closes an era in which great things have been done. In no other country, not in the most advanced of the communities of the old world, are law and order more assured, public tranquillity less disturbed, the standard of living for the whole people higher, provision for education more liberal; in none is self-government, the distinctive gift of our race, more admirably illustrated. Statesmanship, eloquence, sound common sense, lofty patriotism, have never been wanting even in the smallest of the Australian Parliaments; and now, looking forward to the future, and remembering all you have done in the past under difficult circumstances and the rivalry of separation, who shall measure the achievements which may be accomplished by your united efforts? You will be greatly strengthened for defence, your trade will grow by leaps and bounds, common credit will sensibly lighten the public charge, all petty jealousies will disappear. Time would fail me were I to attempt to enumerate the advantages certain to accrue in the near future from federation. I rejoice that the closing stage of my public life has been associated with a movement which, as far as in me lay, I have earnestly strived to help forward. It has had from Lady Brassey and myself the heartiest good wishes. Unless it had been so, I should have been no fitting representative of the Queen and her people in the United Kingdom. All your hopes for the future are fully shared in your old Motherland, and as in coming years you become in an increasing degree a powerful and prosperous State, the possession of a happy and contented people, supreme in these Southern Seas, there will be no envious feelings. Your own greatness will reflect glory on the home of your fathers, and there, as here, it will be said now and for all time and with a full heart, 'Advance Australia!'"

Compare with the above the following, extracted from a typical anti-federal lecture, delivered at Perth, Western Australia, June 29, 1899. The speaker, a man of the would-be professional politician class from New South Wales, and probably an agent of the anti-federal party there, alleged that "the strings of the movement were being pulled by Imperial Statesmen. It was easier to govern these colonies by one Governor and one Premier than through many Governors and Premiers. One head of all the defence forces would make insurrection or revolution more difficult, and independence, with a republican flag, practically impossible, and it would find another billet for a British aristocrat. Lord Brassey was of opinion that we should get a specimen of the royal blood imported, and he mentioned the Marquis of Lorne and the Duke of Fife, who have the good fortune to be married to British princesses, as likely for the post. This might add a glare of splendour to the Commonwealth capital, but would it especially benefit the people? One thing was certain, such a Government would render reforms in the direction of land nationalisation, socialism, the equality of women as voters with men, and the establishment of an independent nation under its own flag infinitely more remote and difficult than under existing conditions. It would be far more arduous to move the Federation Parliament, with its senate of rich Conservatives, than to stir the local Parliaments in the direction of progress." The last sentence, and indeed the whole utterance, is encouraging; to all except political experimentalists.

On July 7, the same speaker ridiculed the statement of Mr G. H. Reid, the Premier of New South Wales, that the other States as a Commonwealth would defend Western Australia from foreign invasion with their last shilling and their last man. It was the British Empire, he said, upon which they would have to rely in such circumstances. These are the methods of the paid agitator.

APPENDIX D

OLD-AGE PENSIONS IN PRACTICE IN NEW ZEALAND

From a Report presented in the Statement for the Year ended 31st March 1899.

THE REGISTRAR, OLD-AGE PENSIONS, TO THE
HON. THE COLONIAL TREASURER.

OLD-AGE PENSIONS OFFICE,
WELLINGTON, 19th June 1899.

"I have the honour to make the following report for your information.

"The Act came into force on the first day of November 1898. In the same month a Registrar was appointed, and in December old-age pension districts were constituted, deputy registrars were appointed, and notices were issued throughout the colony that forms of claim were obtainable at all post-offices.

"The number of pensions granted during January 1899, in respect of which payments were made up to the 31st day of

March 1899, inclusive, was 2,133, and the amount paid in respect thereof was £3,124, 1s. 8d. The amount paid in respect of other than pensions up to the 31st day of March 1899, inclusive, was £510, 8s. 1d.

"The total number of pensions granted up to the 31st day of March 1899, inclusive, was 7,487, representing a yearly payment of £128,082; the average pension being about £17, 2s.

"The amount of absolutely forfeited instalments up to the 31st day of March 1899, inclusive, was £12, 5s.

"The number of pensioners who died before the 31st day of March 1899, inclusive, was thirty-eight, and the number of pensions cancelled up to that date was six, representing altogether a yearly payment of £763.

"The number of pension certificates transferred from one old-age pension district to another, up to the 31st day of March 1899, inclusive, was twenty-three.

"It is scarcely to be expected that the administration of a new measure will be altogether smooth at first. It is, therefore, a matter for congratulation that few difficulties have presented themselves, and that an entirely new experience had been generally anticipated in the detailed provisions of the Act and regulations.

"Under the existing Act no provision is made for any payment to the representatives of a deceased pensioner. It seems reasonable that the portion of an instalment accrued up to the date of the pensioner's death should be paid to the person who has defrayed the expenses of burial. It seems desirable also that near relatives from whom a pensioner may legally claim maintenance should not be relieved by the Old-age Pensions Act of such responsibility. I recommend also that the Colonial Treasurer should be empowered to pay an instalment of pension which has been forfeited through non-delivery of the pension certificate or other cause, not being the fault or neglect of the pensioner.

"Sub-section (3) of section 13, relating to the method of calculating the joint income of husband and wife, has not been uniformly interpreted. It might be well to remove all doubt as to the intention of this provision.

"The claims of some persons, who are otherwise qualified, have been rejected on the ground that they have not been naturalised subjects for five years, as prescribed by section 64 of the Act. I suggest some modification of this disability," etc. (*The remainder is unimportant, except following.*)

RETURN SHOWING COST OF ADMINISTRATION OF "THE OLD-AGE PENSIONS ACT, 1898," FOR THE FINANCIAL YEAR ENDED 31ST MARCH 1899.

	£	s.	d.	£	s.	d.
Salaries—						
Registrar	100	1	1			
Deputy Registrars	40	3	10			
				140	4	11
Other Expenses—						
Advertising and printing	16	6	0			
Clerical assistance	247	18	0			
Interpreting	7	9	3			
Shorthand-writer	19	0	0			
Travelling allowance and expenses	76	2	2			
Sundries	3	7	9			
				370	3	2
Total				£510	8	1

THE TREASURY, 23rd *June* 1899.

APPENDIX E

OLD AGE PENSIONS IN NEW SOUTH WALES

In the *Report on Old-age Pensions, etc., in England and on the Continent of Europe* [by Lieut.-Col. J. C. Neild, New South Wales Commissioner: By Authority, Sydney, 1898] Col. Neild recommends the payment of a minimum pension of 7s. 6d. weekly (in case of *"unmerited misfortune,"* 11s. 3d.) to persons over fifty-five; "necessity to be a condition precedent to pension." The Report is a large 8vo of 450 pages, and is worth perusal.

§ 786 is particularly interesting, giving a range of examples from (1) "*Individuals with no personal income, or personal income not exceeding* 10s. *per week*, weekly pension 7s. 6d."; to (30) "*Married couples, having two children, with weekly personal income of* 30s., weekly pension 2s. 6d."; and (yet further) to the maximum pension payable to the victims of "*unmerited misfortune*" — "*Married couples, with two children*, per week, 26s. 3d."

"It will be seen," says the *Report*, § 788, "that these proposals offer considerable inducement towards thrift"; *how*, is not over clear.

"The source from which the pensions are to be provided" is admitted to be "of paramount importance."

A tax on tea is recommended as likely to be sufficient (§ 795).

But, if the Federal Government takes the tea tax, "probably an impost upon flour would be an alternative." (§ 796).

§ 797. "It is quite possible that this suggestion will be made the subject of thoughtless objection, as a tax of any kind on bread is necessarily unpopular, but I submit that there is an immense, and an essential, distinction between a tax on bread for ordinary purposes of Government, *and a tax on bread to provide bread for the aged, the helpless, and the indigent.*"

"Such an objection, too, would be sentimental rather than practical, for wharfage dues upon breadstuffs are universal . . . while lands occupied with wheat are largely the subject of taxation."

A royalty upon mining profits is further recommended (§ 800), on the ground, apparently, that it would be paid chiefly by London companies.

ADVANCED AUSTRALIA

APPENDIX F

RETURNS OF IMPORTS AND EXPORTS, QUEENSLAND, 1899
SHEWING THE RATE PER HEAD OF THE POPULATION.

	1897.	1898.
Population on December 31st	478,440	492,602
Imports	£5,429,191	£6,007,266
Imports per head of population	£11, 6s. 11½d.	£12, 3s. 11d.

EXPORTS.

Classification of Articles, &c.	1897.	1898.
	£	£
Gold, in Dust and Bars	2,568,702	2,855,781
Specie (Coin)	60,254	218,547
Silver Lead Bullion and Silver Gold Bullion, and Silver Precipitates	55,785	41,951
Silver Ore and Gold Ore Slag	10,863	23,037
Copper—Ore, Regulus, Smelted and Matté	21,388	6,430
Tin—Ore, Slag, and Smelted	36,670	31,871
Drapery, Apparel, Silks, &c.	14,835	12,006
Shell Fish (Oysters) and Bêche-de-mer	24,265	16,069
Fruit—Green	87,450	96,313
Grain, Pulse, &c.	17,887	5,222
Hides and Skins	438,211	466,265
Live Stock by Sea	7,980	16,487
Live Stock Overland (Horses, Cattle and Sheep)	821,526	798,949
Pearl Shell and Tortoise Shell	130,053	111,975
Preserved Meat (Salt Meat, &c.)	365,045	482,676
Frozen Meat	662,994	676,698
Rum (Colonial)	1,900	2,081
Sugar (Colonial)	681,038	1,329,876
Tallow	272,528	328,531
Timber	7,791	8,254
Wool	2,509,342	3,018,098
All Other	295,050	309,010
TOTALS	£9,091,557	£10,856,127
Exports per head of Population	£ s. d. 19 0 0½	£ s. d. 22 0 9

APPENDIX

RETURN SHOWING THE TOTAL VALUE OF IMPORTS INTO AND EXPORTS FROM THE VARIOUS PORTS OF QUEENSLAND, ALSO BORDERWISE, DURING THE YEAR ENDED 31st DECEMBER 1898.

Ports.	Imports.	Exports.	Total Trade.
ESTIMATED MEAN POPULATION, 492,602.			
	£	£	£
Brisbane	3,333,740	2,490,001	5,823,741
Ipswich	69,725	—	69,725
Maryborough . . .	164,194	98,200	262,394
Bundaberg . . .	93,754	466,123	559,877
Gladstone . . .	10,737	127,365	138,102
Rockhampton . . .	622,061	2,434,287	3,056,348
St Lawrence . . .	740	28,791	29,531
Mackay	107,533	382,878	490,411
Bowen	24,091	230,906	254,997
Townsville . . .	875,175	2,616,511	3,491,686
Dungeness . . .	21,004	171,757	192,761
Geraldton . . .	11,429	119,019	130,448
Cairns	91,333	193,210	284,543
Port Douglas . . .	7,597	35,423	43,020
Cooktown	53,648	85,534	139,182
Thursday Island . .	60,342	128,047	188,389
Normanton . . .	38,244	154,566	192,810
Burketown . . .	3,205	17,518	20,723
Total Seaward . .	5,588,552	9,780,136	15,368,688
Across the Border (including Live Stock)	418,714	1,075,991	1,494,705
	£6,007,266	£10,856,127	£16,863,393

Imports, Exports, and Total Trade per head

Imports.　　　　Exports.　　　　Total.
£12, 3s. 11d.　£22, 0s. 9d.　£34, 4s. 8d.

J. C. KENT, *for Collector of Customs.*

CUSTOMS, BRISBANE,
23rd May 1899.

APPENDIX G
NEW ZEALAND GOLD OUTPUT 1899

	ozs.	Value.			ozs.	Value.
January .	33,049	£130,207	April .		33,343	£130,509
February	21,729	. 81,984	May .		25,962	. 100,161
March .	36,843	. 143,821	June .		41,547	. 161,924

APPENDIX H
POPULATION OF AUSTRALASIA

The Australasian Colonies as a whole contained a population on the 31st December 1898 estimated at 4,476,985 persons, with an average total annual increase of merely 1½ per cent.

AUSTRALASIAN COLONIES.

Colony.	Population on 31st December 1898.			Rate of Increase during 1898.		
	Males.	Females.	Total.	Males.	Females.	Total.
	No.	No.	No.	per cent.	per cent.	per cent.
New South Wales	721,335	624,905	1,346,240	1·69	1·76	1·72
Victoria . .	593,446	582,044	1,175,490	—0·33	0·21	—0·06
Queensland . .	279,670	218,853	498,523	3·06	2·59	2·85
South Australia (including Northern Territory) . .	191,745	176,055	367,800	1·81	0·77	1·31
Western Australia	112,054	56,075	168,129	1·54	8·75	3·83
Tasmania . .	95,632	81,709	177,341	4·39	1·99	3·27
New Zealand (exclusive of 39,854 Maoris) . .	392,124	351,339	743,463	1·93	2·03	1·98
Australasia . .	2,386,006	2,090,980	4,476,986	1·48	1·55	1·52

EMIGRATION FROM UNITED KINGDOM TO AUSTRALASIA.

1893	.	11,412	1895	.	10,809	1896	.	10,710
1894	.	11,151				1897	.	12,396

A statement is added giving the arrivals and departures for each of the Australasian Colonies during the year 1898. The figures are Mr Coghlan's, and the result is shown to be a net gain of 7,670 persons :—

Colony	Arrivals			Departures			Excess of Arrivals over Departures		
	Males. No.	Females. No.	Total. No.	Males. No.	Females. No.	Total. No.	Males. No.	Females. No.	Total. No.
New South Wales	89,495	49,613	139,108	86,590	49,285	135,875	2,905	328	3,233
Victoria	64,026	30,410	94,436	70,914	35,784	106,698	—6,888	—5,374	—12,262
Queensland	23,999	10,244	34,243	19,013	9,097	28,110	4,986	1,147	6,133
South Australia	64,245	30,452	94,697	62,783	31,396	94,179	1,462	—944	518
Western Australia	22,683	10,026	32,709	21,769	6,987	28,756	914	3,039	3,953
Tasmania	16,270	7,804	24,074	13,340	7,335	20,675	2,930	469	3,399
New Zealand	12,524	6,331	18,855	10,438	5,721	16,159	2,086	610	2,696
Australasia	293,242	144,880	438,122	284,847	145,605	430,452	8,395	—725	7,670

APPENDIX I
WESTERN AUSTRALIA
Return showing Gold Produce of Colony entered for Export; also at Royal Mint, Perth.

MONTH.	1894. Quantity.	1894. Value.	1897. Quantity.	1897. Value.	1898. Quantity.	1898. Value.
	ozs. dwts. grs.	£ s. d.	ozs. dwts. grs.	£ s. d.	ozs. dwts. grs.	£ s. d.
January	⎫	⎫	40,385 14 3	153,469 9 8	93,395 8 19	354,902 13 5
February	⎬ 35,367 18 13	⎬ 134,398 2 5	32,526 0 0	123,598 16 0	53,739 3 14	204,208 17 8
March	⎭	⎭	40,296 7 12	153,126 4 6	75,380 0 21	286,444 3 4
	35,367 18 13	134,398 2 5	113,209 1 15	430,194 10 2	222,514 13 6	845,555 14 5
April	⎫	⎫	39,660 7 12	150,709 8 6	84,082 12 16	319,514 0 2
May	⎬ 40,450 0 5	⎬ 153,710 0 10	59,111 15 3	224,624 13 6	83,346 18 18	316,718 7 3
June	⎭	⎭	53,348 14 20	202,725 4 4	80,749 12 20	306,848 12 9
	75,817 18 18	288,108 3 3	265,329 19 2	1,008,253 16 6	470,693 17 12	1,788,636 14 7
July	⎫	⎫	48,811 4 17	185,482 13 10	76,980 15 9	292,526 18 5
August	⎬ 62,846 6 16	⎬ 238,816 1 4	65,129 3 10	247,490 17 0	89,395 9 10	339,702 15 9
September	⎭	⎭	71,776 11 6	272,750 18 9	89,179 4 4	338,880 19 10
	138,664 5 10	526,924 4 7	451,046 18 11	1,713,978 6 1	726,249 6 11	2,759,747 8 7
October	17,453 6 20	66,322 14 0	75,690 3 15	287,622 13 10	116,824 12 5	443,933 10 5
November	23,628 7 5	89,787 15 5	75,845 0 15	288,211 2 5	111,793 2 2	424,813 17 6
December	27,385 6 19	104,064 5 10	72,411 14 9	275,164 10 7	95,316 10 22	362,202 17 6
TOTAL	207,131 6 6	787,098 19 10	674,993 17 2	2,564,976 12 2	1,050,183 11 23	3,999,697 13 6

NOTE.—As the returns in the last quarter of the year are usually the heaviest, the yield for 1899 considerably more than 1½ million ounces, or say 6 millions sterling.

APPENDIX J
TRADE PER HEAD OF THE POPULATION IN 1897

Colony.	Mean Population.	Imports.	Exports.	Total Trade.
		£ s. d.	£ s. d.	£ s. d.
Queensland	478,440	11 6 11	19 0 1	30 7 0
New South Wales	1,310,550	16 11 10	18 2 6	34 14 4
Victoria	1,172,790	13 3 7	14 5 6	27 9 1
South Australia	353,518	20 3 2	19 11 11	39 15 1
Western Australia	155,749	41 4 2	25 5 11	66 10 1
Tasmania	168,916	8 1 11	10 6 6	18 8 5
New Zealand (exclusive of Maoris)	721,609	11 3 3	13 7 8	25 0 11

But the values of the exports of the Australian Colonies, more especially New South Wales, Victoria, and South Australia, are largely increased by the inclusion of articles the produce or manufacture of other colonies and countries.

The value of home productions or manufactures exported from each colony in 1897, and the rate per head of mean population, were as follows :—

Colony.	Home Produce exported.	Per Head of Population.
Queensland	£8,831,450	£18 9 2
New South Wales	17,057,543	13 0 4
Victoria	12,829,394	10 18 9
South Australia	2,484,140	7 0 6
Western Australia	3,218,569	20 13 4
Tasmania	1,721,959	10 3 11
New Zealand	9,596,267	13 6 0

The next table sets forth the amount of the trade of each of the above-named colonies with the United Kingdom in 1897 :—

Colony.	Imports from the United Kingdom.	Exports to the United Kingdom.	Total Trade with the United Kingdom.
	£	£	£
Queensland	2,501,952	3,322,703	5,824,655
New South Wales	7,557,069	8,728,828	16,285,897
Victoria	6,004,798	9,559,249	15,564,047
South Australia	2,057,567	2,182,946	4,240,513
Western Australia	2,624,086	1,736,205	4,360,291
Tasmania	397,510	274,497	672,007
New Zealand	5,392,738	8,168,123	13,560,861

ADVANCED AUSTRALIA

The statement appended shows the relative importance of the Australasian Colonies as a market for the productions of the United Kingdom :—

EXPORTS OF HOME PRODUCTIONS FROM THE UNITED KINGDOM IN 1896, TO—

	£
British India and Ceylon	31,103,596
Germany	22,244,405
Australasia	21,888,292
U.S.A.	20,424,225
France	14,151,512
South Africa	13,821,357
Holland	8,333,935
Belgium	7,816,152

Other countries—less than £700,000 in each case.

The Australasian Colonies, with a population of 4½ millions, thus take third place as consumers of our produce, the exports thereto being more that two-thirds the value of those to British India, with 290 million inhabitants.

A CATALOGUE OF BOOKS AND ANNOUNCEMENTS OF METHUEN AND COMPANY PUBLISHERS : LONDON 36 ESSEX STREET W.C.

CONTENTS

	PAGE
FORTHCOMING BOOKS,	2
POETRY,	13
BELLES LETTRES, ANTHOLOGIES, ETC.,	14
ILLUSTRATED BOOKS,	15
HISTORY,	15
BYZANTINE TEXTS,	17
BIOGRAPHY,	18
TRAVEL, ADVENTURE AND TOPOGRAPHY,	18
NAVAL AND MILITARY,	21
GENERAL LITERATURE,	21
SCIENCE AND TECHNOLOGY,	23
PHILOSOPHY,	24
THEOLOGY,	24
FICTION,	27
BOOKS FOR BOYS AND GIRLS,	35
THE PEACOCK LIBRARY,	35
UNIVERSITY EXTENSION SERIES,	36
SOCIAL QUESTIONS OF TO-DAY	37
CLASSICAL TRANSLATIONS'	37
EDUCATIONAL BOOKS,	38

NOVEMBER 1899

NOVEMBER 1899.

MESSRS. METHUEN'S ANNOUNCEMENTS

Travel and Adventure

THE HIGHEST ANDES. By E. A. FITZGERALD. With Two Maps, 51 Illustrations, 13 of which are Photogravures, and a Panorama. *Royal 8vo.* 30s. *net.*

Also, a Small Edition on Handmade Paper, limited to 50 Copies, 4to. £5, 5s.

A narrative of the highest climb yet accomplished. The illustrations have been reproduced with the greatest care, and the book, in addition to its adventurous interest, contains appendices of great scientific value. It also contains a very elaborate map, and a panorama.

THROUGH ASIA. By SVEN HEDIN. With 300 Illustrations from Photographs and Sketches by the Author, and 3 Maps. Second and cheaper Edition in 16 Fortnightly Parts at 1s. each net; or in two volumes. *Royal 8vo.* 20s. *net.*

Extracts from reviews of this great book, which *The Times* has called 'one of the best books of the century,' will be found on p. 15. The present form of issue places it within the reach of buyers of moderate means.

THE CAROLINE ISLANDS By F. W. CHRISTIAN. With many Illustrations and Maps. *Demy 8vo.* 12s. 6d. *net.*

This book contains a history and complete description of these islands—their physical features, fauna, flora; the habits, and religious beliefs of the inhabitants. It is the result of many years' residence among the natives, and is the only worthy work on the subject.

THREE YEARS IN SAVAGE AFRICA. By LIONEL DECLE. With 100 Illustrations and 5 Maps. Cheaper Edition. *Demy 8vo.* 10s. 6d. *net.*

A NEW RIDE TO KHIVA. By R. L. JEFFERSON. With 51 Illustrations. *Crown 8vo.* 6s.

The account of an adventurous ride on a bicycle through Russia and the deserts of Asia to Khiva.

Poetry

PRESENTATION EDITIONS

BARRACK-ROOM BALLADS. By RUDYARD KIPLING. 60*th Thousand.* *Crown 8vo. Leather, gilt top,* 6s. *net.*

THE SEVEN SEAS. By RUDYARD KIPLING. 50*th Thousand.* *Crown 8vo. Leather, gilt top,* 6s. *net.*

ENGLISH LYRICS. Selected and arranged by W. E. HENLEY. Second and cheaper Edition. *Crown 8vo.* 3s. 6d.

LYRA FRIVOLA. By A. D. GODLEY, M.A., Fellow of Magdalen College, Oxford. *Pott 8vo.* 2s. 6d.

A little volume of occasional verse, chiefly academic.

The Works of Shakespeare

General Editor, EDWARD DOWDEN, Litt. D.

MESSRS. METHUEN have in preparation an Edition of Shakespeare in single Plays. Each play will be edited with a full Introduction, Textual Notes, and a Commentary at the foot of the page.

The first volume will be:

HAMLET. Edited by EDWARD DOWDEN. *Demy 8vo.* 3s. 6d.

History and Biography

THE LETTERS OF ROBERT LOUIS STEVENSON. Arranged and Edited with Notes by SIDNEY COLVIN. *Demy 8vo.* 2 *vols.* 25s. *net.*

These highly important and interesting volumes contain the correspondence of Robert Louis Stevenson from his eighteenth year to almost the last day of his life, selected and edited, with notes and introductions, by Mr. Sidney Colvin, his most intimate friend. The letters are very various in subject and character, being addressed partly to his family and private friends, and partly to such well known living or lately deceased men of letters as Mr. Hamerton, Mr. J. A. Symonds, Mr. Henry James, Mr. James Payn, Dr. Conan Doyle, Mr. J. M. Barrie, Mr. Edmund Gosse, Mr. F. Locker-Lampson, Mr. Cosmo Monkhouse, Mr. Andrew Lang, Mr. W. E. Henley, and the Editor himself. They present a vivid and brilliant autobiographical picture of the mind and character of the distinguished author. It was originally intended that a separate volume containing a full narrative and critical Life by the Editor should appear simultaneously with the letters, and form part of the work; but the publication of this has for various reasons been postponed.

THE LIFE AND LETTERS OF SIR JOHN EVERETT MILLAIS, President of the Royal Academy. By his Son, J. G. MILLAIS. With over 300 Illustrations, of which 9 are in photogravure. *Two volumes. Royal 8vo.* 32s. *net.*

An edition limited to 350 copies will also be printed. This will contain 22 of Millais' great paintings reproduced in photogravure, with a case containing an extra set of these Photogravures pulled on India paper. The price of this edition will be £4, 4s. *net.*

In these two magnificent volumes is contained the authoritative biography of the most distinguished and popular painter of the last half of the century. They contain the story of his extraordinary boyhood, of his early struggles and triumphs, of the founding of the Pre-Raphaelite Brotherhood, now first given to the world in authentic detail, of the painting of most of his famous pictures, of his friendships with many of the most distinguished men of the day in art, letters, and politics, of his home life, and of his sporting tastes. There are a large number of letters to his wife describing the circumstances under which his pictures were painted, letters from Her Majesty the Queen, Lord Beaconsfield, Mr. Gladstone, Mr. Watts, Sir William Harcourt, Lord Rosebery, Lord Leighton, etc., etc. Among them are several illustrated letters from Landseer, Leech, Du Maurier, and Mike Halliday. The last letter that Lord Beaconsfield wrote before his death is reproduced in fac-simile. Mr. Val Prinsep contributes his reminiscences of Millais in a long and most interesting chapter.

Not the least attractive and remarkable feature of this book will be the magnificence of its illustrations. No more complete representation of the art of any painter has ever been produced on the same scale. The owners of Sir John Millais' most famous pictures and their copyrights have generously given their consent to their reproduction in his biography, and, in addition to those pictures with which the public is familiar, over two hundred pictures and sketches which have never been reproduced before, and which, in all probability, will never be seen again by the general public, will appear in these pages. The early chapters contain sketches made by Millais at the age of seven. There follow some exquisite drawings made by him during his Pre-Raphaelite period, a large number of sketches and studies made for his great pictures, water colour sketches, pen-and-ink sketches, and drawings, humorous and serious. There are ten portraits of Millais himself, including two by Mr. Watts and Sir Edward Burne Jones. There is a portrait of Dickens, taken after death, and a sketch of D. G. Rossetti. Thus the book will be not only a biography of high interest and an important contribution to the history of English art, but in the best sense of the word, a beautiful picture book.

THE EXPANSION OF EGYPT. A Political and Historical Survey. By A. SILVA WHITE. With four Special Maps. *Demy 8vo.* 15s. *net.*

This is an account of the political situation in Egypt, and an elaborate description of the Anglo-Egyptian Administration. It is a comprehensive treatment of the whole Egyptian problem by one who has studied every detail on the spot.

THE VICAR OF MORWENSTOW. A Biography. By S. BARING GOULD, M.A. A new and revised Edition. With Portrait. *Crown 8vo.* 3s. 6d.

This is a completely new edition of the well known biography of R. S. Hawker.

A CONSTITUTIONAL AND POLITICAL HISTORY OF ROME. By T. M. TAYLOR, M.A., Fellow of Gonville and Caius College, Cambridge, Senior Chancellor's Medallist for Classics, Porson University Scholar, etc., etc. *Crown 8vo.* 7s. 6d.

An account of the origin and growth of the Roman Institutions, and a discussion of the various political movements in Rome from the earliest times to the death of Augustus.

A HISTORY OF THE CHURCH OF CYPRUS. By JOHN HACKETT, M.A. With Maps and Illustrations. *Demy 8vo.* 12s. 6d. *net.*

A work which brings together all that is known on the subject from the introduction of Christianity to the commencement of the British occupation. A separate division deals with the local Latin Church during the period of the Western Supremacy.

BISHOP LATIMER. By A. J. CARLYLE, M.A. *Crown 8vo.* 3s. 6d. [*Leaders of Religion Series.*

MESSRS. METHUEN'S ANNOUNCEMENTS 5

Theology

CHRISTIAN MYSTICISM. The Bampton Lectures for 1899. By W. R. INGE, M.A., Fellow and Tutor of Hertford College, Oxford. *Demy 8vo.* 12s. 6d. *net.*

A complete survey of the subject from St. John and St. Paul to modern times, covering the Christian Platonists, Augustine, the Devotional Mystics, the Mediæval Mystics, and the Nature Mystics and Symbolists, including Böhme and Wordsworth.

A BIBLICAL INTRODUCTION. By W. H. BENNETT, M.A., and W. F. ADENEY, M.A. *Crown 8vo.* 7s. 6d.

This volume furnishes students with the latest results in biblical criticism, arranged methodically. Each book is treated separately as to date, authorship, etc.

ST. PAUL, THE MASTER-BUILDER. By WALTER LOCK, D.D., Warden of Keble College. *Crown 8vo.* 3s. 6d.

An attempt to popularise the recent additions to our knowledge of St. Paul as a missionary, a statesman and an ethical teacher.

THE OECUMENICAL DOCUMENTS OF THE FAITH. Edited with Introductions and Notes by T. HERBERT BINDLEY, B.D., Merton College, Oxford, Principal of Codrington College and Canon of Barbados, and sometime Examining Chaplain to the Lord Bishop. *Crown 8vo.* 6s.

THE CREED OF NICAEA.   THE TOME OF LEO.
THREE EPISTLES OF CYRIL. THE CHALCEDONIAN DEFINITION.

The Churchman's Bible

General Editor, J. H. BURN, B.D., Examining Chaplain to the Bishop of Aberdeen.

Messrs. METHUEN propose to issue a series of expositions upon most of the books of the Bible. The volumes will be practical and devotional rather than critical in their purpose, and the text of the authorised version will be explained in sections or paragraphs, which will correspond as far as possible with the divisions of the Church Lectionary.

THE EPISTLE OF ST. PAUL TO THE GALATIANS. Explained by A. W. ROBINSON, B.D., Vicar of All Hallows, Barking. *Fcap. 8vo.* 1s. 6d. *net. Leather,* 2s. 6d. *net.*

ECCLESIASTES. Explained by W. A. STREANE, M.A. *Fcp. 8vo.* 1s. 6d. *net. Leather,* 2s. 6d. *net.*

The Churchman's Library

Edited by J. H. BURN, B.D.

THE WORKMANSHIP OF THE PRAYER BOOK: Its Literary and Liturgical Aspects. By J. DOWDEN, D.D., Lord Bishop of Edinburgh. *Crown 8vo.* 3s. 6d.

This volume, avoiding questions of controversy, exhibits the liturgical aims and literary methods of the authors of the Prayer Book.

Messrs. Methuen's Announcements

The Library of Devotion
Pott 8vo. Cloth 2s.; leather 2s. 6d. net.

NEW VOLUMES.

A SERIOUS CALL TO A DEVOUT AND HOLY LIFE.
By WILLIAM LAW. Edited, with an Introduction by C. BIGG, D.D., late Student of Christ Church.

This is a reprint, word for word and line for line, of the *Editio Princeps.*

THE TEMPLE. By GEORGE HERBERT. Edited, with an Introduction and Notes, by E. C. S. GIBSON, D.D., Vicar of Leeds.

This edition contains Walton's Life of Herbert, and the text is that of the first edition.

Science

THE SCIENTIFIC STUDY OF SCENERY. By J. E. MARR, Fellow of St John's College, Cambridge. Illustrated. *Crown 8vo.* 6s.

An elementary treatise on geomorphology—the study of the earth's outward forms. It is for the use of students of physical geography and geology, and will also be highly interesting to the general reader.

A HANDBOOK OF NURSING. By M. N. OXFORD, of Guy's Hospital. *Crown 8vo.* 3s. 6d.

This is a complete guide to the science and art of nursing, containing copious instruction both general and particular.

Classical

THE NICOMACHEAN ETHICS OF ARISTOTLE. Edited, with an Introduction and Notes by JOHN BURNET, M.A., Professor of Greek at St. Andrews. *Demy 8vo.* 15s. net.

This edition contains parallel passages from the Eudemian Ethics, printed under the text, and there is a full commentary, the main object of which is to interpret difficulties in the light of Aristotle's own rules.

THE CAPTIVI OF PLAUTUS. Edited, with an Introduction, Textual Notes, and a Commentary, by W. M. LINDSAY, Fellow of Jesus College, Oxford. *Demy 8vo.* 10s. 6d. net.

For this edition all the important MSS. have been re-collated. An appendix deals with the accentual element in early Latin verse. The Commentary is very full.

ZACHARIAH OF MITYLENE. Translated into English by F. J. HAMILTON, D.D., and E. W. BROOKS. *Demy 8vo.* 12s. 6d. net. [*Byzantine Texts.*

MESSRS. METHUEN'S ANNOUNCEMENTS 7

Sport

The Library of Sport

THE ART AND PRACTICE OF HAWKING. By E. B. MITCHELL. Illustrated by G. E. LODGE and others. *Demy 8vo.* 10s. 6d.

A complete description of the Hawks, Falcons, and Eagles used in ancient and modern times, with directions for their training and treatment. It is not only a historical account, but a complete practical guide.

THOUGHTS ON HUNTING. By PETER BECKFORD. Edited by J. OTHO PAGET, and Illustrated by G. H. JALLAND. *Demy 8vo.* 10s. 6d.

This edition of one of the most famous classics of sport contains an introduction and many footnotes by Mr. Paget, and is thus brought up to the standard of modern knowledge.

General Literature

THE BOOK OF THE WEST. By S. BARING GOULD. With numerous Illustrations. *Two volumes.* Vol. I. Devon. Vol. II. Cornwall. *Crown 8vo.* 6s. each.

PONS ASINORUM; OR, A GUIDE TO BRIDGE. By A. HULME BEAMAN. *Fcap. 8vo.* 2s.

A practical guide, with many specimen games, to the new game of Bridge.

TENNYSON AS A RELIGIOUS TEACHER. By CHARLES F. G. MASTERMAN. *Crown 8vo.* 6s.

The Little Guides

Pott 8vo, cloth 3s. ; *leather,* 3s. 6d. *net.*

NEW VOLUME.

SHAKESPEARE'S COUNTRY. By B. C. WINDLE, F.R.S., M.A. Illustrated by E. H. NEW.

Uniform with Mr. Wells' 'Oxford' and Mr. Thomson's 'Cambridge.

Methuen's Standard Library

THE DECLINE AND FALL OF THE ROMAN EMPIRE. By EDWARD GIBBON. Edited by J. B. BURY, LL.D., Fellow of Trinity College, Dublin. *In Seven Volumes. Demy 8vo, gilt top.* 8s. 6d. *each. Crown 8vo.* 6s. *each. Vol. VII.*

The concluding Volume of this Edition.

THE DIARY OF THOMAS ELLWOOD. Edited by G. C. CRUMP, M.A. *Crown 8vo.* 6s.

This edition is the only one which contains the complete book as originally published. It contains a long introduction and many footnotes.

8   MESSRS. METHUEN'S ANNOUNCEMENTS

LA COMMEDIA DI DANTE ALIGHIERI. Edited by PAGET TOYNBEE, M.A. *Crown 8vo.* 6s.
This edition of the Italian text of the Divine Comedy, founded on Witte's minor edition, carefully revised, is issued in commemoration of the sixth century of Dante's journey through the three kingdoms of the other world.

Illustrated and Gift Books

THE LIVELY CITY OF LIGG. By GELLETT BURGESS. With many Illustrations by the Author. *Small 4to.* 3s. 6d.

THE PHIL MAY ALBUM. *4to.* 7s. 6d. *net.*
This highly interesting volume contains 100 drawings by Mr. Phil May, and is representative of his earliest and finest work.

ULYSSES; OR, DE ROUGEMONT OF TROY. Described and depicted by A. H. MILNE. *Small quarto.* 3s. 6d.
The adventures of Ulysses, told in humorous verse and pictures.

THE CROCK OF GOLD. Fairy Stories told by S. BARING GOULD, and Illustrated by F. D. BEDFORD. *Crown 8vo.* 6s.

TOMMY SMITH'S ANIMALS. By EDMUND SELOUS. Illustrated by G. W. ORD. *Fcp. 8vo.* 2s. 6d.
A little book designed to teach children respect and reverence for animals.

A BIRTHDAY BOOK. With a Photogravure Frontispiece. *Demy 8vo.* 10s. 6d.
This is a birthday-book of exceptional dignity, and the extracts have been chosen with particular care.
The three passages for each day bear a certain relation to each other, and form a repertory of sententious wisdom from the best authors living or dead.

Educational

PRACTICAL PHYSICS. By H. STROUD, D. Sc., M.A., Professor of Physics in the Durham College of Science, Newcastle-on-Tyne. Fully illustrated. *Crown 8vo.* 3s. 6d.
[*Textbooks of Technology.*

GENERAL ELEMENTARY SCIENCE. By J. T. DUNN, D.Sc., and V. A. MUNDELLA. With many Illustrations. *Crown 8vo.* 3s. 6d.
[*Methuen's Science Primers.*

MESSRS. METHUEN'S ANNOUNCEMENTS

THE METRIC SYSTEM. By LEON DELBOS. *Crown 8vo.* 2s.
A theoretical and practical guide, for use in elementary schools and by the general reader.

A SOUTH AFRICAN ARITHMETIC. By HENRY HILL, B.A., Assistant Master at Worcester School, Cape Colony. *Crown 8vo.* 3s. 6d.
This book has been specially written for use in South African schools.

A KEY TO STEDMAN'S EASY LATIN EXERCISES. By C. G. BOTTING, M.A. *Crown 8vo.* 3s. *net.*

NEW TESTAMENT GREEK. A Course for Beginners. By G. RODWELL, B.A. With a Preface by WALTER LOCK, D.D., Warden of Keble College. *Fcap. 8vo.* 3s. 6d.

EXAMINATION PAPERS IN ENGLISH HISTORY. By J. TAIT WARDLAW, B.A., King's College, Cambridge. *Crown 8vo.* 2s. 6d. [*School Examination Series.*

A GREEK ANTHOLOGY. Selected by E. C. MARCHANT, M.A., Fellow of Peterhouse, Cambridge, and Assistant Master at St. Paul's School. *Crown 8vo.* 3s. 6d.

CICERO DE OFFICIIS. Translated by G. B. GARDINER, M.A. *Crown 8vo.* 2s. 6d. [*Classical Translations.*

The Novels of Charles Dickens

Crown 8vo. Each Volume, cloth 3s., leather 4s. 6d. net.

Messrs. METHUEN have in preparation an edition of those novels of Charles Dickens which have now passed out of copyright. Mr. George Gissing, whose critical study of Dickens is both sympathetic and acute, has written an Introduction to each of the books, and a very attractive feature of this edition will be the illustrations of the old houses, inns, and buildings, which Dickens described, and which have now in many instances disappeared under the touch of modern civilisation. Another valuable feature will be a series of topographical and general notes to each book by Mr. F. G. Kitton. The books will be produced with the greatest care as to printing, paper and binding.

The first volumes will be:

THE PICKWICK PAPERS. With Illustrations by E. H. NEW. *Two Volumes.*

NICHOLAS NICKLEBY. With Illustrations by R. J. WILLIAMS. *Two Volumes.*

BLEAK HOUSE. With Illustrations by BEATRICE ALCOCK. *Two Volumes.*

OLIVER TWIST. With Illustrations by E. H. NEW. *Two Volumes.*

MESSRS. METHUEN'S ANNOUNCEMENTS

The Little Library

Pott 8vo. Each Volume, cloth 1s. 6d. *net. ; leather* 2s. 6d. *net.*

Messrs. METHUEN intend to produce a series of small books under the above title, containing some of the famous books in English and other literatures, in the domains of fiction, poetry, and belles lettres. The series will also contain several volumes of selections in prose and verse.

The books will be edited with the most sympathetic and scholarly care. Each one will contain an Introduction which will give (1) a short biography of the author, (2) a critical estimate of the book. Where they are necessary, short notes will be added at the foot of the page.

The Little Library will ultimately contain complete sets of the novels of W. M. Thackeray, Jane Austen, the sisters Brontë, Mrs. Gaskell and others. It will also contain the best work of many other novelists whose names are household words.

Each book will have a portrait or frontispiece in photogravure, and the volumes will be produced with great care in a style uniform with that of 'The Library of Devotion.'

The first volumes will be:

A LITTLE BOOK OF ENGLISH LYRICS. With Notes.

PRIDE AND PREJUDICE. By JANE AUSTEN. With an Introduction and Notes by E. V. LUCAS. *Two Volumes.*

VANITY FAIR. By W. M. THACKERAY. With an Introduction by S. GWYNN. *Three Volumes.*

PENDENNIS. By W. M. THACKERAY. With an Introduction by S. GWYNN. *Three volumes.*

EOTHEN. By A. W. KINGLAKE. With an Introduction and Notes.

CRANFORD. By Mrs. GASKELL. With an Introduction and Notes by E. V. LUCAS.

THE INFERNO OF DANTE. Translated by H. F. CARY. With an Introduction and Notes by PAGET TOYNBEE.

JOHN HALIFAX, GENTLEMAN. By MRS. CRAIK. With an Introduction by ANNIE MATHESON. *Two volumes.*

THE EARLY POEMS OF ALFRED, LORD TENNYSON. Edited by J. C. COLLINS, M.A.

THE PRINCESS. By ALFRED, LORD TENNYSON. Edited by ELIZABETH WORDSWORTH.

MAUD, AND OTHER POEMS. By ALFRED, LORD TENNYSON. Edited by ELIZABETH WORDSWORTH.

IN MEMORIAM. By ALFRED, LORD TENNYSON. Edited by H. C. BEECHING, M.A.

A LITTLE BOOK OF SCOTTISH LYRICS. Arranged and Edited by T. F. HENDERSON.

Fiction

THE KING'S MIRROR. By ANTHONY HOPE. *Crown 8vo.* 6s.

THE CROWN OF LIFE. By GEORGE GISSING, Author of 'Demos,' 'The Town Traveller,' etc. *Crown 8vo.* 6s.

A NEW VOLUME OF WAR STORIES. By STEPHEN CRANE, Author of 'The Red Badge of Courage.' *Crown 8vo.* 6s.

THE STRONG ARM. By ROBERT BARR. *Crown 8vo.* 6s.

TO LONDON TOWN. By ARTHUR MORRISON, Author of 'Tales of Mean Streets,' 'A Child of the Jago,' etc. *Crown 8vo.* 6s.

ONE HOUR AND THE NEXT. By THE DUCHESS OF SUTHERLAND. *Crown 8vo.* 6s.

SIREN CITY. By BENJAMIN SWIFT, Author of 'Nancy Noon.' *Crown 8vo.* 6s.

VENGEANCE IS MINE. By ANDREW BALFOUR, Author of 'By Stroke of Sword.' Illustrated. *Crown 8vo.* 6s.

PRINCE RUPERT THE BUCCANEER. By C. J. CUTCLIFFE HYNE, Author of 'Captain Kettle,' etc. *Crown 8vo.* 6s.

PABO THE PRIEST. By S. BARING GOULD, Author of 'Mehalah,' etc. Illustrated. *Crown 8vo.* 6s.

GILES INGILBY. By W. E. NORRIS. Illustrated. *Crown 8vo.* 6s.

THE PATH OF A STAR. By SARA JEANETTE DUNCAN, Author of 'A Voyage of Consolation.' Illustrated. *Crown 8vo.* 6s.

THE HUMAN BOY. By EDEN PHILPOTTS, Author of 'Children of the Mist.' With a Frontispiece. *Crown 8vo.* 6s.

A series of English schoolboy stories, the result of keen observation, and of a most engaging wit.

THE HUMAN INTEREST. By VIOLET HUNT, Author of 'A Hard Woman,' etc. *Crown 8vo.* 6s.

MESSRS. METHUEN'S ANNOUNCEMENTS

AN ENGLISHMAN. By MARY L. PENDERED. *Crown 8vo.* 6s.

A GENTLEMAN PLAYER. By R. N. STEPHENS, Author of 'An Enemy to the King.' *Crown 8vo.* 6s.

DANIEL WHYTE. By A. J. DAWSON, Author of 'Bismillah.' *Crown 8vo.* 6s.

A New Edition of the Novels of Marie Corelli

This New Edition is in a more convenient form than the Library Edition, and is issued in a new and specially designed cover.

In Crown 8vo, Cloth, 6s. Leather, 6s. net.

A ROMANCE OF TWO WORLDS.	THE SOUL OF LILITH.
VENDETTA.	WORMWOOD.
THELMA.	BARABBAS: A DREAM OF THE
ARDATH: THE STORY OF A	WORLD'S TRAGEDY.
DEAD SELF.	THE SORROWS OF SATAN.

The Novelist

MESSRS. METHUEN are making an interesting experiment which constitutes a fresh departure in publishing. They are issuing under the above general title a Monthly Series of New Fiction by popular authors at the price of Sixpence. Each Number is as long as the average Six Shilling Novel. The first numbers of 'THE NOVELIST' are as follows:—

I. DEAD MEN TELL NO TALES. E. W. HORNUNG. [*Ready.*

II. JENNIE BAXTER, JOURNALIST. ROBERT BARR. [*Ready.*

III. THE INCA'S TREASURE. ERNEST GLANVILLE. [*Ready.*

IV. A SON OF THE STATE. W. PETT RIDGE. [*Ready.*

V. FURZE BLOOM. S. BARING GOULD. [*Ready.*

VI. BUNTER'S CRUISE. C. GLEIG. [*Ready.*

VII. THE GAY DECEIVERS. ARTHUR MOORE. [*November.*

VIII. A NEW NOVEL. MRS. MEADE. [*December.*

A CATALOGUE OF

MESSRS. METHUEN'S
PUBLICATIONS

Poetry

Rudyard Kipling. BARRACK-ROOM BALLADS. By RUDYARD KIPLING. 60*th Thousand. Crown 8vo.* 6*s.*
'Mr. Kipling's verse is strong, vivid, full of character. . . . Unmistakeable genius rings in every line.'—*Times.*
'The ballads teem with imagination, they palpitate with emotion. We read them with laughter and tears; the metres throb in our pulses, the cunningly ordered words tingle with life; and if this be not poetry, what is?'—*Pall Mall Gazette.*

Rudyard Kipling. THE SEVEN SEAS. By RUDYARD KIPLING. 50*th Thousand. Cr. 8vo. Buckram, gilt top.* 6*s.*
'The new poems of Mr. Rudyard Kipling have all the spirit and swing of their predecessors. Patriotism is the solid concrete foundation on which Mr. Kipling has built the whole of his work.'—*Times.*
'The Empire has found a singer; it is no depreciation of the songs to say that statesmen may have, one way or other, to take account of them.'—*Manchester Guardian.*
'Animated through and through with indubitable genius.'—*Daily Telegraph.*

"Q." POEMS AND BALLADS. By "Q." *Crown 8vo.* 3*s.* 6*d.*
'This work has just the faint, ineffable touch and glow that make poetry.'—*Speaker.*

"Q." GREEN BAYS: Verses and Parodies. By "Q." *Second Edition. Crown 8vo.* 3*s.* 6*d.*

E. Mackay. A SONG OF THE SEA. By ERIC MACKAY. *Second Edition. Fcap. 8vo.* 5*s.*
'Everywhere Mr. Mackay displays himself the master of a style marked by all the characteristics of the best rhetoric.'—*Globe.*

H. Ibsen. BRAND. A Drama by HENRIK IBSEN. Translated by WILLIAM WILSON. *Third Edition. Crown 8vo.* 3*s.* 6*d.*
'The greatest world-poem of the nineteenth century next to "Faust." It is in the same set with "Agamemnon," with "Lear," with the literature that we now instinctively regard as high and holy.'—*Daily Chronicle.*

"A. G." VERSES TO ORDER. By "A. G." *Crown 8vo.* 2*s.* 6*d. net.*
'A capital specimen of light academic poetry.'—*St. James's Gazette.*

James Williams. VENTURES IN VERSE. By JAMES WILLIAMS, Fellow of Lincoln College, Oxford. *Crown 8vo.* 3*s.* 6*d.*
'In matter and manner the book is admirable.'—*Glasgow Herald.*

J. G. Cordery. THE ODYSSEY OF HOMER. A Translation by J. G. CORDERY. *Crown 8vo.* 7*s.* 6*d.*
'A spirited, accurate, and scholarly piece of work.'—*Glasgow Herald.*

Belles Lettres, Anthologies, etc.

R. L. Stevenson. VAILIMA LETTERS. By ROBERT LOUIS STEVENSON. With an Etched Portrait by WILLIAM STRANG. *Second Edition. Crown 8vo. Buckram. 6s.*

'A fascinating book.'—*Standard.*
'Full of charm and brightness.'—*Spectator.*
'A gift almost priceless.'—*Speaker.*
'Unique in Literature.'—*Daily Chronicle.*

G. Wyndham. THE POEMS OF WILLIAM SHAKESPEARE. Edited with an Introduction and Notes by GEORGE WYNDHAM, M.P. *Demy 8vo. Buckram, gilt top. 10s. 6d.*

This edition contains the 'Venus,' 'Lucrece,' and Sonnets, and is prefaced with an elaborate introduction of over 140 pp.
'One of the most serious contributions to Shakespearian criticism that have been published for some time.'—*Times.*
'We have no hesitation in describing Mr. George Wyndham's introduction as a masterly piece of criticism, and all who love our Elizabethan literature will find a very garden of delight in it.'—*Spectator.*
'Mr. Wyndham's notes are admirable, even indispensable.'—*Westminster Gazette.*

W. E. Henley. ENGLISH LYRICS. Selected and Edited by W. E. HENLEY. *Crown 8vo. Buckram, gilt top. 6s.*

'It is a body of choice and lovely poetry.—*Birmingham Gazette.*

Henley and Whibley. A BOOK OF ENGLISH PROSE. Collected by W. E. HENLEY and CHARLES WHIBLEY. *Crown 8vo. Buckram, gilt top. 6s.*

'Quite delightful. A greater treat for those not well acquainted with pre-Restoration prose could not be imagined.'—*Athenæum.*

H. C. Beeching. LYRA SACRA: An Anthology of Sacred Verse. Edited by H. C. BEECHING, M.A. *Crown 8vo. Buckram. 6s.*

'A charming selection, which maintains a lofty standard of excellence.'—*Times.*

"Q." THE GOLDEN POMP. A Procession of English Lyrics. Arranged by A. T. QUILLER COUCH. *Crown 8vo. Buckram. 6s.*

'A delightful volume: a really golden "Pomp."'—*Spectator.*

W. B. Yeats. AN ANTHOLOGY OF IRISH VERSE. Edited by W. B. YEATS. *Crown 8vo. 3s. 6d.*

'An attractive and catholic selection.—*Times.*

G. W. Steevens. MONOLOGUES OF THE DEAD. By G. W. STEEVENS. *Foolscap 8vo. 3s. 6d.*

'The effect is sometimes splendid, sometimes bizarre, but always amazingly clever.'—*Pall Mall Gazette.*

W. M. Dixon. A PRIMER OF TENNYSON. By W. M. DIXON, M.A. *Cr. 8vo. 2s. 6d.*

'Much sound and well-expressed criticism. The bibliography is a boon.'—*Speaker.*

W. A. Craigie. A PRIMER OF BURNS. By W. A. CRAIGIE. *Crown 8vo. 2s. 6d.*

'A valuable addition to the literature of the poet.'—*Times.*

L. Magnus. A PRIMER OF WORDSWORTH. By LAURIE MAGNUS. *Crown 8vo. 2s. 6d.*

'A valuable contribution to Wordsworthian literature.'—*Literature.*

Sterne. THE LIFE AND OPINIONS OF TRISTRAM SHANDY. By LAWRENCE STERNE. With an Introduction by CHARLES WHIBLEY, and a Portrait. *2 vols. 7s.*

'Very dainty volumes are these: the paper, type, and light-green binding are all very agreeable to the eye.'—*Globe.*

Congreve. THE COMEDIES OF WILLIAM CONGREVE. With an Introduction by G. S. STREET, and a Portrait. *2 vols. 7s.*

Morier. THE ADVENTURES OF HAJJI BABA OF ISPAHAN. By JAMES MORIER. With an Introduction by E. G. BROWNE, M.A., and a Portrait. *2 vols. 7s.*

Walton. THE LIVES OF DONNE, WOTTON, HOOKER, HERBERT AND SANDERSON. By IZAAK WALTON. With an Introduction by VERNON BLACKBURN, and a Portrait. 3s. 6d.

Johnson. THE LIVES OF THE ENGLISH POETS. By SAMUEL JOHNSON, LL.D. With an Introduction by J. H. MILLAR, and a Portrait. 3 vols. 10s. 6d.

Burns. THE POEMS OF ROBERT BURNS. Edited by ANDREW LANG and W. A. CRAIGIE. With Portrait. *Second Edition. Demy 8vo, gilt top.* 6s.

This edition contains a carefully collated Text, numerous Notes, critical and textual, a critical and biographical Introduction, and a Glossary.

'Among editions in one volume, this will take the place of authority.'—*Times.*

F. Langbridge. BALLADS OF THE BRAVE; Poems of Chivalry, Enterprise, Courage, and Constancy. Edited by Rev. F. LANGBRIDGE. *Second Edition. Cr. 8vo. 3s. 6d.* School Edition. 2s. 6d.

'A very happy conception happily carried out. These "Ballads of the Brave" are intended to suit the real tastes of boys, and will suit the taste of the great majority.'—*Spectator.*

'The book is full of splendid things.'—*World.*

Illustrated Books

John Bunyan. THE PILGRIM'S PROGRESS. By JOHN BUNYAN. Edited, with an Introduction, by C. H. FIRTH, M.A. With 39 Illustrations by R. ANNING BELL. *Crown 8vo.* 6s.

This book contains a long Introduction by Mr. Firth, whose knowledge of the period is unrivalled; and it is lavishly illustrated.

'The best "Pilgrim's Progress."'—*Educational Times.*

F. D. Bedford. NURSERY RHYMES. With many Coloured Pictures by F. D. BEDFORD. *Super Royal 8vo.* 5s.

'An excellent selection of the best known rhymes, with beautifully coloured pictures exquisitely printed.'—*Pall Mall Gazette.*

S. Baring Gould. A BOOK OF FAIRY TALES retold by S. BARING GOULD. With numerous Illustrations and Initial Letters by ARTHUR J. GASKIN. *Second Edition. Cr. 8vo. Buckram.* 6s.

'Mr. Baring Gould is deserving of gratitude, in re-writing in simple style the old stories that delighted our fathers and grandfathers.'—*Saturday Review.*

S. Baring Gould. OLD ENGLISH FAIRY TALES. Collected and edited by S. BARING GOULD. With Numerous Illustrations by F. D. BEDFORD. *Second Edition. Cr. 8vo. Buckram.* 6s.

'A charming volume.'—*Guardian.*

S. Baring Gould. A BOOK OF NURSERY SONGS AND RHYMES. Edited by S. BARING GOULD, and Illustrated by the Birmingham Art School. *Buckram, gilt top. Crown 8vo.* 6s.

H. C. Beeching. A BOOK OF CHRISTMAS VERSE. Edited by H. C. BEECHING, M.A., and Illustrated by WALTER CRANE. *Cr. 8vo, gilt top. 3s. 6d.*

An anthology which, from its unity of aim and high poetic excellence, has a better right to exist than most of its fellows.'—*Guardian.*

History

Gibbon. THE DECLINE AND FALL OF THE ROMAN EMPIRE. By EDWARD GIBBON. A New Edition, Edited with Notes, Appendices, and Maps, by J. B. BURY, LL.D., Fellow of Trinity College, Dublin. *In Seven Volumes. Demy 8vo. Gilt top. 8s. 6d. each. Also Cr. 8vo.* 6s.

each. Vols. *I., II., III., IV., V.,* and *VI.*
'The time has certainly arrived for a new edition of Gibbon's great work.... Professor Bury is the right man to undertake this task. His learning is amazing, both in extent and accuracy. The book is issued in a handy form, and at a moderate price, and it is admirably printed.'—*Times.*
'The standard edition of our great historical classic.'—*Glasgow Herald.*
'At last there is an adequate modern edition of Gibbon. ... The best edition the nineteenth century could produce.'—*Manchester Guardian.*

Flinders Petrie. A HISTORY OF EGYPT, FROM THE EARLIEST TIMES TO THE PRESENT DAY. Edited by W. M. FLINDERS PETRIE, D.C.L., LL.D., Professor of Egyptology at University College. *Fully Illustrated. In Six Volumes. Cr.* 8vo. 6s. *each.*
VOL. I. PREHISTORIC TIMES TO XVITH DYNASTY. W. M. F. Petrie. *Fourth Edition.*
VOL. II. THE XVIITH AND XVIIITH DYNASTIES. W. M. F. Petrie. *Third Edition.*
VOL. IV. THE EGYPT OF THE PTOLEMIES. J. P. Mahaffy.
VOL. V. ROMAN EGYPT. J. G. Milne.
'A history written in the spirit of scientific precision so worthily represented by Dr. Petrie and his school cannot but promote sound and accurate study, and supply a vacant place in the English literature of Egyptology.'—*Times.*

Flinders Petrie. RELIGION AND CONSCIENCE IN ANCIENT EGYPT. By W. M. FLINDERS PETRIE, D.C.L., LL.D. Fully Illustrated. *Crown* 8vo. 2s. 6d.
'The lectures will afford a fund of valuable information for students of ancient ethics.'—*Manchester Guardian.*

Flinders Petrie. SYRIA AND EGYPT, FROM THE TELL EL AMARNA TABLETS. By W. M. FLINDERS PETRIE, D.C.L., LL.D. *Crown* 8vo. 2s. 6d.
'A marvellous record. The addition made to our knowledge is nothing short of amazing.'—*Times.*

Flinders Petrie. EGYPTIAN TALES. Edited by W. M. FLINDERS PETRIE. Illustrated by TRISTRAM ELLIS. *In Two Volumes. Cr.* 8vo. 3s. 6d. *each.*
'Invaluable as a picture of life in Palestine and Egypt.'—*Daily News.*

Flinders Petrie. EGYPTIAN DECORATIVE ART. By W. M. FLINDERS PETRIE. With 120 Illustrations. *Cr.* 8vo. 3s. 6d.
'In these lectures he displays rare skill in elucidating the development of decorative art in Egypt.'—*Times.*

C. W. Oman. A HISTORY OF THE ART OF WAR. Vol. II.: The Middle Ages, from the Fourth to the Fourteenth Century. By C. W. OMAN, M.A., Fellow of All Souls', Oxford. Illustrated. *Demy* 8vo. 21s.
'The book is based throughout upon a thorough study of the original sources, and will be an indispensable aid to all students of mediæval history.'—*Athenæum.*
'The whole art of war in its historic evolution has never been treated on such an ample and comprehensive scale, and we question if any recent contribution to the exact history of the world has possessed more enduring value.'—*Daily Chronicle.*

S. Baring Gould. THE TRAGEDY OF THE CÆSARS. With numerous Illustrations from Busts, Gems, Cameos, etc. By S. BARING GOULD. *Fourth Edition. Royal* 8vo. 15s.
'A most splendid and fascinating book on a subject of undying interest. The great feature of the book is the use the author has made of the existing portraits of the Caesars and the admirable critical subtlety he has exhibited in dealing with this line of research. It is brilliantly written, and the illustrations are supplied on a scale of profuse magnificence.' —*Daily Chronicle.*

F. W. Maitland. CANON LAW IN ENGLAND. By F. W. MAITLAND, LL.D., Downing Professor of the Laws of England in the University of Cambridge. *Royal* 8vo. 7s. 6d.
'Professor Maitland has put students of English law under a fresh debt. These essays are landmarks in the study of the history of Canon Law.'—*Times.*

MESSRS. METHUEN'S CATALOGUE 17

H. de B. Gibbins. INDUSTRY IN ENGLAND : HISTORICAL OUTLINES. By H. DE B. GIBBINS, Litt.D., M.A. With 5 Maps. *Second Edition. Demy 8vo.* 10s. 6d.

H. E. Egerton. A HISTORY OF BRITISH COLONIAL POLICY. By H. E. EGERTON, M.A. *Demy 8vo.* 12s. 6d.

'It is a good book, distinguished by accuracy in detail, clear arrangement of facts, and a broad grasp of principles.'— *Manchester Guardian.*

'Able, impartial, clear. . . . A most valuable volume.'—*Athenæum.*

Albert Sorel. THE EASTERN QUESTION IN THE EIGHTEENTH CENTURY. By ALBERT SOREL, of the French Academy. Translated by F. C. BRAMWELL, M.A. With a Map. *Cr. 8vo.* 3s. 6d.

C. H. Grinling. A HISTORY OF THE GREAT NORTHERN RAILWAY, 1845-95. By CHARLES H. GRINLING. With Maps and Illustrations. *Demy 8vo.* 10s. 6d.

'Mr. Grinling has done for a Railway what Macaulay did for English History.'— *The Engineer.*

W. Sterry. ANNALS OF ETON COLLEGE. By W. STERRY, M.A. With numerous Illustrations. *Demy 8vo.* 7s. 6d.

'A treasury of quaint and interesting reading. Mr. Sterry has by his skill and vivacity given these records new life.'— *Academy.*

Fisher. ANNALS OF SHREWSBURY SCHOOL. By G. W. FISHER, M.A., late Assistant Master. With numerous Illustrations. *Demy 8vo.* 10s. 6d.

'This careful, erudite book.'—*Daily Chronicle.*

'A book of which Old Salopians are sure to be proud.'—*Globe.*

J. Sargeaunt. ANNALS OF WESTMINSTER SCHOOL. By J. SARGEAUNT, M.A., Assistant Master. With numerous Illustrations. *Demy 8vo.* 7s. 6d.

A. Clark. THE COLLEGES OF OXFORD: Their History and their Traditions. By Members of the University. Edited by A. CLARK, M.A., Fellow and Tutor of Lincoln College. *8vo.* 12s. 6d.

'A work which will be appealed to for many years as the standard book.'— *Athenæum.*

J. Wells. A SHORT HISTORY OF ROME. By J. WELLS, M.A., Fellow and Tutor of Wadham Coll., Oxford. *Second and Revised Edition.* With 3 Maps. *Crown 8vo.* 3s. 6d.

This book is intended for the Middle and Upper Forms of Public Schools and for Pass Students at the Universities. It contains copious Tables, etc.

'An original work written on an original plan, and with uncommon freshness and vigour.'—*Speaker.*

O. Browning. A SHORT HISTORY OF MEDIÆVAL ITALY, A.D. 1250-1530. By OSCAR BROWNING, Fellow and Tutor of King's College, Cambridge. *In Two Volumes. Cr. 8vo.* 5s. *each.*

VOL. I. 1250-1409.—Guelphs and Ghibellines.

VOL. II. 1409-1530.—The Age of the Condottieri.

O'Grady. THE STORY OF IRELAND. By STANDISH O'GRADY, Author of 'Finn and his Companions.' *Crown 8vo.* 2s. 6d.

Byzantine Texts
Edited by J. B. BURY, M.A.

EVAGRIUS. Edited by Professor LÉON PARMENTIER of Liége and M. BIDEZ of Gand. *Demy 8vo.* 10s. 6d.

THE HISTORY OF PSELLUS. By C. SATHAS. *Demy 8vo.* 15s. net.

Biography

S. Baring Gould. THE LIFE OF NAPOLEON BONAPARTE. By S. BARING GOULD. With over 450 Illustrations in the Text and 12 Photogravure Plates. *Large quarto. Gilt top.* 36s.

'The best biography of Napoleon in our tongue, nor have the French as good a biographer of their hero. A book very nearly as good as Southey's "Life of Nelson."'—*Manchester Guardian.*

'The main feature of this gorgeous volume is its great wealth of beautiful photogravures and finely-executed wood engravings, constituting a complete pictorial chronicle of Napoleon I.'s personal history from the days of his early childhood at Ajaccio to the date of his second interment.'—*Daily Telegraph.*

P. H. Colomb. MEMOIRS OF ADMIRAL SIR A. COOPER KEY. By Admiral P. H. COLOMB. With a Portrait. *Demy 8vo.* 16s.

'An interesting and adequate biography. The whole book is one of the greatest interest.'—*Times.*

Morris Fuller. THE LIFE AND WRITINGS OF JOHN DAVENANT, D.D. (1571-1641), Bishop of Salisbury. By MORRIS FULLER, B.D. *Demy 8vo.* 10s. 6d.

J. M. Rigg. ST. ANSELM OF CANTERBURY: A CHAPTER IN THE HISTORY OF RELIGION. By J. M. RIGG. *Demy 8vo.* 7s. 6d.

F. W. Joyce. THE LIFE OF SIR FREDERICK GORE OUSELEY. By F. W. JOYCE, M.A. 7s. 6d.

'This book has been undertaken in quite the right spirit, and written with sympathy, insight, and considerable literary skill.'—*Times.*

W. G. Collingwood. THE LIFE OF JOHN RUSKIN. By W. G. COLLINGWOOD, M.A. With Portraits, and 13 Drawings by Mr. Ruskin. *Second Edition.* 2 vols. *8vo.* 32s.

'No more magnificent volumes have been published for a long time.'—*Times.*

'It is long since we had a biography with such delights of substance and of form. Such a book is a pleasure for the day, and a joy for ever.'—*Daily Chronicle.*

C. Waldstein. JOHN RUSKIN. By CHARLES WALDSTEIN, M.A. With a Photogravure Portrait. *Post 8vo.* 5s.

'A thoughtful and well-written criticism of Ruskin's teaching.'—*Daily Chronicle.*

A. M. F. Darmesteter. THE LIFE OF ERNEST RENAN. By MADAME DARMESTETER. With Portrait. *Second Edition. Cr. 8vo.* 6s.

'A polished gem of biography, superior in its kind to any attempt that has been made of recent years in England, Madame Darmesteter has indeed written for English readers "*The* Life of Ernest Renan."'—*Athenæum.*

W. H. Hutton. THE LIFE OF SIR THOMAS MORE. By W. H. HUTTON, M.A. With Portraits. *Cr. 8vo.* 5s.

'The book lays good claim to high rank among our biographies. It is excellently even lovingly, written.'—*Scotsman.*

Travel, Adventure and Topography

Sven Hedin. THROUGH ASIA. By SVEN HEDIN, Gold Medallist of the Royal Geographical Society. With 300 Illustrations from Sketches and Photographs by the Author, and Maps. 2 vols. *Royal 8vo.* 20s. net.

'One of the greatest books of the kind issued during the century. It is impossible to give an adequate idea of the richness of the contents of this book,

nor of its abounding attractions as a story of travel unsurpassed in geographical and human interest. Much of it is a revelation. Altogether the work is one which in solidity, novelty, and interest must take a first rank among publications of its class.'—*Times*.
'In these magnificent volumes we have the most important contribution to Central Asian geography made for many years. Intensely interesting as a tale of travel.' —*Spectator*.

F. H. Skrine and E. D. Ross. THE HEART OF ASIA. By F. H. SKRINE and E. D. ROSS. With Maps and many Illustrations by VERESTCHAGIN. *Large Crown 8vo.* 10s. 6d. *net.*
'This volume will form a landmark in our knowledge of Central Asia. . . . Illuminating and convincing. For the first time we are enabled clearly to understand not only how Russia has established her rule in Central Asia, but what that rule actually means to the Central Asian peoples. This book is not only *felix opportunitate*, but of enduring value.'—*Times*.

R. E. Peary. NORTHWARD OVER THE GREAT ICE. By R. E. PEARY, Gold Medallist of the Royal Geographical Society. With over 800 Illustrations. *2 vols. Royal 8vo.* 32s. *net.*
'The book is full of interesting matter—a tale of brave deeds simply told; abundantly illustrated with prints and maps.' —*Standard*.
'His book will take its place among the permanent literature of Arctic exploration.' —*Times*.

G. S. Robertson. CHITRAL: The Story of a Minor Siege. By Sir G. S. ROBERTSON, K.C.S.I. With numerous Illustrations, Map and Plans. *Second Edition. Demy 8vo.* 10s. 6d.
'It is difficult to imagine the kind of person who could read this brilliant book without emotion. The story remains immortal—a testimony imperishable. We are face to face with a great book.'—*Illustrated London News*.
'A book which the Elizabethans would have thought wonderful. More thrilling, more piquant, and more human than any novel.'—*Newcastle Chronicle*.
'One of the most stirring military narratives written in our time.'—*Times*.
'As fascinating as Sir Walter Scott's best fiction.'—*Daily Telegraph*.
'A noble story, nobly told.'—*Punch*.

H. H. Johnston. BRITISH CENTRAL AFRICA. By Sir H. H. JOHNSTON, K.C.B. With nearly Two Hundred Illustrations, and Six Maps. *Second Edition. Crown 4to.* 18s. *net.*
'A fascinating book, written with equal skill and charm—the work at once of a literary artist and of a man of action who is singularly wise, brave, and experienced. It abounds in admirable sketches from pencil.' — *Westminster Gazette*.

L. Decle. THREE YEARS IN SAVAGE AFRICA. By LIONEL DECLE. With 100 Illustrations and 5 Maps. *Second Edition. Demy 8vo.* 10s. 6d. *net.*
'A fine, full book.'—*Pall Mall Gazette*.
'Its bright pages give a better general survey of Africa from the Cape to the Equator than any single volume that has yet been published.'—*Times*.

A. Hulme Beaman. TWENTY YEARS IN THE NEAR EAST. By A. HULME BEAMAN. *Demy 8vo.* With Portrait. 10s. 6d.
'One of the most entertaining books that we have had in our hands for a long time. It is unconventional in a high degree; it is written with sagacious humour; it is full of adventures and anecdotes.'—*Daily Chronicle*.

Henri of Orleans. FROM TONKIN TO INDIA. By PRINCE HENRI OF ORLEANS. Translated by HAMLEY BENT, M.A. With 100 Illustrations and a Map. *Cr. 4to, gilt top.* 25s.

R. S. S. Baden-Powell. THE DOWNFALL OF PREMPEH. A Diary of Life in Ashanti, 1895. By Colonel BADEN-POWELL. With 21 Illustrations and a Map. *Cheaper Edition. Large Crown 8vo.* 6s.

R. S. S. Baden-Powell. THE MATABELE CAMPAIGN, 1896. By Col. BADEN-POWELL. With nearly 100 Illustrations. *Cheaper Edition. Large Crown 8vo.* 6s.

S. L. Hinde. THE FALL OF THE CONGO ARABS. By S. L. HINDE. With Plans, etc. *Demy 8vo.* 12s. 6d.

A. St. H. Gibbons. EXPLORATION AND HUNTING IN CENTRAL

AFRICA. By Major A. ST. H. GIBBONS. With full-page Illustrations by C. WHYMPER, and Maps. *Demy 8vo.* 15*s.*

'His book is a grand record of quiet, unassuming, tactful resolution. His adventures were as various as his sporting exploits were exciting.'—*Times.*

E. H. Alderson. WITH THE MASHONALAND FIELD FORCE, 1896. By Lieut.-Colonel ALDERSON. With numerous Illustrations and Plans. *Demy 8vo.* 10*s.* 6*d.*

'A clear, vigorous, and soldier-like narrative.'—*Scotsman.*

Fraser. ROUND THE WORLD ON A WHEEL. By JOHN FOSTER FRASER. With 100 Illustrations. *Crown 8vo.* 6*s.*

'A very entertaining book of travel.'—*Spectator.*
The story is told with delightful gaiety, humour, and crispness. There has rarely appeared a more interesting tale of modern travel.'—*Scotsman.*
'A classic of cycling, graphic and witty.'—*Yorkshire Post.*

Seymour Vandeleur. CAMPAIGNING ON THE UPPER NILE AND NIGER. By Lieut. SEYMOUR VANDELEUR. With an Introduction by Sir G. GOLDIE, K.C.M.G. With 4 Maps, Illustrations, and Plans. *Large Crown 8vo.* 10*s.* 6*d.*

'Upon the African question there is no book procurable which contains so much of value as this one.'—*Guardian.*

Lord Fincastle. A FRONTIER CAMPAIGN. By Viscount FINCASTLE, V.C., and Lieut. P. C. ELLIOTT-LOCKHART. With a Map and 16 Illustrations. *Second Edition. Crown 8vo.* 6*s.*

'An admirable book, and a really valuable treatise on frontier war.'—*Athenæum.*

E. N. Bennett. THE DOWNFALL OF THE DERVISHES: A Sketch of the Sudan Campaign of 1898. By E. N. BENNETT, Fellow of Hertford College. With Four Maps and a Photogravure Portrait of the Sirdar. *Third Edition. Crown 8vo.* 3*s* 6*d.*

J. K. Trotter. THE NIGER SOURCES. By Colonel J. K. TROTTER, R.A. With a Map and Illustrations. *Crown 8vo.* 5*s.*

Michael Davitt. LIFE AND PROGRESS IN AUSTRALASIA. By MICHAEL DAVITT, M.P. 500 pp. With 2 Maps. *Crown 8vo.* 6*s.*

W. Crooke. THE NORTH-WESTERN PROVINCES OF INDIA: THEIR ETHNOLOGY AND ADMINISTRATION. By W. CROOKE. With Maps and Illustrations. *Demy 8vo.* 10*s.* 6*d.*

'A carefully and well-written account of one of the most important provinces of the Empire. Mr. Crooke deals with the land in its physical aspect, the province under Hindoo and Mussulman rule, under British rule, its ethnology and sociology, its religious and social life, the land and its settlement, and the native peasant.'—*Manchester Guardian.*

A. Boisragon. THE BENIN MASSACRE. By CAPTAIN BOISRAGON. *Second Edition. Cr. 8vo.* 3*s.* 6*d.*

'If the story had been written four hundred years ago it would be read to-day as an English classic.'—*Scotsman.*

H. S. Cowper. THE HILL OF THE GRACES: OR, THE GREAT STONE TEMPLES OF TRIPOLI. By H. S. COWPER, F.S.A. With Maps, Plans, and 75 Illustrations. *Demy 8vo.* 10*s.* 6*d.*

W. Kinnaird Rose. WITH THE GREEKS IN THESSALY. By W. KINNAIRD ROSE, Reuter's Correspondent. With Plans and 23 Illustrations. *Crown 8vo.* 6*s.*

W. B. Worsfold. SOUTH AFRICA. By W. B. WORSFOLD, M.A. *With a Map. Second Edition. Cr. 8vo.* 6*s.*

'A monumental work compressed into a very moderate compass.'—*World.*

Naval and Military

G. W. Steevens. NAVAL POLICY: By G. W. STEEVENS. *Demy 8vo. 6s.*

This book is a description of the British and other more important navies of the world, with a sketch of the lines on which our naval policy might possibly be developed.
'An extremely able and interesting work.' —*Daily Chronicle.*

D. Hannay. A SHORT HISTORY OF THE ROYAL NAVY, FROM EARLY TIMES TO THE PRESENT DAY. By DAVID HANNAY. Illustrated. 2 *Vols. Demy 8vo. 7s. 6d. each.* Vol. I., 1200-1688.

'We read it from cover to cover at a sitting, and those who go to it for a lively and brisk picture of the past, with all its faults and its grandeur, will not be disappointed. The historian is endowed with literary skill and style.'—*Standard.*
'We can warmly recommend Mr. Hannay's volume to any intelligent student of naval history. Great as is the merit of Mr. Hannay's historical narrative, the merit of his strategic exposition is even greater.'—*Times.*

C. Cooper King. THE STORY OF THE BRITISH ARMY. By Colonel COOPER KING. Illustrated. *Demy 8vo. 7s. 6d.*

'An authoritative and accurate story of England's military progress.'—*Daily Mail.*

R. Southey. ENGLISH SEAMEN (Howard, Clifford, Hawkins, Drake, Cavendish). By ROBERT SOUTHEY. Edited, with an Introduction, by DAVID HANNAY. *Second Edition. Crown 8vo. 6s.*
'A brave, inspiriting book.'—*Black and White.*

W. Clark Russell. THE LIFE OF ADMIRAL LORD COLLINGWOOD. By W. CLARK RUSSELL. With Illustrations by F. BRANGWYN. *Third Edition. Crown 8vo. 6s.*
'A book which we should like to see in the hands of every boy in the country.'—*St. James's Gazette.*
'A really good book.'—*Saturday Review.*

E. L. S. Horsburgh. THE CAMPAIGN OF WATERLOO. By E. L. S. HORSBURGH, B.A. With Plans. *Crown 8vo. 5s.*
'A brilliant essay—simple, sound, and thorough.'—*Daily Chronicle.*

H. B. George. BATTLES OF ENGLISH HISTORY. By H. B. GEORGE, M.A., Fellow of New College, Oxford. With numerous Plans. *Third Edition. Cr. 8vo. 6s.*
'Mr. George has undertaken a very useful task—that of making military affairs intelligible and instructive to non-military readers—and has executed it with a large measure of success.'—*Times.*

General Literature

S. Baring Gould. OLD COUNTRY LIFE. By S. BARING GOULD. With Sixty-seven Illustrations. *Large Cr. 8vo. Fifth Edition. 6s.*
'"Old Country Life," as healthy wholesome reading, full of breezy life and movement, full of quaint stories vigorously told, will not be excelled by any book to be published throughout the year. Sound, hearty, and English to the core.' —*World.*

S. Baring Gould. AN OLD ENGLISH HOME. By S. BARING GOULD. With numerous Plans and Illustrations. *Crown 8vo. 6s.*
'The chapters are delightfully fresh, very informing, and lightened by many a good story. A delightful fireside companion.' —*St. James's Gazette.*

S. Baring Gould. HISTORIC ODDITIES AND STRANGE

EVENTS. By S. BARING GOULD. *Fourth Edition. Crown 8vo. 6s.*

S. Baring Gould. FREAKS OF FANATICISM. By S. BARING GOULD. *Third Edition. Cr. 8vo. 6s.*

S. Baring Gould. A GARLAND OF COUNTRY SONG: English Folk Songs with their Traditional Melodies. Collected and arranged by S. BARING GOULD and H. F. SHEPPARD. *Demy 4to. 6s.*

S. Baring Gould. SONGS OF THE WEST: Traditional Ballads and Songs of the West of England, with their Melodies. Collected by S. BARING GOULD, M.A., and H. F. SHEPPARD, M.A. In 4 Parts. *Parts I., II., III.*, 3s. each. *Part IV.*, 5s. *In one Vol., French morocco,* 15s.
'A rich collection of humour, pathos, grace, and poetic fancy.'—*Saturday Review.*

S. Baring Gould. YORKSHIRE ODDITIES AND STRANGE EVENTS. By S. BARING GOULD. *Fourth Edition. Crown 8vo. 6s.*

S. Baring Gould. STRANGE SURVIVALS AND SUPERSTITIONS. By S. BARING GOULD. *Cr. 8vo. Second Edition. 6s.*

S. Baring Gould. THE DESERTS OF SOUTHERN FRANCE. By S. BARING GOULD. 2 *vols. Demy 8vo.* 32s.

Cotton Minchin. OLD HARROW DAYS. By J. G. COTTON MINCHIN. *Cr. 8vo. Second Edition.* 5s.
'This book is an admirable record.'—*Daily Chronicle.*

W. E. Gladstone. THE SPEECHES OF THE RT. HON. W. E. GLADSTONE, M.P. Edited by A. W. HUTTON, M.A., and H. J. COHEN M.A. With Portraits, *Demy 8vo. Vols. IX. and X.,* 12s. 6d. each.

E. V. Zenker. ANARCHISM. By E. V. ZENKER. *Demy 8vo. 7s. 6d.*
'Herr Zenker has succeeded in producing a careful and critical history of the growth of Anarchist theory.'

H. G. Hutchinson. THE GOLFING PILGRIM. By HORACE G. HUTCHINSON. *Crown 8vo. 6s.*
'Full of useful information with plenty of good stories.'—*Truth.*
'Without this book the golfer's library will be incomplete.'—*Pall Mall Gazette.*
'It will charm all golfers.'—*Times.*

J. Wells. OXFORD AND OXFORD LIFE. By Members of the University. Edited by J. WELLS, M.A., Fellow and Tutor of Wadham College. *Third Edition. Cr. 8vo. 3s. 6d.*
'We congratulate Mr. Wells on the production of a readable and intelligent account of Oxford as it is at the present time, written by persons who are possessed of a close acquaintance with the system and life of the University.'—*Athenæum.*

J. Wells. OXFORD AND ITS COLLEGES. By J. WELLS, M.A., Fellow and Tutor of Wadham College. Illustrated by E. H. NEW. *Third Edition. Fcap. 8vo. 3s. Leather. 3s 6d. net.*
'An admirable and accurate little treatise, attractively illustrated.'—*World.*
'A luminous and tasteful little volume.'—*Daily Chronicle.*
'Exactly what the intelligent visitor wants.'—*Glasgow Herald.*

A. H. Thompson. CAMBRIDGE AND ITS COLLEGES. By A. HAMILTON THOMPSON. With Illustrations by E. H. NEW. *Pott 8vo. 3s. Leather.* 3s. 6d. *net.*
This book is uniform with Mr. Wells' very successful book, 'Oxford and its Colleges.'
'It is brightly written and learned, and is just such a book as a cultured visitor needs.'—*Scotsman.*

C. G. Robertson. VOCES ACADEMICÆ. By C. GRANT ROBERTSON, M.A., Fellow of All Souls', Oxford. *With a Frontispiece. Pott 8vo.* 3s. 6d.
'Decidedly clever and amusing.'—*Athenæum.*

Rosemary Cotes. DANTE'S GARDEN. By ROSEMARY COTES. With a Frontispiece. *Second Edition. Fcp. 8vo. 2s. 6d. Leather, 3s. 6d. net.*
'A charming collection of legends of the flowers mentioned by Dante.'—*Academy.*

MESSRS. METHUEN'S CATALOGUE   23

Clifford Harrison. READING AND READERS. By CLIFFORD HARRISON. *Fcp. 8vo.* 2s. 6d.

'We recommend schoolmasters to examine its merits, for it is at school that readers are made.'—*Academy.*
'An extremely sensible little book.'—*Manchester Guardian.*

L. Whibley. GREEK OLIGARCHIES: THEIR ORGANISATION AND CHARACTER. By L. WHIBLEY, M.A., Fellow of Pembroke College, Cambridge. *Crown 8vo.* 6s.

'An exceedingly useful handbook: a careful and well-arranged study.'—*Times.*

L. L. Price. ECONOMIC SCIENCE AND PRACTICE. By L. L. PRICE,

M.A., Fellow of Oriel College, Oxford. *Crown 8vo.* 6s.

J. S. Shedlock. THE PIANOFORTE SONATA: Its Origin and Development. By J. S. SHEDLOCK. *Crown 8vo.* 5s.

'This work should be in the possession of every musician and amateur. A concise and lucid history and a very valuable work for reference.'—*Athenæum.*

E. M. Bowden. THE EXAMPLE OF BUDDHA: Being Quotations from Buddhist Literature for each Day in the Year. Compiled by E. M. BOWDEN. *Third Edition.* 16mo. 2s. 6d.

Science and Technology

Freudenreich. DAIRY BACTERIOLOGY. A Short Manual for the Use of Students. By Dr. ED. VON FREUDENREICH, Translated by J. R. AINSWORTH DAVIS, M.A. *Crown 8vo.* 2s. 6d.

Chalmers Mitchell. OUTLINES OF BIOLOGY. By P. CHALMERS MITCHELL, M.A. *Illustrated. Cr. 8vo.* 6s.

A text-book designed to cover the new Schedule issued by the Royal College of Physicians and Surgeons.

G. Massee. A MONOGRAPH OF THE MYXOGASTRES. By GEORGE MASSEE. With 12 Coloured Plates. *Royal 8vo.* 18s. net.

'A work much in advance of any book in the language treating of this group of organisms. Indispensable to every student of the Myxogastres.'—*Nature.*

Stephenson and Suddards. ORNAMENTAL DESIGN FOR WOVEN FABRICS. By C. STEPHENSON, of The Technical College, Bradford, and F. SUDDARDS, of The Yorkshire College, Leeds. With 65 full-page plates. *Demy 8vo.* 7s. 6d.

'The book is very ably done, displaying an intimate knowledge of principles, good taste, and the faculty of clear exposition.'—*Yorkshire Post.*

TEXTBOOKS OF TECHNOLOGY. Edited by PROFESSORS GARNETT and WERTHEIMER.

HOW TO MAKE A DRESS By J. A. E. WOOD. *Illustrated. Cr. 8vo.* 1s. 6d.

'Though primarily intended for students, Miss Wood's dainty little manual may be consulted with advantage by any girls who want to make their own frocks. The directions are simple and clear, and the diagrams very helpful.'—*Literature.*

CARPENTRY AND JOINERY. By F. C. WEBBER. With many Illustrations. *Cr. 8vo.* 3s. 6d.

'An admirable elementary text-book on the subject.'—*Builder.*

PRACTICAL MECHANICS. By SIDNEY H. WELLS. With 75 Illustrations and Diagrams. *Crown 8vo.* 3s. 6d.

Philosophy

L. T. Hobhouse. THE THEORY OF KNOWLEDGE. By L. T. HOBHOUSE, Fellow of C.C.C., Oxford. *Demy 8vo.* 21s.

'The most important contribution to English philosophy since the publication of Mr. Bradley's "Appearance and Reality."'—*Glasgow Herald.*
'A brilliantly written volume.'—*Times.*

W. H. Fairbrother. THE PHILOSOPHY OF T. H. GREEN. By W. H. FAIRBROTHER, M.A. *Cr. 8vo.* 3s. 6d.

'In every way an admirable book.'—*Glasgow Herald.*

F. W. Bussell. THE SCHOOL OF PLATO. By F. W. BUSSELL, D.D., Fellow of Brasenose College, Oxford. *Demy 8vo.* 10s. 6d.

'A clever and stimulating book.'—*Manchester Guardian.*

F. S. Granger. THE WORSHIP OF THE ROMANS. By F. S. GRANGER, M.A., Litt.D. *Crown 8vo.* 6s.

'A scholarly analysis of the religious ceremonies, beliefs, and superstitions of ancient Rome, conducted in the new light of comparative anthropology.'—*Times.*

Theology

S. R. Driver. SERMONS ON SUBJECTS CONNECTED WITH THE OLD TESTAMENT. By S. R. DRIVER, D.D., Canon of Christ Church, Regius Professor of Hebrew in the University of Oxford. *Cr. 8vo.* 6s.

'A welcome companion to the author's famous "Introduction."'—*Guardian.*

T. K. Cheyne. FOUNDERS OF OLD TESTAMENT CRITICISM. By T. K. CHEYNE, D.D., Oriel Professor at Oxford. *Large Crown 8vo.* 7s. 6d.

A historical sketch of O. T. Criticism.
'A very learned and instructive work.'—*Times.*

H. Rashdall. DOCTRINE AND DEVELOPMENT. By HASTINGS RASHDALL, M.A., Fellow and Tutor of New College, Oxford. *Cr. 8vo.* 6s.

'A very interesting attempt to restate some of the principal doctrines of Christianity, in which Mr. Rashdall appears to us to have achieved a high measure of success. He is often learned, almost always sympathetic, and always singularly lucid.'—*Manchester Guardian.*

H. H. Henson. APOSTOLIC CHRISTIANITY: As Illustrated by the Epistles of St. Paul to the Corinthians. By H. H. HENSON, M.A., Fellow of All Souls', Oxford. *Cr. 8vo.* 6s.

'A worthy contribution towards same solution of the great religious problems of the present day.'—*Scotsman.*

H. H. Henson. DISCIPLINE AND LAW. By H. HENSLEY HENSON, B.D., Fellow of All Souls', Oxford. *Fcap. 8vo.* 2s. 6d.

H. H. Henson. LIGHT AND LEAVEN : HISTORICAL AND SOCIAL SERMONS. By H. H. HENSON, M.A. *Crown 8vo.* 6s.

W. H. Bennett. A PRIMER OF THE BIBLE. By W. H. BENNETT. *Second Edition. Cr. 8vo.* 2s. 6d.

'The work of an honest, fearless, and sound critic, and an excellent guide in a small compass to the books of the Bible.'—*Manchester Guardian.*

William Harrison. CLOVELLY SERMONS. By WILLIAM HARRISON, M.A., late Rector of Clovelly. With a Preface by 'LUCAS MALET.' *Cr. 8vo.* 3s. 6d.

Cecilia Robinson. THE MINISTRY OF DEACONESSES. By Deacon-

MESSRS. METHUEN'S CATALOGUE 25

ness CECILIA ROBINSON. With an Introduction by the Lord Bishop of Winchester. *Cr. 8vo.* 3s. 6d.
'A learned and interesting book.'—*Scotsman.*

E. B. Layard. RELIGION IN BOYHOOD. Notes on the Religious Training of Boys. By E. B. LAYARD, M.A. 18mo. 1s.

W. Yorke Fausset. THE *DE CATECHIZANDIS RUDIBUS* OF ST. AUGUSTINE. Edited, with Introduction, Notes, etc., by W. YORKE FAUSSET, M.A. *Cr. 8vo.* 3s. 6d.

F. Weston. THE HOLY SACRIFICE. By F. WESTON, M.A., Curate of St. Matthew's, Westminster. *Pott 8vo.* 6d. net.
A small volume of devotions at the Holy Communion, especially adapted to the needs of servers and those who do not communicate.

À Kempis. THE IMITATION OF CHRIST. By THOMAS À KEMPIS. With an Introduction by DEAN FARRAR. Illustrated by C. M. GERE. *Second Edition. Fcap. 8vo.* 3s. 6d. *Padded morocco,* 5s.
'Amongst all the innumerable English editions of the "Imitation," there can have been few which were prettier than this one, printed in strong and handsome type, with all the glory of red initials.'—*Glasgow Herald.*

J. Keble. THE CHRISTIAN YEAR. By JOHN KEBLE. With an Introduction and Notes by W. LOCK, D.D., Warden of Keble College. Illustrated by R. ANNING BELL. *Second Edition. Fcap. 8vo.* 3s. 6d. *Padded morocco.* 5s.
'The present edition is annotated with all the care and insight to be expected from Mr. Lock.'—*Guardian.*

Oxford Commentaries

General Editor, WALTER LOCK, D.D., Warden of Keble College, Dean Ireland's Professor of Exegesis in the University of Oxford.
THE BOOK OF JOB. Edited, with Introduction and Notes, by E. C. S. GIBSON, D.D., Vicar of Leeds. *Demy 8vo.* 6s.

Handbooks of Theology

General Editor, A. ROBERTSON, D.D., Principal of King's College, London.

THE XXXIX. ARTICLES OF THE CHURCH OF ENGLAND. Edited with an Introduction by E. C. S. GIBSON, D.D., Vicar of Leeds, late Principal of Wells Theological College. *Second and Cheaper Edition in One Volume. Demy 8vo.* 12s. 6d.
'We welcome with the utmost satisfaction a new, cheaper, and more convenient edition of Dr. Gibson's book. It was greatly wanted. Dr. Gibson has given theological students just what they want, and we should like to think that it was in the hands of every candidate for orders.'—*Guardian.*

AN INTRODUCTION TO THE HISTORY OF RELIGION. By F. B. JEVONS, M.A., Litt.D., Principal of Bishop Hatfield's Hall. *Demy 8vo.* 10s. 6d.
'The merit of this book lies in the penetration, the singular acuteness and force of the author's judgment. He is at once critical and luminous, at once just and suggestive. A comprehensive and thorough book.'—*Birmingham Post.*

THE DOCTRINE OF THE INCARNATION. By R. L. OTTLEY, M.A., late fellow of Magdalen College, Oxon., and Principal of Pusey House. *In Two Volumes. Demy 8vo.* 15s.
'A clear and remarkably full account of the main currents of speculation. Scholarly precision . . . genuine tolerance . . . intense interest in his subject—are Mr. Ottley's merits.'—*Guardian.*

AN INTRODUCTION TO THE HISTORY OF THE CREEDS. By A. E. BURNS, Examining Chaplain to the Bishop of Lichfield. *Demy 8vo.* 10s. 6d.
'This book may be expected to hold its place as an authority on its subject.'—*Spectator.*
'It is an able and learned treatise, and contains a mass of information which will be most useful to scholars.'—*Glasgow Herald.*

The Churchman's Library
Edited by J. H. BURN, B.D.

THE BEGINNINGS OF ENGLISH CHRISTIANITY. By W. E. COLLINS, M.A. With Map. *Cr. 8vo.* 3*s.* 6*d.*

An investigation in detail, based upon original authorities, of the beginnings of the English Church, with a careful account of earlier Celtic Christianity.
'An excellent example of thorough and fresh historical work.'—*Guardian.*

SOME NEW TESTAMENT PROBLEMS. By ARTHUR WRIGHT, Fellow of Queen's College, Cambridge. *Crown 8vo.* 6*s.*

THE KINGDOM OF HEAVEN HERE AND HEREAFTER. By CANON WINTERBOTHAM, M.A., B.SC., LL.B. *Cr. 8vo.* 3*s.* 6*d.*

'A most able book, at once exceedingly thoughtful and richly suggestive.'—*Glasgow Herald.*

The Library of Devotion
Pott 8vo, cloth, 2*s.; leather,* 2*s.* 6*d. net.*

'This series is excellent.'—THE BISHOP OF LONDON.
'A very delightful edition.'—THE BISHOP OF BATH AND WELLS.
'Well worth the attention of the Clergy.'—THE BISHOP OF LICHFIELD.
'The new "Library of Devotion" is excellent.'—THE BISHOP OF PETERBOROUGH.
'Charming.'—*Record.*
'Delightful.'—*Church Bells.*

THE CONFESSIONS OF ST. AUGUSTINE. Newly Translated, with an Introduction and Notes, by C. BIGG, D.D., late Student of Christ Church. *Second Edition.*
'The translation is an excellent piece of English, and the introduction is a masterly exposition. We augur well of a series which begins so satisfactorily.'—*Times.*

THE CHRISTIAN YEAR. By JOHN KEBLE. With Introduction and Notes by WALTER LOCK, D.D., Warden of Keble College, Ireland Professor at Oxford.
'The volume is very prettily bound and printed, and may fairly claim to be an advance on any previous editions.'—*Guardian.*

THE IMITATION OF CHRIST. A Revised Translation, with an Introduction, by C. BIGG, D.D., late Student of Christ Church.
A practically new translation of this book, which the reader has, almost for the first time, exactly in the shape in which it left the hands of the author.
'A beautiful and scholarly production.'—*Speaker.*
'A nearer approach to the original than has yet existed in English.'—*Academy.*

A BOOK OF DEVOTIONS. By J. W. STANBRIDGE, M.A., Rector of Bainton, Canon of York, and sometime Fellow of St. John's College, Oxford.
It is probably the best book of its kind. It deserves high commendation.'—*Church Gazette.*

LYRA INNOCENTIUM. By JOHN KEBLE. Edited, with Introduction and Notes, by WALTER LOCK, D.D., Warden of Keble College, Oxford.

Leaders of Religion
Edited by H. C. BEECHING, M.A. *With Portraits, Crown 8vo.* 3*s.* 6*d.*

A series of short biographies of the most prominent leaders of religious life and thought of all ages and countries.

The following are ready—

CARDINAL NEWMAN. By R. H. HUTTON.
JOHN WESLEY. By J. H. OVERTON, M.A.
BISHOP WILBERFORCE. By G. W. DANIELL, M.A.
CARDINAL MANNING. By A. W. HUTTON, M.A.

CHARLES SIMEON. By H. C. G. MOULE, D.D.
JOHN KEBLE. By WALTER LOCK, D.D.
THOMAS CHALMERS. By Mrs. OLIPHANT.
LANCELOT ANDREWES. By R. L. OTTLEY, M.A.
AUGUSTINE OF CANTERBURY. By E. L. CUTTS, D.D.
WILLIAM LAUD. By W. H. HUTTON, B.D.
JOHN KNOX. By F. MACCUNN.
JOHN HOWE. By R. F. HORTON, D.D.
BISHOP KEN. By F. A. CLARKE, M.A.
GEORGE FOX, THE QUAKER. By T. HODGKIN, D.C.L.
JOHN DONNE. By AUGUSTUS JESSOPP, D.D.
THOMAS CRANMER. By. A. J. MASON.

Other volumes will be announced in due course.

Fiction

SIX SHILLING NOVELS
Marie Corelli's Novels
Large crown 8vo. 6s. each.

A ROMANCE OF TWO WORLDS. *Nineteenth Edition.*
VENDETTA. *Fifteenth Edition.*
THELMA. *Twenty-first Edition.*
ARDATH: THE STORY OF A DEAD SELF. *Eleventh Edition.*
THE SOUL OF LILITH, *Ninth Edition.*
WORMWOOD. *Ninth Edition.*
BARABBAS: A DREAM OF THE WORLD'S TRAGEDY. *Thirty-fourth Edition.*
'The tender reverence of the treatment and the imaginative beauty of the writing have reconciled us to the daring of the conception, and the conviction is forced on us that even so exalted a subject cannot be made too familiar to us, provided it be presented in the true spirit of Christian faith. The amplifications of the Scripture narrative are often conceived with high poetic insight, and this "Dream of the World's Tragedy" is a lofty and not inadequate paraphrase of the supreme climax of the inspired narrative.'—*Dublin Review.*

THE SORROWS OF SATAN. *Forty-first Edition.*
'A very powerful piece of work.... The conception is magnificent, and is likely to win an abiding place within the memory of man.... The author has immense command of language, and a limitless audacity.... This interesting and remarkable romance will live long after much of the ephemeral literature of the day is forgotten.... A literary phenomenon ... novel, and even sublime.'—W. T. STEAD in the *Review of Reviews.*

Anthony Hope's Novels
Crown 8vo. 6s. each.

THE GOD IN THE CAR. *Eighth Edition.*
'A very remarkable book, deserving of critical analysis impossible within our limit; brilliant, but not superficial; well considered, but not elaborated; constructed with the proverbial art that conceals, but yet allows itself to be enjoyed by readers to whom fine literary method is a keen pleasure.'—*The World.*

A CHANGE OF AIR. *Fifth Edition.*
'A graceful, vivacious comedy, true to human nature. The characters are traced with a masterly hand.'—*Times.*

A MAN OF MARK. *Fifth Edition.*
'Of all Mr. Hope's books, "A Man of Mark" is the one which best compares with "The Prisoner of Zenda."'—*National Observer.*

THE CHRONICLES OF COUNT ANTONIO. *Fourth Edition.*
'It is a perfectly enchanting story of love and chivalry, and pure romance. The Count is the most constant, desperate, and modest and tender of lovers, a peerless gentleman, an intrepid fighter, a faithful friend, and a magnanimous foe.'—*Guardian.*

PHROSO. Illustrated by H. R. MILLAR. *Fourth Edition.*
'The tale is thoroughly fresh, quick with vitality, stirring the blood.'—*St. James's Gazette.*

'A story of adventure, every page of which is palpitating with action.'—*Speaker.*
'From cover to cover "Phroso" not only engages the attention, but carries the reader in little whirls of delight from adventure to adventure.'—*Academy.*

SIMON DALE. Illustrated. *Third Edition.*

'"Simon Dale" is one of the best historical romances that have been written for a long while.'—*St. James's Gazette.*
'A brilliant novel. The story is rapid and most excellently told. As for the hero, he is a perfect hero of romance'—*Athenæum.*
'There is searching analysis of human nature, with a most ingeniously constructed plot. Mr. Hope has drawn the contrasts of his women with marvellous subtlety and delicacy.'—*Times.*

Gilbert Parker's Novels
Crown 8vo. 6s. each.

PIERRE AND HIS PEOPLE. *Fifth Edition.*
'Stories happily conceived and finely executed. There is strength and genius in Mr. Parker's style.'—*Daily Telegraph.*

MRS. FALCHION. *Fourth Edition.*
'A splendid study of character.'—*Athenæum.*
'A very striking and admirable novel.'—*St. James's Gazette.*

THE TRANSLATION OF A SAVAGE.
'The plot is original and one difficult to work out; but Mr. Parker has done it with great skill and delicacy. The reader who is not interested in this original, fresh, and well-told tale must be a dull person indeed.'—*Daily Chronicle.*

THE TRAIL OF THE SWORD. Illustrated. *Sixth Edition.*
'A rousing and dramatic tale. A book like this, in which swords flash, great surprises are undertaken, and daring deeds done, in which men and women live and love in the old passionate way, is a joy inexpressible.'—*Daily Chronicle.*

WHEN VALMOND CAME TO PONTIAC: The Story of a Lost Napoleon. *Fourth Edition.*
'Here we find romance—real, breathing, living romance. The character of Valmond is drawn unerringly. The book must be read, we may say re-read, for any one thoroughly to appreciate Mr. Parker's delicate touch and innate sympathy with humanity.'—*Pall Mall Gazette.*

AN ADVENTURER OF THE NORTH: The Last Adventures of 'Pretty Pierre.' *Second Edition.*
'The present book is full of fine and moving stories of the great North, and it will add to Mr. Parker's already high reputation.'—*Glasgow Herald.*

THE SEATS OF THE MIGHTY. Illustrated. *Tenth Edition.*
'The best thing he has done; one of the best things that any one has done lately.'—*St. James's Gazette.*
'Mr. Parker seems to become stronger and easier with every serious novel that he attempts. He shows the matured power which his former novels have led us to expect, and has produced a really fine historical novel.'—*Athenæum.*
'A great book.'—*Black and White.*

THE POMP OF THE LAVILETTES. *Second Edition.* 3s. 6d.
'Living, breathing romance, genuine and unforced pathos, and a deeper and more subtle knowledge of human nature than Mr. Parker has ever displayed before. It is, in a word, the work of a true artist.'—*Pall Mall Gazette.*

THE BATTLE OF THE STRONG: a Romance of Two Kingdoms. Illustrated. *Fourth Edition.*
'Such a splendid story, so splendidly told, will be read with avidity, and will add new honour even to Mr. Parker's reputation.'—*St. James's Gazette.*
'No one who takes a pleasure in literature but will read Mr. Gilbert Parker's latest romance with keen enjoyment. The mere writing is so good as to be a delight in itself, apart altogether from the interest of the tale.'—*Pall Mall Gazette.*
'Nothing more vigorous or more human has come from Mr. Gilbert Parker than this novel. It has all the graphic power of his last book, with truer feeling for the romance, both of human life and wild nature. There is no character without its unique and picturesque interest. Mr. Parker's style, especially his descriptive style, has in this book, perhaps even more than elsewhere, aptness and vitality.'—*Literature.*

S. Baring Gould's Novels

Crown 8vo. 6s. each.

'To say that a book is by the author of "Mehalah" is to imply that it contains a story cast on strong lines, containing dramatic possibilities, vivid and sympathetic descriptions of Nature, and a wealth of ingenious imagery.'—*Speaker.*

'That whatever Mr. Baring Gould writes is well worth reading, is a conclusion that may be very generally accepted. His views of life are fresh and vigorous, his language pointed and characteristic, the incidents of which he makes use are striking and original, his characters are life-like, and though somewhat exceptional people, are drawn and coloured with artistic force. Add to this that his descriptions of scenes and scenery are painted with the loving eyes and skilled hands of a master of his art, that he is always fresh and never dull, and it is no wonder that readers have gained confidence in his power of amusing and satisfying them, and that year by year his popularity widens.'—*Court Circular.*

ARMINELL. *Fourth Edition.*
URITH. *Fifth Edition.*
IN THE ROAR OF THE SEA. *Sixth Edition.*
MRS. CURGENVEN OF CURGENVEN. *Fourth Edition.*
CHEAP JACK ZITA. *Fourth Edition.*
THE QUEEN OF LOVE. *Fourth Edition.*
MARGERY OF QUETHER. *Third Edition.*
JACQUETTA. *Third Edition.*

KITTY ALONE. *Fifth Edition.*
NOÉMI. Illustrated. *Fourth Edition.*
THE BROOM-SQUIRE. Illustrated. *Fourth Edition.*
THE PENNYCOMEQUICKS. *Third Edition.*
DARTMOOR IDYLLS.
GUAVAS THE TINNER. Illustrated. *Second Edition.*
BLADYS. Illustrated. *Second Edition.*
DOMITIA. Illustrated. *Second Edition.*

Conan Doyle. ROUND THE RED LAMP. By A. CONAN DOYLE. *Sixth Edition. Crown 8vo. 6s.*

'The book is far and away the best view that has been vouchsafed us behind the scenes of the consulting-room.'—*Illustrated London News.*

Stanley Weyman. UNDER THE RED ROBE. By STANLEY WEYMAN, Author of 'A Gentleman of France.' With Illustrations by R. C. WOODVILLE. *Fifteenth Edition. Crown 8vo. 6s.*

'Every one who reads books at all must read this thrilling romance, from the first page of which to the last the breathless reader is haled along. An inspiration of manliness and courage.'—*Daily Chronicle.*

Lucas Malet. THE WAGES OF SIN. By LUCAS MALET. *Thirteenth Edition. Crown 8vo. 6s.*

Lucas Malet. THE CARISSIMA. By LUCAS MALET, Author of 'The Wages of Sin,' etc. *Third Edition. Crown 8vo. 6s.*

George Gissing. THE TOWN TRAVELLER. By GEORGE GISSING, Author of 'Demos,' 'In the Year of Jubilee,' etc. *Second Edition. Cr. 8vo. 6s.*

'It is a bright and witty book above all things. Polly Sparkes is a splendid bit of work.'—*Pall Mall Gazette.*
'The spirit of Dickens is in it.'—*Bookman.*

S. R. Crockett. LOCHINVAR. By S. R. CROCKETT, Author of 'The Raiders,' etc. Illustrated. *Second Edition. Crown 8vo. 6s.*

'Full of gallantry and pathos, of the clash of arms, and brightened by episodes of humour and love. . . .'—*Westminster Gazette.*

S. R. Crockett. THE STANDARD BEARER. By S. R. CROCKETT. *Crown 8vo. 6s.*

'A delightful tale in his best style.'—*Speaker.*
'Mr. Crockett at his best.'—*Literature.*

Arthur Morrison. TALES OF MEAN STREETS. By ARTHUR MORRISON. *Fifth Edition. Cr. 8vo. 6s.*

'Told with consummate art and extraordinary detail. In the true humanity of the book lies its justification, the permanence of its interest, and its indubitable triumph.'—*Athenæum.*
'A great book. The author's method is amazingly effective, and produces a thrilling sense of reality. The writer lays upon us a master hand. The book is simply appalling and irresistible in its interest. It is humorous also; without humour it would not make the mark it is certain to make.'—*World.*

Arthur Morrison. A CHILD OF THE JAGO. By ARTHUR MORRISON. *Third Edition. Cr. 8vo. 6s.*
'The book is a masterpiece.'—*Pall Mall Gazette.*
'Told with great vigour and powerful simplicity.'—*Athenæum.*

Mrs. Clifford. A FLASH OF SUMMER. By Mrs. W. K. CLIFFORD, Author of 'Aunt Anne,' etc. *Second Edition. Crown 8vo. 6s.*
'The story is a very beautiful one, exquisitely told.'—*Speaker.*

Emily Lawless. HURRISH. By the Honble. EMILY LAWLESS, Author of 'Maelcho,' etc. *Fifth Edition. Cr. 8vo. 6s.*

Emily Lawless. MAELCHO: a Sixteenth Century Romance. By the Honble. EMILY LAWLESS. *Second Edition. Crown 8vo. 6s.*
'A really great book.'—*Spectator.*
'There is no keener pleasure in life than the recognition of genius. A piece of work of the first order, which we do not hesitate to describe as one of the most remarkable literary achievements of this generation.'—*Manchester Guardian.*

Emily Lawless. TRAITS AND CONFIDENCES. By the Honble. EMILY LAWLESS. *Crown 8vo. 6s.*

E. W. Hornung. THE AMATEUR CRACKSMAN. By E. W. HORNUNG. *Crown 8vo. 6s.*
'An audaciously entertaining volume.'—*Spectator.*
'Fascinating and entertaining in a supreme degree.'—*Daily Mail.*
'We are fascinated by the individuality, the daring, and the wonderful coolness of Raffles the resourceful, and follow him breathlessly in his career.'—*World.*

Jane Barlow. A CREEL OF IRISH STORIES. By JANE BARLOW, Author of 'Irish Idylls.' *Second Edition. Crown 8vo. 6s.*
'Vivid and singularly real.'—*Scotsman.*

Jane Barlow. FROM THE EAST UNTO THE WEST. By JANE BARLOW. *Crown 8vo. 6s.*
'The genial humour and never-failing sympathy recommend the book to those who like healthy fiction.'—*Scotsman.*

Mrs. Caffyn. ANNE MAULEVERER. By Mrs. CAFFYN (Iota), Author of 'The Yellow Aster.' *Second Edition. Crown 8vo. 6s.*
'The author leaves with us a most delectable addition to the heroines in modern fiction, and she has established herself as one of the leading women novelists of the day.'—*Daily Chronicle.*
'A fine conception and absorbingly interesting.'—*Athenæum.*

Dorothea Gerard. THINGS THAT HAVE HAPPENED. By DOROTHEA GERARD, Author of 'Lady Baby.' *Crown 8vo. 6s.*
'All the stories are delightful.'—*Scotsman.*

J. H. Findlater. THE GREEN GRAVES OF BALGOWRIE. By JANE H. FINDLATER. *Fourth Edition. Crown 8vo. 6s.*
'A powerful and vivid story.'—*Standard.*
'A beautiful story, sad and strange as truth itself.'—*Vanity Fair.*
'A very charming and pathetic tale.'—*Pall Mall Gazette.*
'A singularly original, clever, and beautiful story.'—*Guardian.*
'Reveals to us a new writer of undoubted faculty and reserve force.'—*Spectator.*
'An exquisite idyll, delicate, affecting, and beautiful.'—*Black and White.*

J. H. Findlater. A DAUGHTER OF STRIFE. By JANE HELEN FINDLATER. *Crown 8vo. 6s.*
'A story of strong human interest.'—*Scotsman.*

J. H. Findlater. RACHEL. By JANE H. FINDLATER. *Second Edition. Crown 8vo. 6s.*
'Powerful and sympathetic.'—*Glasgow Herald.*
'A not unworthy successor to "The Green Graves of Balgowrie."'—*Critic.*

Mary Findlater. OVER THE HILLS. By MARY FINDLATER. *Second Edition. Cr. 8vo. 6s.*
'A strong and fascinating piece of work.'—*Scotsman.*

'A charming romance, and full of incident. The book is fresh and strong.'—*Speaker.*
'A strong and wise book of deep insight and unflinching truth.'—*Birmingham Post.*

Mary Findlater. BETTY MUSGRAVE. By MARY FINDLATER. *Second Edition. Crown 8vo. 6s.*
'Handled with dignity and delicacy.... A most touching story.'—*Spectator.*
'Told with great skill, and the pathos of it rings true and unforced throughout.'—*Glasgow Herald.*

Alfred Ollivant. OWD BOB, THE GREY DOG OF KENMUIR. By ALFRED OLLIVANT. *Second Edition. Cr. 8vo. 6s.*
'Weird, thrilling, strikingly graphic.'—*Punch.*
'We admire this book.... It is one to read with admiration and to praise with enthusiasm.'—*Bookman.*
'It is a fine, open-air, blood-stirring book, to be enjoyed by every man and woman to whom a dog is dear.'—*Literature.*

B. M. Croker. PEGGY OF THE BARTONS. By B. M. CROKER, Author of 'Diana Barrington.' *Fourth Edition. Crown 8vo. 6s.*
Mrs. Croker excels in the admirably simple, easy, and direct flow of her narrative, the briskness of her dialogue, and the geniality of her portraiture.'—*Spectator.*
'All the characters, indeed, are drawn with clearness and certainty; and it would be hard to name any quality essential to first-class work which is lacking from this book.'—*Saturday Review.*

H. G. Wells. THE STOLEN BACILLUS, and other Stories. By H. G. WELLS. *Second Edition. Crown 8vo. 6s.*
'They are the impressions of a very striking imagination, which, it would seem, has a great deal within its reach.'—*Saturday Review.*

H. G. Wells. THE PLATTNER STORY AND OTHERS. By H. G. WELLS. *Second Edition. Cr. 8vo. 6s.*
'Weird and mysterious, they seem to hold the reader as by a magic spell.'—*Scotsman.*

Sara Jeanette Duncan. A VOYAGE OF CONSOLATION. By SARA JEANETTE DUNCAN, Author of 'An American Girl in London.' Illustrated. *Third Edition. Cr. 8vo. 6s.*

'A most delightfully bright book.'—*Daily Telegraph.*
'The dialogue is full of wit.'—*Globe.*
'Laughter lurks in every page.'—*Daily News.*

C. F. Keary. THE JOURNALIST. By C. F. KEARY. *Cr. 8vo. 6s.*
'It is rare indeed to find such poetical sympathy with Nature joined to close study of character and singularly truthful dialogue: but then "The Journalist" is altogether a rare book.'—*Athenæum.*

E. F. Benson. DODO: A DETAIL OF THE DAY. By E. F. BENSON. *Sixteenth Edition. Cr. 8vo. 6s.*
'A perpetual feast of epigram and paradox.'—*Speaker.*

E. F. Benson. THE VINTAGE. By E. F. BENSON. Author of 'Dodo.' Illustrated by G. P. JACOMB-HOOD. *Third Edition. Crown 8vo. 6s.*
'Full of fire, earnestness, and beauty.'—*The World.*

E. F. Benson. THE CAPSINA. By E. F. BENSON, Author of 'Dodo.' With Illustrations by G. P. JACOMB-HOOD. *Second Edition. Cr. 8vo. 6s.*
'The story moves through an atmosphere of heroism and adventure.'—*Manchester Guardian.*

Mrs. Oliphant. SIR ROBERT'S FORTUNE. By. Mrs. OLIPHANT. *Crown 8vo. 6s.*

Mrs. Oliphant. THE TWO MARYS. By Mrs. OLIPHANT. *Second Edition. Crown 8vo. 6s.*

Mrs. Oliphant. THE LADY'S WALK. By Mrs. OLIPHANT. *Second Edition. Crown 8vo. 6s.*

W. E. Norris. MATTHEW AUSTIN. By W. E. NORRIS, Author of 'Mademoiselle de Mersac,' etc. *Fourth Edition. Crown 8vo. 6s.*
'An intellectually satisfactory and morally bracing novel.'—*Daily Telegraph.*

W. E. Norris. HIS GRACE. By W. E. NORRIS. *Third Edition. Crown 8vo. 6s.*
'Mr. Norris has drawn a really fine character in the Duke.'—*Athenæum.*

W. E. Norris. THE DESPOTIC LADY AND OTHERS. By W. E. NORRIS. *Crown 8vo. 6s.*
'A budget of good fiction of which no one will tire.'—*Scotsman.*

MESSRS. METHUEN'S CATALOGUE

W. E. Norris. CLARISSA FURIOSA. By W. E. NORRIS. *Cr. 8vo. 6s.*
'As a story it is admirable, as a *jeu d'esprit* it is capital, as a lay sermon studded with gems of wit and wisdom it is a model.'—*The World.*

W. Clark Russell. MY DANISH SWEETHEART. By W. CLARK RUSSELL. *Illustrated. Fourth Edition. Crown 8vo. 6s.*

Robert Barr. IN THE MIDST OF ALARMS. By ROBERT BARR. *Third Edition. Cr. 8vo. 6s.*
'A book which has abundantly satisfied us by its capital humour.'—*Daily Chronicle.*
'Mr. Barr has achieved a triumph.'—*Pall Mall Gazette.*

Robert Barr. THE MUTABLE MANY. By ROBERT BARR. *Second Edition. Crown 8vo. 6s.*
'Very much the best novel that Mr. Barr has yet given us. There is much insight in it, and much excellent humour.'—*Daily Chronicle.*

Robert Barr. THE COUNTESS TEKLA. By ROBERT BARR. *Second Edition. Crown 8vo. 6s.*
'Thrilling and brilliant.'—*Critic.*
'Such a tale as Mr. Barr's would ever receive a hearty welcome. Of these mediæval romances, which are now gaining ground, "The Countess Tekla" is the very best we have seen. The story is written in clear English, and a picturesque, moving style.'—*Pall Mall Gazette.*

Andrew Balfour. BY STROKE OF SWORD. By ANDREW BALFOUR. Illustrated. *Fourth Edition. Cr. 8vo. 6s.*
'A banquet of good things.'—*Academy.*
'A recital of thrilling interest, told with unflagging vigour.'—*Globe.*
An unusually excellent example of a semi-historic romance.'—*World.*

Andrew Balfour. TO ARMS! By ANDREW BALFOUR. Illustrated. *Second Edition. Crown 8vo. 6s.*
'The marvellous perils through which Allan passes are told in powerful and lively fashion.'—*Pall Mall Gazette.*

R. B. Townshend. LONE PINE: A Romance of Mexican Life. By R. B. TOWNSHEND. *Crown 8vo. 6s.*
'It is full of incident and adventure. The great fight is as thrilling a bit of fighting as we have read for many a day.'—*Speaker.*

'The volume is evidently the work of a clever writer and of an educated and experienced traveller.'—*Athenæum.*

J. Maclaren Cobban. THE KING OF ANDAMAN: A Saviour of Society. By J. MACLAREN COBBAN. *Crown 8vo. 6s.*
'An unquestionably interesting book. It contains one character, at least, who has in him the root of immortality.'—*Pall Mall Gazette.*

J. Maclaren Cobban. WILT THOU HAVE THIS WOMAN? By J. MACLAREN COBBAN. *Cr. 8vo. 6s.*

J. Maclaren Cobban. THE ANGEL OF THE COVENANT. By J. MACLAREN COBBAN. *Cr. 8vo. 6s.*
'Mr. Cobban has achieved a work of such rare distinction that there is nothing comparable with it in recent Scottish romance. It is a great historical picture, in which fact and fancy are welded together in a fine realisation of the spirit of the times.'—*Pall Mall Gazette.*

Marshall Saunders. ROSE À CHARLITTE: A Romantic Story of Acadie. By MARSHALL SAUNDERS. *Crown 8vo. 6s.*
'Graceful and well written.'—*Saturday Review.*
'Charmingly told.'—*Manchester Guardian.*

R. N. Stephens. AN ENEMY TO THE KING. By R. N. STEPHENS. *Second Edition. Cr. 8vo. 6s.*
'It is full of movement, and the movement is always buoyant.'—*Scotsman.*
'A stirring story with plenty of movement.'—*Black and White.*

Robert Hichens. BYEWAYS. By ROBERT HITCHINS. Author of 'Flames, etc.' *Second Edition. Cr. 8vo. 6s.*
'The work is undeniably that of a man of striking imagination.'—*Daily News.*

Percy White. A PASSIONATE PILGRIM. By PERCY WHITE, Author of 'Mr. Bailey-Martin.' *Cr. 8vo. 6s.*

W. Pett Ridge. SECRETARY TO BAYNE, M.P. By W. PETT RIDGE. *Crown 8vo. 6s.*

E. Dawson and A. Moore. ADRIAN ROME. By E. DAWSON and A. MOORE, Authors of 'A Comedy of Masks.' *Crown 8vo. 6s.*
'A clever novel dealing with youth and genius.'—*Academy.*

J. S. Fletcher. THE BUILDERS. By J. S. FLETCHER, Author of 'When Charles I. was King.' Second Edition. Cr. 8vo. 6s.

J. S. Fletcher. THE PATHS OF THE PRUDENT. By J. S. FLETCHER. Crown 8vo. 6s.
'The story has a curious fascination for the reader, and the theme and character are handled with rare ability.'—Scotsman.
'Dorinthia is charming. The story is told with great humour.'—Pall Mall Gazette.

J. B. Burton. IN THE DAY OF ADVERSITY. By J. BLOUNDELLE-BURTON. Second Edition. Cr. 8vo. 6s.
'Unusually interesting and full of highly dramatic situations. —Guardian.

J. B. Burton. DENOUNCED. By J. BLOUNDELLE-BURTON. Second Edition. Crown 8vo. 6s.
'A fine, manly, spirited piece of work.'—World.

J. B. Burton. THE CLASH OF ARMS. By J. BLOUNDELLE-BURTON. Second Edition. Cr. 8vo. 6s.
'A brave story—brave in deed, brave in word, brave in thought.'—St. James's Gazette.

J. B. Burton. ACROSS THE SALT SEAS. By J. BLOUNDELLE-BURTON. Second Edition. Crown 8vo. 6s.
'The very essence of the true romantic spirit.'—Truth.

R. Murray Gilchrist. WILLOW-BRAKE. By R. MURRAY GILCHRIST. Crown 8vo. 6s.
'It is a singularly pleasing and eminently wholesome volume, with a decidedly charming note of pathos at various points.'—Athenæum.

W. C. Scully. THE WHITE HECATOMB. By W. C. SCULLY, Author of 'Kafir Stories.' Cr. 8vo. 6s.
'Reveals a marvellously intimate understanding of the Kaffir mind.'—African Critic.

W. C. Scully. BETWEEN SUN AND SAND. By W. C. SCULLY, Author of 'The White Hecatomb.' Cr. 8vo. 6s.
'The reader passes at once into the very atmosphere of the African desert: the inexpressible space and stillness swallow him up, and there is no world for him but that immeasurable waste.'—Athenæum.

M. M. Dowie. GALLIA. By MÉNIE MURIEL DOWIE, Author of 'A Girl in the Karpathians.' Third Edition. Cr. 8vo. 6s.

M. M. Dowie. THE CROOK OF THE BOUGH. By MÉNIE MURIEL DOWIE. Cr. 8vo. 6s.

Julian Corbett. A BUSINESS IN GREAT WATERS. By JULIAN CORBETT. Second Edition. Cr. 8vo. 6s.

OTHER SIX-SHILLING NOVELS

Crown 8vo.

MISS ERIN. By M. E. FRANCIS.
ANANIAS. By the Hon. Mrs. ALAN BRODRICK.
CORRAGEEN IN '98. By Mrs. ORPEN.
THE PLUNDER PIT. By J. KEIGHLEY SNOWDEN.
CROSS TRAILS. By VICTOR WAITE.
SUCCESSORS TO THE TITLE. By Mrs. WALFORD.
KIRKHAM'S FIND. By MARY GAUNT.
DEADMAN'S. By MARY GAUNT.
CAPTAIN JACOBUS: A ROMANCE OF THE ROAD. By L. COPE CORNFORD.
SONS OF ADVERSITY. By L. COPE CORNFORD.
THE KING OF ALBERIA. By LAURA DAINTREY.
THE DAUGHTER OF ALOUETTE. By MARY A. OWEN.
CHILDREN OF THIS WORLD. By ELLEN F. PINSENT.
AN ELECTRIC SPARK. By G. MANVILLE FENN.
UNDER SHADOW OF THE MISSION. By L. S. MCCHESNEY.
THE SPECULATORS. By J. F. BREWER.
THE SPIRIT OF STORM. By RONALD ROSS.

THE QUEENSBERRY CUP. By CLIVE P. WOLLEY.
A HOME IN INVERESK. By T. L. PATON.
MISS ARMSTRONG'S AND OTHER CIRCUMSTANCES. By JOHN DAVIDSON.
DR. CONGALTON'S LEGACY. By HENRY JOHNSTON.
TIME AND THE WOMAN. By RICHARD PRYCE.
THIS MAN'S DOMINION. By the Author of 'A High Little World.'
DIOGENES OF LONDON. By H. B. MARRIOTT WATSON.
THE STONE DRAGON. By MURRAY GILCHRIST.
A VICAR'S WIFE. By EVELYN DICKINSON.
ELSA. By E. M'QUEEN GRAY.
THE SINGER OF MARLY. By I. HOOPER.
THE FALL OF THE SPARROW. By M. C. BALFOUR.
A SERIOUS COMEDY. By HERBERT MORRAH.
THE FAITHFUL CITY. By HERBERT MORRAH.
IN THE GREAT DEEP. By J. A. BARRY.
BIJLI, THE DANCER. By JAMES BLYTHE PATTON.
JOSIAH'S WIFE. By NORMA LORIMER.
THE PHILANTHROPIST. By LUCY MAYNARD.
VAUSSORE. By FRANCIS BRUNE.

THREE-AND-SIXPENNY NOVELS
Crown 8vo.

DERRICK VAUGHAN, NOVELIST. 42nd thousand. By EDNA LYALL.
THE KLOOF BRIDE. By ERNEST GLANVILLE.
A VENDETTA OF THE DESERT. By W. C. SCULLY.
SUBJECT TO VANITY. By MARGARET BENSON.
THE SIGN OF THE SPIDER. By BERTRAM MITFORD.
THE MOVING FINGER. By MARY GAUNT.
JACO TRELOAR. By J. H. PEARCE.
THE DANCE OF THE HOURS. By 'VERA.'
A WOMAN OF FORTY. By ESMÉ STUART.
A CUMBERER OF THE GROUND. By CONSTANCE SMITH.
THE SIN OF ANGELS. By EVELYN DICKINSON.
AUT DIABOLUS AUT NIHIL. By X. L.
THE COMING OF CUCULAIN. By STANDISH O'GRADY.
THE GODS GIVE MY DONKEY WINGS. By ANGUS EVAN ABBOTT.
THE STAR GAZERS. By G. MANVILLE FENN.
THE POISON OF ASPS. By R. ORTON-PROWSE.
THE QUIET MRS. FLEMING. By R. PRYCE.
DISENCHANTMENT. By F. MABEL ROBINSON.
THE SQUIRE OF WANDALES. By A. SHIELD.
A REVEREND GENTLEMAN. By J. M. COBBAN.
A DEPLORABLE AFFAIR. By W. E. NORRIS.
A CAVALIER'S LADYE. By Mrs. DICKER.
THE PRODIGALS. By Mrs. OLIPHANT.
THE SUPPLANTER. By P. NEUMANN.
A MAN WITH BLACK EYELASHES. By H. A. KENNEDY.
A HANDFUL OF EXOTICS. By S. GORDON.
AN ODD EXPERIMENT. By HANNAH LYNCH.
TALES OF NORTHUMBRIA. By HOWARD PEASE.

HALF-CROWN NOVELS
Crown 8vo.

HOVENDEN, V.C. By F. MABEL ROBINSON.
THE PLAN OF CAMPAIGN. By F. MABEL ROBINSON.
MR. BUTLER'S WARD. By F. MABEL ROBINSON.
ELI'S CHILDREN. By G. MANVILLE FENN.
A DOUBLE KNOT. By G. MANVILLE FENN.
DISARMED. By M. BETHAM EDWARDS.
A MARRIAGE AT SEA. By W. CLARK RUSSELL.
IN TENT AND BUNGALOW. By the Author of 'Indian Idylls.'
MY STEWARDSHIP. By E. M'QUEEN GRAY.
JACK'S FATHER. By W. E. NORRIS.
A LOST ILLUSION. By LESLIE KEITH.

THE TRUE HISTORY OF JOSHUA DAVIDSON, Christian and Communist. By E. LYNN LYNTON. *Eleventh Edition. Post 8vo.* 1s.

Books for Boys and Girls
A Series of Books by well-known Authors, well illustrated.

THREE-AND-SIXPENCE EACH

THE ICELANDER'S SWORD. By S. BARING GOULD.
TWO LITTLE CHILDREN AND CHING. By EDITH E. CUTHELL.
TODDLEBEN'S HERO. By M. M. BLAKE.
ONLY A GUARD-ROOM DOG. By EDITH E. CUTHELL.
THE DOCTOR OF THE JULIET. By HARRY COLLINGWOOD.
MASTER ROCKAFELLAR'S VOYAGE. By W. CLARK RUSSELL.
SYD BELTON: Or, The Boy who would not go to Sea. By G. MANVILLE FENN.
THE WALLYPUG IN LONDON. By G. E. FARROW.
ADVENTURES IN WALLYPUG LAND. By G. E. FARROW. 5s.

The Peacock Library
A Series of Books for Girls by well-known Authors, handsomely bound, and well illustrated.

THREE-AND-SIXPENCE EACH

A PINCH OF EXPERIENCE. By L. B. WALFORD.
THE RED GRANGE. By Mrs. MOLESWORTH.
THE SECRET OF MADAME DE MONLUC. By the Author of 'Mdle. Mori.'
OUT OF THE FASHION. B L. T. MEADE.
DUMPS. By Mrs. PARR.
A GIRL OF THE PEOPLE. By L. T. MEADE.
HEPSY GIPSY. By L. T. MEADE. 2s. 6d.
THE HONOURABLE MISS. By L. T. MEADE.
MY LAND OF BEULAH. By Mrs. LEITH ADAMS.

University Extension Series

A series of books on historical, literary, and scientific subjects, suitable for extension students and home-reading circles. Each volume is complete in itself, and the subjects are treated by competent writers in a broad and philosophic spirit.

Edited by J. E. SYMES, M.A.,
Principal of University College, Nottingham.
Crown 8vo. Price (with some exceptions) 2s. 6d.

The following volumes are ready:—

THE INDUSTRIAL HISTORY OF ENGLAND. By H. DE B. GIBBINS, Litt.D., M.A., late Scholar of Wadham College, Oxon., Cobden Prizeman. *Sixth Edition, Revised. With Maps and Plans.* 3s.

A HISTORY OF ENGLISH POLITICAL ECONOMY. By L. L. PRICE, M.A., Fellow of Oriel College, Oxon. *Second Edition.*

PROBLEMS OF POVERTY: An Inquiry into the Industrial Conditions of the Poor. By J. A. HOBSON, M.A. *Fourth Edition.*

VICTORIAN POETS. By A. SHARP.

THE FRENCH REVOLUTION. By J. E. SYMES, M.A.

PSYCHOLOGY. By F. S. GRANGER, M.A. *Second Edition.*

THE EVOLUTION OF PLANT LIFE: Lower Forms. By G. MASSEE. *With Illustrations.*

AIR AND WATER. By V. B. LEWES, M.A. *Illustrated.*

THE CHEMISTRY OF LIFE AND HEALTH. By C. W. KIMMINS, M.A. *Illustrated.*

THE MECHANICS OF DAILY LIFE. By V. P. SELLS, M.A. *Illustrated.*

ENGLISH SOCIAL REFORMERS. By H. DE B. GIBBINS, D.Litt., M.A.

ENGLISH TRADE AND FINANCE IN THE SEVENTEENTH CENTURY. By W. A. S. HEWINS, B.A.

THE CHEMISTRY OF FIRE. The Elementary Principles of Chemistry. By M. M. PATTISON MUIR, M.A. *Illustrated.*

A TEXT-BOOK OF AGRICULTURAL BOTANY. By M. C. POTTER, M.A., F.L.S. *Illustrated.* 3s. 6d.

THE VAULT OF HEAVEN. A Popular Introduction to Astronomy. By R. A. GREGORY. *With numerous Illustrations.*

METEOROLOGY. The Elements of Weather and Climate. By H. N. DICKSON, F.R.S.E., F.R. Met. Soc. *Illustrated.*

A MANUAL OF ELECTRICAL SCIENCE. By GEORGE J. BURCH, M.A. *With numerous Illustrations.* 3s.

THE EARTH. An Introduction to Physiography. By EVAN SMALL, M.A. *Illustrated.*

INSECT LIFE. By F. W. THEOBALD, M.A. *Illustrated.*

ENGLISH POETRY FROM BLAKE TO BROWNING. By W. M. DIXON, M.A.

ENGLISH LOCAL GOVERNMENT. By E. JENKS, M.A., Professor of Law at University College, Liverpool.

THE GREEK VIEW OF LIFE. By G. L. DICKINSON, Fellow of King's College, Cambridge. *Second Edition.*

Social Questions of To-day

Edited by H. DE B. GIBBINS, Litt.D., M.A.

Crown 8vo. 2s. 6d.

A series of volumes upon those topics of social, economic, and industrial interest that are at the present moment foremost in the public mind. Each volume of the series is written by an author who is an acknowledged authority upon the subject with which he deals.

The following Volumes of the Series are ready:—

TRADE UNIONISM—NEW AND OLD. By G. HOWELL. *Second Edition.*

THE CO-OPERATIVE MOVEMENT TO-DAY. By G. J. HOLYOAKE. *Second Edition.*

MUTUAL THRIFT. By Rev. J. FROME WILKINSON, M.A.

PROBLEMS OF POVERTY. By J. A. HOBSON, M.A. *Fourth Edition.*

THE COMMERCE OF NATIONS. By C. F. BASTABLE, M.A., Professor of Economics at Trinity College, Dublin. *Second Edition.*

THE ALIEN INVASION. By W. H. WILKINS, B.A.

THE RURAL EXODUS. By P. ANDERSON GRAHAM.

LAND NATIONALIZATION. By HAROLD COX, B.A.

A SHORTER WORKING DAY. By H. DE B. GIBBINS, D.Litt., M.A., and R. A. HADFIELD, of the Hecla Works, Sheffield.

BACK TO THE LAND: An Inquiry into the Cure for Rural Depopulation. By H. E. MOORE.

TRUSTS, POOLS AND CORNERS. By J. STEPHEN JEANS.

THE FACTORY SYSTEM. By R. W. COOKE-TAYLOR.

THE STATE AND ITS CHILDREN. By GERTRUDE TUCKWELL.

WOMEN'S WORK. By LADY DILKE, Miss BULLEY, and Miss WHITLEY.

MUNICIPALITIES AT WORK. The Municipal Policy of Six Great Towns, and its Influence on their Social Welfare. By FREDERICK DOLMAN.

SOCIALISM AND MODERN THOUGHT. By M. KAUFMANN.

THE HOUSING OF THE WORKING CLASSES. By E. BOWMAKER.

MODERN CIVILIZATION IN SOME OF ITS ECONOMIC ASPECTS. By W. CUNNINGHAM, D.D., Fellow of Trinity College, Cambridge.

THE PROBLEM OF THE UNEMPLOYED. By J. A. HOBSON, B.A.

LIFE IN WEST LONDON. By ARTHUR SHERWELL, M.A. *Second Edition.*

RAILWAY NATIONALIZATION. By CLEMENT EDWARDS.

WORKHOUSES AND PAUPERISM. By LOUISA TWINING.

UNIVERSITY AND SOCIAL SETTLEMENTS. By W. REASON, M.A.

Classical Translations

Edited by H. F. FOX, M.A., Fellow and Tutor of Brasenose College, Oxford.

ÆSCHYLUS — Agamemnon, Chöephoroe, Eumenides. Translated by LEWIS CAMPBELL, LL.D., late Professor of Greek at St. Andrews. 5s.

CICERO—De Oratore I. Translated by E. N. P. MOOR, M.A. 3s. 6d.

CICERO—Select Orations (Pro Milone, Pro Murena, Philippic II., In Catilinam). Translated by H. E. D. BLAKISTON, M.A., Fellow and Tutor of Trinity College, Oxford. 5s.

CICERO—De Natura Deorum. Translated by F. BROOKS, M.A., late Scholar of Balliol College, Oxford. 3s. 6d.

HORACE: THE ODES AND EPODES. Translated by A.

GODLEY, M.A., Fellow of Magdalen College, Oxford. 2s.

LUCIAN—Six Dialogues (Nigrinus, Icaro - Menippus, The Cock, The Ship, The Parasite, The Lover of Falsehood). Translated by S. T. IRWIN, M.A., Assistant Master at Clifton; late Scholar of Exeter College, Oxford. 3s. 6d.

SOPHOCLES — Electra and Ajax. Translated by E. D. A. MORSHEAD, M.A., Assistant Master at Winchester. 2s. 6d.

TACITUS—Agricola and Germania. Translated by R. B. TOWNSHEND, late Scholar of Trinity College, Cambridge. 2s. 6d.

Educational Books

CLASSICAL

PLAUTI BACCHIDES. Edited with Introduction, Commentary, and Critical Notes by J. M'COSH, M.A. Fcap. 4to. 12s. 6d.

PASSAGES FOR UNSEEN TRANSLATION. By E. C. MARCHANT, M.A., Fellow of Peterhouse, Cambridge; and A. M. COOK, M.A., late Scholar of Wadham College, Oxford; Assistant Masters at St. Paul's School. Crown 8vo. 3s. 6d.
'We know no book of this class better fitted for use in the higher forms of schools.'—Guardian.

TACITI AGRICOLA. With Introduction, Notes, Map, etc. By R. F. DAVIS, M.A., Assistant Master at Weymouth College. Crown 8vo. 2s.

TACITI GERMANIA. By the same Editor. Crown 8vo. 2s.

HERODOTUS: EASY SELECTIONS. With Vocabulary. By A. C. LIDDELL, M.A. Fcap. 8vo. 1s. 6d.

SELECTIONS FROM THE ODYSSEY. By E. D. STONE, M.A., late Assistant Master at Eton. Fcap. 8vo. 1s. 6d.

PLAUTUS: THE CAPTIVI. Adapted for Lower Forms by J. H. FREESE, M.A., late Fellow of St. John's, Cambridge. 1s. 6d.

DEMOSTHENES AGAINST CONON AND CALLICLES. Edited with Notes and Vocabulary, by F. DARWIN SWIFT, M.A. Fcap. 8vo. 2s.

EXERCISES IN LATIN ACCIDENCE. By S. E. WINBOLT, Assistant Master in Christ's Hospital. Crown 8vo. 1s. 6d.
An elementary book adapted for Lower Forms to accompany the shorter Latin primer.

NOTES ON GREEK AND LATIN SYNTAX. By G. BUCKLAND GREEN, M.A., Assistant Master at Edinburgh Academy, late Fellow of St. John's College, Oxon. Crown 8vo. 3s. 6d.
Notes and explanations on the chief difficulties of Greek and Latin Syntax, with numerous passages for exercise.

GERMAN

A COMPANION GERMAN GRAMMAR. By H. DE B. GIBBINS, D.Litt., M.A., Assistant Master at Nottingham High School. Crown 8vo. 1s. 6d.

GERMAN PASSAGES FOR UNSEEN TRANSLATION. By E. M'QUEEN GRAY. Crown 8vo. 2s. 6d.

SCIENCE

THE WORLD OF SCIENCE. Including Chemistry, Heat, Light, Sound, Magnetism, Electricity, Botany, Zoology, Physiology, Astronomy, and Geology. By R. ELLIOTT STEEL, M.A., F.C.S. 147 Illustrations. Second Edition. Cr. 8vo. 2s. 6d.

ELEMENTARY LIGHT. By R. E. STEEL. With numerous Illustrations. Crown 8vo. 4s. 6d.

VOLUMETRIC ANALYSIS. By J. B. RUSSELL, B.Sc., Science Master at Burnley Grammar School. Cr. 8vo. 1s. 6d.
'A collection of useful, well-arranged notes.'—School Guardian.

ENGLISH

ENGLISH RECORDS. A Companion to the History of England. By H. E. MALDEN, M A. *Crown 8vo. 3s. 6d.*
A book which aims at concentrating information upon dates, genealogy officials, constitutional documents, etc., which is usually found scattered in different volumes.

THE ENGLISH CITIZEN: HIS RIGHTS AND DUTIES. By H. E. MALDEN, M.A. *1s. 6d.*

A DIGEST OF DEDUCTIVE LOGIC. By JOHNSON BARKER, B.A. *Crown 8vo. 2s. 6d.*

A CLASS-BOOK OF DICTATION PASSAGES. By W. WILLIAMSON, M.A. *Second Edition, Crown 8vo. 1s. 6d.*

TEST CARDS IN EUCLID AND ALGEBRA. By D. S. CALDERWOOD, Headmaster of the Normal School, Edinburgh. In three packets of 40, with Answers. *1s.*

METHUEN'S COMMERCIAL SERIES

Edited by H. DE B. GIBBINS, Litt.D., M.A.

BRITISH COMMERCE AND COLONIES FROM ELIZABETH TO VICTORIA. By H. DE B. GIBBINS, Litt.D., M.A. *Third Edition. 2s.*

COMMERCIAL EXAMINATION PAPERS. By H. DE B. GIBBINS, Litt.D., M.A. *1s. 6d.*

THE ECONOMICS OF COMMERCE. By H. DE B. GIBBINS, Litt.D., M.A. *1s. 6d.*

FRENCH COMMERCIAL CORRESPONDENCE. By S. E. BALLY, Master at the Manchester Grammar School. *Second Edition. 2s.*

GERMAN COMMERCIAL CORRESPONDENCE. By S. E. BALLY. *2s. 6d.*

A FRENCH COMMERCIAL READER. By S. E. BALLY. *2s.*

COMMERCIAL GEOGRAPHY, with special reference to the British Empire. By L. W. LYDE, M.A. *Second Edition. 2s.*

A PRIMER OF BUSINESS. By S. JACKSON, M.A. *Second Edition. 1s. 6d.*

COMMERCIAL ARITHMETIC. By F. G. TAYLOR, M.A. *Second Edition. 1s. 6d.*

PRÉCIS WRITING AND OFFICE CORRESPONDENCE. By E. E. WHITFIELD, M.A. *2s.*

A GUIDE TO PROFESSIONS AND BUSINESS. By HENRY JONES. *1s. 6d.*

WORKS BY A. M. M. STEDMAN, M.A.

INITIA LATINA: Easy Lessons on Elementary Accidence. *Third Edition. Fcap. 8vo. 1s.*

FIRST LATIN LESSONS. *Fifth Edition. Crown 8vo. 2s.*

FIRST LATIN READER. With Notes adapted to the Shorter Latin Primer and Vocabulary. *Fourth Edition revised. 18mo. 1s. 6d.*

EASY SELECTIONS FROM CÆSAR. Part 1. The Helvetian War. *Second Edition. 18mo. 1s.*

EASY SELECTIONS FROM LIVY. Part I. The Kings of Rome. *18mo. 1s. 6d.*

EASY LATIN PASSAGES FOR UNSEEN TRANSLATION. *Sixth Edition. Fcap. 8vo. 1s. 6d.*

EXEMPLA LATINA. First Lessons in Latin Accidence. With Vocabulary. *Crown 8vo. 1s.*

EASY LATIN EXERCISES ON THE SYNTAX OF THE SHORTER AND REVISED LATIN PRIMER. With Vocabulary. *Seventh and cheaper Edition, re-written. Crown 8vo. 1s. 6d.* Issued with the consent of Dr. Kennedy.

THE LATIN COMPOUND SENTENCE: Rules and Exercises.

Crown 8vo. 1s. 6d. With Vocabulary. 2s.
NOTANDA QUAEDAM: Miscellaneous Latin Exercises on Common Rules and Idioms. *Third Edition.* Fcap. 8vo. 1s. 6d. With Vocabulary. 2s.
LATIN VOCABULARIES FOR REPETITION: Arranged according to Subjects. *Eighth Edition.* Fcap. 8vo. 1s. 6d.
A VOCABULARY OF LATIN IDIOMS. 18mo. *Second Edition.* 1s.
STEPS TO GREEK. 18mo. 1s.
A SHORTER GREEK PRIMER. Crown 8vo. 1s. 6d.
EASY GREEK PASSAGES FOR UNSEEN TRANSLATION. *Third Edition Revised.* Fcap. 8vo. 1s. 6d.
GREEK VOCABULARIES FOR REPETITION. Arranged according to Subjects. *Second Edition.* Fcap. 8vo. 1s. 6d.
GREEK TESTAMENT SELECTIONS. For the use of Schools. *Third Edition.* With Introduction, Notes, and Vocabulary. Fcap. 8vo. 2s. 6d.
STEPS TO FRENCH. *Fourth Edition.* 18mo. 8d.
FIRST FRENCH LESSONS. *Fourth Edition Revised.* Crown 8vo. 1s.
EASY FRENCH PASSAGES FOR UNSEEN TRANSLATION. *Third Edition revised.* Fcap. 8vo. 1s. 6d.
EASY FRENCH EXERCISES ON ELEMENTARY SYNTAX. With Vocabulary. *Second Edition.* Crown 8vo. 2s. 6d. KEY 3s. net.
FRENCH VOCABULARIES FOR REPETITION: Arranged according to Subjects. *Seventh Edition.* Fcap. 8vo. 1s.

SCHOOL EXAMINATION SERIES

EDITED BY A. M. M. STEDMAN, M.A. Crown 8vo. 2s. 6d.

FRENCH EXAMINATION PAPERS IN MISCELLANEOUS GRAMMAR AND IDIOMS. By A. M. M. STEDMAN, M.A. *Tenth Edition.*
A KEY, issued to Tutors and Private Students only, to be had on application to the Publishers. *Fourth Edition.* Crown 8vo. 6s. net.
LATIN EXAMINATION PAPERS IN MISCELLANEOUS GRAMMAR AND IDIOMS. By A. M. M. STEDMAN, M.A. *Ninth Edition.*
KEY (*Fourth Edition*) issued as above. 6s. net.
GREEK EXAMINATION PAPERS IN MISCELLANEOUS GRAMMAR AND IDIOMS. By A. M. M. STEDMAN, M.A. *Fifth Edition.*
KEY (*Second Edition*) issued as above. 6s. net.

GERMAN EXAMINATION PAPERS IN MISCELLANEOUS GRAMMAR AND IDIOMS. By R. J. MORICH, Manchester. *Fifth Edition.*
KEY (*Second Edition*) issued as above. 6s. net.
HISTORY AND GEOGRAPHY EXAMINATION PAPERS. By C. H. SPENCE, M.A., Clifton College. *Second Edition.*
SCIENCE EXAMINATION PAPERS. By R. E. STEEL, M.A., F.C.S. *In two vols.*
Part I. Chemistry; Part II. Physics.
GENERAL KNOWLEDGE EXAMINATION PAPERS. By A. M. M. STEDMAN, M.A. *Third Edition.*
KEY (*Second Edition*) issued as above. 7s. net.

www.ingramcontent.com/pod-product-compliance
Lightning Source LLC
Chambersburg PA
CBHW022006220426
43663CB00007B/978